PLAY IN A GODLESS WORLD

The Theory and Practice of Play in Shakespeare, Nietzsche and Freud

Catherine Bates

OPEN GATE PRESS
LONDON

First published in 1999 by Open Gate Press
51 Achilles Road, London NW6 1DZ

British Library Cataloguing-in-Publication Programme
A catalogue reference for this book is available from the
British Library.

ISBN: 1 871871 47 6

Passages from The Standard Edition of the
Complete Psychological Works of Sigmund Freud are quoted by
arrangement with Mark Paterson & Associates

The author is grateful to the editors of
Modern Philology for permission to reproduce here a version of
her article, 'The Point of Puns', 96 (1999), 421-38

Printed in Great Britain by
The Cromwell Press, Trowbridge, Wiltshire

PLAY IN A GODLESS WORLD

This book challenges a long and respected tradition which sees human play as the fount of creativity and origin of all civilization. According to this tradition play creates order out of chaos. Play is art, as Friedrich Schiller famously stressed. As a special place and time in which actions are set apart and governed by particular rules, play becomes the testing ground in which human beings first learn to control their environment and master their reality. For Donald Winnicott in *Playing and Reality* (1971) and Roger Caillois in *Man, Play and Games* (1958) healthy play marks the beginning of mature adulthood and ordered society. For Johan Huizinga in *Homo Ludens* (1938) it is in and through play that all human civilization evolves.

For these theorists order is an unquestioned good and the world a place that can be corrected and conquered through human effort and ingenuity. Yet their cheerful narratives of progress seem out of place in today's disillusioned world. They tell us less about play than about their need for a theory that optimistically triumphs social and moral improvement.

This book traces the history of an alternative theory of play in Shakespeare, Nietzsche and Freud. For these writers play is not the starting point for a civilized world so much as an end in itself, a cultivation of aesthetic forms which do nothing to disguise their artificiality and which are loved only for the fictions which they are. Nietzsche, the arch-philosopher of play, Freud, the theoriser of slips and jokes, and Shakespeare, master of the man-made illusions of the play-world, are shown in direct and indirect ways to anticipate the playful philosophy which has become a hallmark of postmodern times.

Play in a Godless World is a *Homo Ludens* for the new century. It is intended for a specific as well as a general readership, appealing to students of Shakespeare and drama as well as to those with a wider interest in play as a more general cultural phenomenon. Its home ground is the point where literature, philosophy and psychoanalysis meet.

Contents

Introduction

This book is about play – child's play, wordplay, stage plays, foul play – too promiscuous a word, you might think, to be the subject of any usefully focused study. Yet through all this diversity there runs a common thread. For whatever form it takes – a sports match, a game of cards, a crossword puzzle, a drama – play creates another world, one which, bounded and complete, stands at one remove from the world of reality. From the most spontaneous improvisations of children to the most formal manoeuverings of chess, play engenders its own space, its own momentum and time. The play-world might correspond to the real world but it does not coincide. It exists in some relation to the real world, though the nature of that relation can vary widely. Play can hold the mirror up to nature; it can caricature or subvert that nature; it can stylize nature out of all recognition, or escape from nature far into fantasy. But whether it reflects, refracts, or retreats from nature, play is always an elsewhere, a second world which exists apart from the real world of work, meaning, exchange. This does not make it any the less intense. The straining efforts of the athlete, the actor's wrenching words, the frantic transactions of the gambler show play to be no less vivid, no less 'real' to those involved, whether they watch or perform. But play remains marked off, separate, and self-contained. And this is understood by everyone, including the players who forget themselves and the children who are lost in their game.

Play takes the vicissitudes of human existence and transmutes them, carries them back to its own designed and designated space where they can be played out to the full and worked over, time and again. Play takes the experiences of uncertainty, shock, reversal, and surprise and creates conditions in which they can be isolated, re-created, and put to the test. In play's purest, most abstract form – the lottery – the experience of utter randomness, of fate at its most capricious and blind, is mathematically simulated and consequences of life-changing importance are attached to the result. Games of sport and games of chance take the sheer open-endedness of things – the simple experience of not knowing what is going to happen – and resolve it with an outcome: a clear and unambiguous either/or which, however arbitrary, is characterized by its decisiveness and irreversibility. The stage plays of mimetic drama reproduce human experience in all its diversity, represent all that life may throw at us. Through the suspension of disbelief and an identification with the characters we experience through them the states of unknowing, confusion or doubt. Yet these experiences are contained – redeemed – from the outset by an ending or the existence of an ending which is known in advance. These experiences may be acute – play can induce pity and terror, exhaustion and stress – but they are never more nor less than factitious, the product of human intervention and devising. In play we are no longer subject to a world that is beyond our control but to a world whose conditions of uncertainty are of our own making.

In play experiences are taken out of time and bracketed off to a safe place where their rehearsal or re-enactment can be carried out under conditions that are strictly controlled. Play is a space where uncertainty can be sampled. It is the laboratory or testing ground in which human beings first objectify their world as unpredictable and unreliable and – by reproducing its uncertainty within the terms of the game – learn ultimately to master nature and control their environment. Play makes order out of chaos, submits chaos to rule and design, and to this extent it is, as Friedrich Schiller famously stressed, only another name for the aesthetic – for art. Writing in 1795 Schiller speaks for a long and respected tradition which sees play as the fount of creativity and origin of all civilization. For Johan Huizinga, writing in *Homo Ludens* (1938), play embodies the human will to order and lies behind every aspect of civilized society from language to law, ritual to philosophy. The most rudimentary play of infants or infant societies incarnates the creative spirit and marks the beginning of a great march of progress that leads – at the far end – to the achievements not only of art but of science and technology as well. For Roger Caillois, writing in *Man, Play and Games* (1958), competitive play productively channels man's otherwise self-destructive rivalries and forms the basis for any meritocratically organized society. And for Donald Winnicott, writing in *Playing and*

Reality (1971), the playing child is father to the civilized man, the timid trials and probings of childhood play creatively mapping out a space between the infant's illusions of omnipotence and a sterner reality.

This tradition tells a noble tale. Play shows man at his best. In its creation of worlds it makes him even god-like – the master of ceremonies and unchallenged king of his self-made world. Yet for all its appeal this story is deceptive. Like any myth of progress, its cheery narrative leaves too much out of the account – like the addictive, compulsive, or neurotic play which doesn't so much master the world as master the player. More to the point, it goes round in circles and ends up telling us less about play than about those who theorize it. For those who celebrate order as an unquestioned good – and progress as anything which leads towards it – have a way of situating themselves at the far end of the triumphal process they describe. At the end of the line there is civilization, order, psychic health, and mature adulthood . . . and here is the theory to prove it. Play is described as a gradual ascent towards moral, social, and intellectual achievement – the very exemplars of which are those who describe it as such. The move is a predictable one. These writers theorize play as the beginning of order because it is in their interests to do so: the coherence of their case and their status as theoreticians rest upon it. But they tend not to ask whose order or whose ideology it is. In celebrating civilization they present themselves – and defend their systems – as the end-products of the process they admire. An ordered theoretical statement thus traces its own evolution and congratulates itself in the process. Huizinga and the others rest their own claims to theoretical order firmly on the belief that order is of the highest value – a strategy which grants their thesis the force of a conclusion devoutly to be wished but which leaves the circularity of their argument curiously unexamined.

This book traces the history of an alternative theory of play – one which fits in better with today's gamesome and ludic world where the best and the worst that can be said about human achievement is that it is only a game. It was Nietzsche, the arch-philosopher of play, who did most to discredit those theoreticians who rested their claims to truth on the habits and patternings of their own minds. In *The Birth of Tragedy* (1872) he excoriated the 'theoretical man' whose puny pretensions to order were based upon little more. Those things which the men of theory held most dear – the cherished principles of logic, rule and law – were for Nietzsche a cause not of celebration but desecration. These were but the internal structures of the mind projected outward to give the world the appearance of intelligibility and man the illusion of power. But such order was a fiction – a 'grand metaphysical illusion' – for all was illusion (*in ludere*), all was play. In Nietzsche's unremittingly nihilistic mind the world in its natural state was nothing but chaos and to say that it was otherwise was to lie. Anything which denied the disorder of things by claiming to find order – and especially anything which laid that order at the door of human brilliance and ingenuity – was mystifying and self-deceived. All human orders were vain attempts to draw a veil over the 'ghastly absurdity of existence', and this was true not only of specific orders – of this cultural institution, or that religious practice, that political concept – but of whole ordering systems: religions, world-views, even language itself. Dismantling the pre-supposition that order and meaning might inhere within the world, Nietzsche pulled the rug from under every theorist's feet, orbiting himself and those who follow him into deconstructive free fall.

Or free play. For play is what he was left with. *The Birth of Tragedy* closes with the image of a child playing in the sand. This play is not ulterior. It does not lead anywhere – towards higher, better, more advanced, or more developed things. It does not symbolize anything either, some deep inner truth. It is completely pointless and mindless, going nowhere and enjoyed purely for itself. In this respect, play perfectly encapsulates the absurdity of existence, the sheer emptiness of things. Order is an illusion, but illusion is all that there is. The mistake of theoretical man – one which went back as far as Plato – was to assume that something must lie beneath the surface of appearance when surface was all there ever was. Theoretical man tried to deny illusion – to say that order lay behind illusion, and that order was substantial, truthful, reliable, good. Often he called that order God. But the child has the wisdom to accept illusion and not to look or ask for more. And the artist – the most childlike of human beings – also recognizes that illusion is all that anything comes down to and so sets about making illusions himself. For Nietzsche there was no better way of spending your time. His cult of illusion found itself exemplified not in the work of theoretical man but in the play of the artist and the child. Play was not the starting point for a civilized world so much as an end in itself, a cultivation of aesthetic forms which do nothing to disguise their artificiality and which are loved only for the illusions that they are.

Later chapters of this book look at two writers who adumbrate this alternative theory of play in particularly interesting ways. These writers are Shakespeare and Freud. Freud discusses play most famously in his account of the *fort! da!* game in *Beyond the Pleasure Principle* (1920) but also in the less well-known *Jokes and Their Relation to the Unconscious* (1905) where he theorizes jokes as 'developed play'. Jokes put adults back in touch with their childish past. They rebel against authority and throw off the shackles of an over-burdened existence, temporarily indulging a taste for infantile nonsense that has long since been repressed. But jokes also restore order by returning us to the sober business of making sense. A joke has to be intelligible – or a good joke does, in any case – for if you don't get a joke, it isn't funny, isn't a joke. As Freud's argument oscillates between nonsense and meaning, it wittily if unwittingly reveals a disconcerting ambivalence about its own theoretical procedures. For, as it strains towards clarity and explication, Freud's theory comes to look increasingly like the jokes it so scrupulously records. This ambivalence seems to have discomfited Freud – for the joke book is one of the few texts which he did not obsessively re-work or revise – but it emerges starkly in those who have commented subsequently on the Freudian text. Ernst Kris and E. H. Gombrich restore substance and seriousness, entirely along the lines of Huizinga and the theoretical men, by seeing in Freud's account of jokes the foundation for a whole psychoanalytical theory of art. Jacques Lacan, by contrast, moves in the opposite direction and follows Nietzsche down the path of unredeemed play, the idea that theory might all be a joke perfectly fitting his theoretical bill.

As for Shakespeare, there were good professional reasons why he should propose that play is all that human endeavour comes down to. In celebrating the man-made illusions of the play-world, it is the playwright who has the last laugh. For the playwright is in a different position from the theorist of play. The theorist tries to distinguish between the seriousness of his own writing and the playfulness he writes about, but is in danger of finding himself inside the magic circle he has drawn and of discovering that everything – including his own claim to credibility – is a game. The playwright, however, wishes for nothing more. What for the theorist is a game of double jeopardy, for the playwright is a *raison d'être*. The playwright fashions plots, constructs myths, and lures players, readers, and spectators into a world that neither conceals its illusoriness nor seeks to propose that there is anything behind or beyond. It is in the playwright's interests to preserve, heighten, and intensify the illusion – the play, after all, is the thing. And never more so than in tragedy, the genre that plays and re-plays death. All play is repetitive – like the little boy's *fort! da!* game, it takes the vagaries of human experience into a world that is denuded of consequence where they can be repeated any number of times. But in play-acting death tragedy specifically repeats the unrepeatable. The actors always revive to please tomorrow's audience, making tragedy – of all forms of play – the ultimate illusion, the ultimate myth. In tragedy everyone and no one is fooled, giving rise to that perverse and peculiar pleasure which, as far back as Aristotle, was recognized as belonging to this kind of play. The last chapter of this book considers *Julius Caesar, Hamlet, Antony and Cleopatra*, and *The Winter's Tale* – four plays which enact the deaths of a king, a father, a queen and a wife. As these deaths are self-consciously re-played – staged as illusions or as works of art – Shakespeare and his characters reflect on tragedy's artistic gamble, and invite the reader or spectator to ask whether it has been or ever can be successfully brought off.

Of Gambling, Creativity, and God

Have you ever wondered why the gambler pays his debts? Not why he loses but why, when he does, there's no letting off – why he actually has to pay up? – why, when die is cast, trump called, or chips down, there can be no nervous backing away, no conniving wink, no impish little grin, as if to say, 'but my friends, *it was only a game*'? That's never been any excuse. There's no getting out of it that way. The loser has always had to pay. But why should this be?

That a person should honour his debts is all very well. But what if he's mortgaged himself in play . . . doesn't that make a difference? Should the same principle necessarily apply? Must he still be called to account? Isn't the whole point of play its separateness from life? It provides a space and a time set apart from reality, governed by the game's own special rules. Why should play carry consequences into real life? Isn't that rather unplayful? Why can't bets be contained within the ludic world where they're made, to be dissolved the moment the players get up and disperse? Can't the spirit of play extend to this point and make light of the final reckoning? It seems hard that the gambler should actually be held to his debts given the setting in which they're made.

You'd think there'd be a special dispensation – that the player would be released from losses incurred in this way – and yet there's no general amnesty at the end of the game. The gambler can look for no relenting, neither the individual nor the gambling institution (not even the casino that's run for profit can increase its profitability by suddenly refusing to pay over the jackpot). The player can, of course, hedge his bets – he can make a bet on one side that will compensate him for possible losses on the other – but this only proves the point. The situation would never arise were he not obliged, as if by a law of iron, to pay the debts that he's incurred in the first place. The sentence is irrevocable. Once a pledge has been made the player can't call it back, can't wriggle out of it. Like it or not, once all the fun is over, the debtor has got to pay up. The final settling of the scores takes place in the real world, beyond the confines of the game, where another mood and a quite different jurisdiction prevail – as separate from the world of the game as is the cold reality of the street to the blinking spectator who emerges from the theatre.

There's no way out. Debts made in play must be paid. But why should this be? The question hardly arises when the stakes are small – the debt's just a minor irritation, begrudged, perhaps, but soon forgotten. But what if a fortune has been lost, if that heart-stopping moment presages no trifling, compassable debt but an entire inheritance gone and, in its wake, truly Hogarthian scenes of ruination? Can one then expect a reprieve? No, even then the game is up. The loser may turn to his confederates in dismay. He may supplicate and implore – 'surely you don't mean to hold me to this?' – but his appeal to solidarity is in vain. The law is on their side. They may choose to show him mercy, but that is a purely an *ad hominem* case. They would be quite within their rights to claim their dues. The loser can't back off, saying it was only a joke. The fact that he's lost at play makes no odds and grants him no right of appeal. Whatever has been pledged must be paid, no matter how frivolous the wager nor how catastrophic the consequences. The gambler can look for no concession, no redress. The loser must pay his dues, if it bankrupts him – and beggars his family – in the process.

Again, why should this be? Perhaps the answer is only too obvious. Doesn't the gambler pay his debts in order to preserve the tension, the sheer excitement of play? If he knew that his debts might be waived wouldn't that remove for ever the thrill of risk? The gambler must be assured that the penalty holds and that he actually stands to lose if he is properly to experience his delirium. There is no other way it can be brought about. Think how attenuated, how miserably thin his pleasure would be if every wager were but an empty threat – a polite fiction, an aesthetic suspending of disbelief – like those feeble fun-fair casinos, barely worthy the name, where players stake only toy money. Their scare is utterly tame, inoculated from the outset by the knowledge that it's not for real. The gambler cares nothing for such cheap thrills. The rule that the loser pay his dues may not protect the player but what it does protect, surely, is the game – the threat of genuine loss and the frisson of real fear without which a game would scarcely be worth playing at all?

Except the question arises again. This may well be true of the small, payable debt – the thrill may be worth every penny. But what about those extremes where whole worlds – family fortunes, personal reputations – have been wagered and . . . well, lost? Isn't that rather a high price – too high a price – for the thrill? Isn't the consequence just out of all proportion to the game? Some consequences are more serious than others. There are degrees of misfortune, and there's a point, surely, at which the gravity of a loss and its long-term consequences begin to outweigh the pleasure of that momentary high? If the requirement that the gambler pay his debts were meant to arouse his pleasure, then this would be the point at which the law could intervene to protect him from pain. Couldn't things be organized in such a way that what ensured the gambler's pleasure – his exhilarating flirtation with risk – could also insure that thrill, preserve the player from a degree of loss that was capable of annihilating that pleasure, of wiping it out at a stroke? A system in which a whole inheritance can be lost at the tables would seem to be in nobody's interests. You'd think there'd be a caveat which recognized the playfulness of the whole occasion and which limited the seriousness of losses there incurred – a set price, a ceiling of acceptable folly, a fixed rate for masochism: a given percentage of the risk-taker's assets, say, which could legally be his to lose but beyond which (some things get beyond a joke, after all) the law would intervene and, in its wisdom, protect the gambler from himself. But apparently not. The gambler is free to risk what he likes and to bring the direst of consequences on his head. There's no protection, no internal mechanism to limit the scale of his self-sought disaster.

So it can't only be a question of pleasure. There must be something else, and perhaps the simplest explanation is the most obvious, namely that it's a matter of fair play. There are winners as well as losers, after all, and if the loser refuses to pay his debts then no one stands to benefit. It's clear that if you are going to play you must take your chances, accept your losses as evenly as your gains, and pay your debts uncomplainingly – as willingly, indeed, as you would wish your partners to pay theirs were the tables turned. In this respect, gambling operates a totally fair exchange, an exemplary transaction, an admirable ethical code. The gambler exercises the same grim courtesy as the chivalrous knight, his engagement in play like an engagement in war where an etiquette of enmity and obedience to rule upholds a similarly exacting code of practice.

On the other hand, fair play has never accounted for everything. Since when has a code of honour held back the truly determined individual? Isn't there such a thing as self-interest? Not every war is conducted according to the rules of fair play. There are those who play dirty or who – truer to their objectives than to some inimical code of honour – fight to win. If the history of war has its guerillas and its terrorists, doesn't the gambling past have its fair quota of cheats? Mightn't the man who faced ruin at the card tables dispense with the polite conventions of fair play for once and cheat his fellows of what he owed them? Why should he abide by the terms of some gentlemanly agreement when it's so manifestly to his disadvantage? Why on earth should he play fair?

Yet it's worth pausing for a moment to consider his case. For the man who neglects to pay his debts is not quite the same as the ordinary cheat. Compare the simple rogue, who cheats at cards but who makes over his losses when required, with the man who might play like an angel but who, though happy enough to pocket his winnings when the going is good, has a way of vanishing into the night when his own debts are called. How differently would the two be treated? The ordinary cheat might be the most abominable villain. He might bamboozle his fellows without compunction. But society has always made room for him – for the opportunist who uses cunning to outwit his more credulous friends. Civilization has always tolerated the cheat, even has a soft spot for him, and has made a place for him all the way from Brer Rabbit back to Odysseus. For the cheat still respects certain things and still abides by the rule that the loser pay his dues. Naturally he would, since it's in his interests to do so. But compare him with that other lucky joe. Imagine the hue and cry that would follow him. Infamy! Daylight robbery! He wouldn't be winked at, deplored but half forgiven with a grudging 'well, but you have to hand it to him'. His dishonesty is of a different order of magnitude. Both men are operating out of self-interest. Both equally stand to become rich at the expense of others. But there is thieving and thieving, it seems. It is one thing to cheat at play, quite another to cheat the players. The ordinary cheat abuses the rules of the game – he might use loaded dice or marked cards. But the opprobrium that meets the other suggests that what he abuses is something altogether different. He might have followed the rules of the game to the letter and played with the utmost scrupulosity – that would be why he'd lost to the other. But this would count for nothing, would mitigate not a fraction of his crime. He would be worse even than the bad sport. The cheat abuses the rules of the game; the bad sport calls the game itself into question. But not even the spoil-sport is an anarchist. Our man would come lowest in the infernal pecking order. For he plays all right. But by defrauding his fellows what he declines to do is to observe a ground rule which even the cheat respects. It's as if he's refusing to play a second game, a game that exists over and above the first, a game whose law is absolute and never put in doubt. It is this which marks him out as diabolical and which puts his *legerdemain* on a quite different value scale.

So to say it's a question of fair play isn't quite to put it strongly enough. The obligation that the loser pay his dues is something more than a polite convention. Conventions can be flouted all too easily, but this rule is a given, an absolute – something so taken for granted that it's observed even by the cheat who plays to win and who otherwise isn't too concerned about flouting all the rules in the book. Given the choice, the cheat gets round the system by abusing the rules of the particular game. He doesn't attempt to abuse the system. It's as if he's calculated that he'd never get away with it. This rule seems to exist on a different level from ordinary morals – from the practical considerations of right and wrong. For it's not only respected by the trickster. It also remains indifferent to the question of whether gambling itself might be wicked. It makes no comment whatever on whether the player should have been gambling in the first place but simply holds him to the consequences he's incurred. Even the spluttering zealot for whom all gambling is the work of the Devil would concede that debts made in play should be paid. Not paying them would only compound, not cancel, the sin.

So what might, on the face of it, have seemed pretty uncontroversial – a mere necessity or matter of fact – begins on reflection to look rather odd. For this obligation that the player pay his dues holds good no matter how playful the bet, no matter how ill-advised, no matter how morally questionable, nor how frankly ruinous the consequences. It's not playful, it's not necessarily pleasurable, it is far from sensible and not greatly advantageous, it's not even particularly ethical, and yet it continues to hold with absolute force. Why should this be?

What is it exactly which this law lays down? In its simplest formulation, it attaches consequences to the outcome of a game. It makes that outcome binding and irreversible and it forces the player to abide absolutely by the result. No matter how trifling the cause nor how disproportionate the effects, this law brooks no exception, no appeal. In the most extreme case, an entire fortune might be lost at the throw of a die or spin of the wheel. Why should such terrible consequences be attached to a game of chance? Life is chancy enough as it is, and the unknown already threatens the player with the most fearful of unforeseen consequences. Fire, flood or fraud might relieve a man of his fortune just as effectively as a game of roulette. But if there's one kind of chance against which he might take every precaution – taking out insurance or seeking legal redress – there is also this other kind against which precautions are not only non-existent but positively disallowed. And the law which, under normal circumstances, would do all it could to save our friend – to protect him from loss and depredation, to preserve his property from accident or theft – when it comes to play, stands back mute and quite impervious. Indeed, it allows the player to expose himself to unlimited risk.

The difference is that the chance in the game is man-made. In life chance is beyond our control. Anything might happen, whether it's predicted, feared, intuited, or wholly unforeseen. We are subject to any eventuality – any category of event – and even the most well-prepared are capable of being taken completely by surprise. The player doesn't submit himself to this kind of chance. Things either happen or they don't. But he will willingly submit himself to a game of chance. For here the chance is artificial and manufactured – engineered with the greatest precision. The game takes the infinity of things that might occur and reduces it to manageable proportions. It narrows contingency down to a single outcome, one that can be calculated in advance and quantified as an acceptable either/or – heads or tails, winning or losing. From the totally unexpected, the game of chance creates a scene of expectation. It doesn't turn an unpleasant surprise into a pleasant one but it brings surprise under control. The player doesn't know what the outcome is going to be but he does know that an outcome will be achieved and roughly of what kind it will be. The game thus converts surprise into expectation. It preserves a measure of uncertainty – but that's precisely what it does: preserve an uncertainty that can be measured. The game of chance samples uncertainty, encloses it within an hour-glass, and creates laboratory conditions in which uncertainty can be taken in hand. In short, the game formalizes chance. It takes something over which we have no control and gives it a form and a shape. It puts uncertainty within our control.

Chance is no less random in the game than it is in life. The game imitates the chanciness of life in such a way that the player has no way of knowing which number is going to come up. But it's he who has narrowed the chances from the open set of all possible occurrences down to a strictly numerical field and who, in so doing, has made himself arbiter of the arbitrary. Playing the game makes him no less prone to vicissitude – life remains as unpredictable as ever, and there's nothing to say that even the playing of the game won't be hijacked by some unforeseen event or other. Nor will playing the game necessarily make him richer. The Lord still moves in mysterious ways, still giveth and taketh away. The gambler may end up no better or worse off than if he'd never gambled in the first place and simply let fate (or the Lord) take its course. But these are not the reasons why he plays. The gambler doesn't play because it will make him richer or render him magically invulnerable to fate. He plays because in the game he willingly submits himself to a chance that's of his own making. It's under his control and so gives him the luxury of experiencing his own mastery. It doesn't give him power over the outcome. He still doesn't know what that's going to be and it's this uncertainty which holds his breath and sets his heart aflutter. But it gives him the power to effect a result, to make an outcome happen. The game of chance doesn't grant him the power of decision – the ability to say who will win – but it does give him the power of decidability – the ability to arrange the circumstances which will decide who the winner is. It doesn't make the player God, able to give and to take away. But it does perhaps make him a god, able to create the conditions in which giving and taking will occur.

In Jorge Luis Borges' short story about the Babylonian lottery it's this power of divine intervention which, once taken into their own hands, so fatally addicts the players of the game. Borges describes an anciently constituted game of chance which, though pretty rudimentary at first, becomes ever more labyrinthine and mandarin. The Babylonians start drawing lots to decide not only fortunate outcomes – the winning of money, an assignation with a beautiful woman – but adverse outcomes as well – a fine, imprisonment, even death. As time goes by they develop more subtle variations on the theme. For, as they reflect on the power the lottery grants them – the power to direct human destiny – they come to realize with a dawning gleam that this power is infinitely extendable, that it has no limit, and that they are, in fact, free to manipulate chance not only at the initial drawing of the lots but at every stage thereafter, right through to the execution of the final sentence. They learn to draw lots on lots, so that any decision or point of action in its turn branches off into further alternatives and those to still more, thus creating an infinite series over which they have unlimited control:

> Let us imagine a first drawing, which eventuates in a sentence of death against some individual. To carry out the sentence, another drawing is set up, and this drawing proposes (let us say) nine possible executioners. Of these executioners, four can initiate a third drawing which will reveal the name of the actual executioner, two others can replace the adverse order with a fortunate order (the finding of a treasure, let us say), another may exacerbate the death sentence (that is: make it infamous or enrich it with torture), still others may refuse to carry it out . . .

The lottery turns man's vulnerability to chance into an exquisite work of art, and it delivers to the Babylonians the power of gods – the power to make things happen. The unsteadying pleasure which this power affords them vastly outweighs the player's little thrill that he might lose or the faint hope that he might win. These small pleasures are as nothing – mere fore-play – to the mighty climax which the gambler feels at playing god. At its most developed, the Babylonian lottery appeals not to mere hope but to 'all the faculties of men', faculties that are engaged – engaged even to the death – by this vertiginous experience of control. For the game grants the players power over causality – a total say over the conditions that will decide what happens next. In this context, the all-binding law which attaches consequences to the outcome of the game makes perfect sense. For it underwrites that power. It enables events of the greatest magnitude to be decided by something that's humanly controlled. It binds cause to effect, and, since it puts humanity in charge of cause, clearly no effect can be too great – the greater the effect, the greater the power to cause it. No wonder there's no limit to what can be lost at play, no officious capping of consequence. No price could be too high. Even a fortune would be cheap at the price, a finite amount to pay for this infinite power. This is a pleasure worth getting addicted to, and it's for the privilege of experiencing it that the gambler is allowed to pay as exorbitantly as he likes. Imagine if the rule did not exist – if, out of some misguided spirit of liberality, we were weakly to relent, to release the player from his debts – think how fatally this would compromise that power, the ability to determine fate and to shape the future with our own hands.

All the same, lotteries – even ones of Babylonian proportions – are not the only kind of game, and there is more to human play than games of chance. There are some games, no less compelling, which combine chance with strategy or skill – a randomly dealt hand of cards, for example, is the player's to wield with all the ingenuity of which he is master. And there are others – tournaments, matches, competitions – which aspire to minimize chance if not to eliminate it altogether. Here the idea is to let the best man win, and it's not chance but experience and expertise – intense training or strenuous exertion – which are to decide the outcome. When two evenly matched teams or individuals pit their strengths – mental and physical – against each other, it's the respective abilities of the two, even if only a hair's-breadth apart, which are to resolve the issue. Games like these aim to neutralize chance and introduce factors which are specifically under human control in order to counterbalance or off-set its effects. Nor does every game involve gambling. The point of a lottery is to take an outcome which in itself is purely formal – the throw of a die or the drawing of a lucky number – and to attach to it consequences that are all too real. Yet there are many games where the outcome is, in practical terms, just as symbolic – a ball in a net, a man past a line – but where no further material consequences are necessarily attached. Sports players and their supporters don't need to have a financial stake in the outcome of the game to feel suspense and anticipation of the most raging kind, nor to experience feelings any less intense than those of the most hardened gambler. There are many games, in other words, where chance has little or nothing to do with it and where no gambling is involved. Do the heady delights of the lottery still apply?

A game of chance creates a degree of uncertainty that is particularly extreme. The dice, balls, or lottery tickets are randomizers – they reproduce chance at its most arbitrary, where neither the players' individual qualities nor anything they may say or do has any bearing on the outcome. The lottery recreates man's helplessness before a fate which comes straight from the blue and which strikes good and bad indiscriminately. It simulates fate at its most freakish, capricious, and blind. Other kinds of game, by contrast, reproduce an uncertainty that is less absolute, where human effort and deserving have at least some contribution to make. In these games the player is not so much a passive victim of chance as an active agent who has the power to intervene and to influence the result, at least to some extent. Personal qualities of experience, fitness, or skill are brought into play to modify or direct the outcome one way or the other. Games like these recreate a world which is closer, perhaps, to the experience of everyday life – where most outcomes are a banal mixture of chance and striving, a product of happy or unhappy accident and the ingenious compromises of human adaptability.

Games vary in the different levels of uncertainty they create. But the difference is one of degree and not of kind. A player may project the outcome differently in a game of chance or a game of sport, but in neither case is that outcome known in advance. The uncertainty may be more or less extreme, but in both cases it is still subject to human control. Both kinds of game take the experience of not knowing what's going to eventuate and create an artificial environment in which an outcome is set up to occur. It doesn't greatly matter, in fact, how that outcome is brought about – whether by the most random drawing of lots or by the most intense application of effort. Both kinds of game provide an arena or field – set apart in space and time – where a transition is staged from a state of not knowing to one of knowing, from the sheer open-endedness of things to the resolution of a final result.

Both sorts of game proffer the same kind of pleasure – the power of effecting an outcome, of making something happen. A game of chance represents the game in its purest form, for it deals with uncertainty at its most extreme and attaches effects of the greatest consequence to a cause of the most undisguised artificiality. But other games are still performing the same basic manoeuvre, still taking uncertainty under control, still bringing an uncertain future to a conclusion, however contrived. It may be that the Babylonian has the edge, that he enjoys this pleasure at its most acute and lies on the very edge of the scale of bliss. But in other games it is still the same scale. Less may hang materially on the outcome of a competition than on a bet. But even in those games where the degree of uncertainty is minimal and the consequences less than all-consuming, the pleasure is still of the same kind – pleasure in the power to take uncertainty in hand and, under conditions of the strictest control, to play it out to a final resolution.

Indeed, the same could be said of almost every kind of activity that might be described as playful. So far I've only considered games with open outcomes. But there are many others where the resolution of the outcome is not in doubt but either predictable or contained within the structure of that particular game. There are all those solitary games, for example, where it's not who is going to win or lose that matters but how laboriously or effortlessly an individual player can bring the game to an end. In the case of puzzles it's not a question of who might be the luckiest or most skilful player – although these can be tied to competitions – but the player's own successful completion of the challenge. The final form of the outcome might still be unknown, as in a crossword where the code remains to be cracked, or it may, as in a jigsaw, be known from the beginning. But, one way or another, both allow the player to move from a state of uncertainty – fragmentariness or confusion – to one of order, understanding, and wholeness.

The crossword or jigsaw rehearse unknowing of a particular kind – not understanding a word, not being able to see the whole picture. But there is nothing to prevent play from imitating life's uncertainty at its most general. Children, for example, are endlessly inventive in acting out variations on what is, for them, a most uncontrolled and unpredictable existence. If children are subject to a mysterious adult world where the control – if not meaning – of events is often beyond them, they re-assert their power in play. They take that set of events – a domestic crisis, a hospital visit – and play it out on their own terms, often creating different outcomes to suit the particular mood of the moment. In other cases, an outcome may be more or less completely closed – held to and repeated with exactitude every time the game is played out. This kind of play, the drama, takes the complete story – uncertainty, resolution, outcome – and treats it as a whole, incorporating all its elements in one sitting. A given set of events is taken out of time – storied, plotted, and staged. And, through what Aristotle saw as a plot's most intrinsic components – reversal and recognition – actors and audience make the same transition the game-player makes, from a state of unknowing to one of knowing, from uncertainty to resolution.

Drama represents human play at its most sophisticated. Here the outcome is by definition closed – already decided and not a matter for uncertainty. Who ever wagered on the ending of *Macbeth*? The pleasure invested in drama is different from that of the puzzle-player who experiences the satisfaction of working through a difficulty by himself, different from that of a sportsman or sports spectator whose every nerve-ending is bound up with the resolution of an unknown outcome, different from that of the lottery player who submits himself to a blind chance of his own making. In drama, the experience of uncertainty is vicarious. The actor or spectator knows as well as anyone else that the play is artificial, the feelings it arouses as factitious as those aroused by a lottery, puzzle, or game of sport. He also knows, as the others do not, that the outcome is scripted, fixed in advance. But, through the suspension of disbelief, he pretends to forget the outcome, and, by identifying himself with the characters in the play, is able to experience through them the passage from perplexity through to resolution. He may not wager on the outcome of *Macbeth*, but it's this ability which makes it possible for the actor or spectator to enter into the experience of a character who does lay so tragic a bet on his own destiny.

The treatment of uncertainty is the basic component of human play, and this is why play takes so many different forms – so general an idea naturally lends itself to endless variation. At one end of the scale lies play at its most life-like: mimetic drama – a medium which could be defined, as it was for Aristotle, as an imitation of life. Drama takes uncertainty as a general phenomenon and plays out variations on the basic human theme of not knowing what's going to happen next. Since the outcome is known ahead of time, these variations alleviate what would otherwise be as boring as watching the same sports match over and over again. But, as a highly developed literary form, the drama also allows for the rehearsal in art of all the complications and par-ticularities of individual human experience. Further along the spectrum lies the kind of play which is equally mimetic, in that it imitates life's general unpredictability, but which allows for greater fluidity in its outcomes – improvisation, say, or children's play. Next in line are those games which take a specific aspect of uncertainty and contrive to recreate it, reproducing within their own format the accidentals of a real-life situation – an election, for example, or a murder investigation, or the vagaries of the money markets. These, in turn, are followed by those games which also select some specific criterion of uncertainty but which enact it with greater abstraction or stylization, rather as chess formalizes the disorder of war, or a game like snakes-and-ladders the experience of unexpected reversal. Here one would include all those games where the uncertainty created is life-like – insofar as its resolution involves a mixture of chance and human effort – but where the form in which that resolution is played out is, as in most sports, strictly symbolic. At the furthest end lies the lottery – the game which shows play in its most abstract form – for the game of chance deals with uncertainty *per se* and with uncertainty in its most radical form.

Seen like this, the spectrum is pretty inclusive. It extends from games with closed to games with open outcomes, from games which simulate the myriad uncertainties of life to those which recreate uncertainty with the greatest stylization, from those which exclude chance altogether to those which are wholly structured around it. With all these variations, the formula is basically the same. Play is an organized response to a frighteningly disorganized world.

Play takes some aspect of human life over which man has little or no say – uncertainty, contingency, chance, ignorance, surprise, reversal, coincidence, loss, disorder, war, fragmentariness, confusion – and submits it to human control. Play takes uncertainty – whether at its most general or most particular – and endows it with a shape and a form, a form that may equally be realistic or highly abstracted. Play creates an artificial stage or field on which the players may either bring an outcome to fruition or repeat, any number of times, an outcome which they know in advance, but where, in either case, the pleasure is basically the same – the pleasure of taking uncertainty and putting under control. That pleasure may take different forms and may be felt with varying degrees of intensity, but in all its forms human play trades in consolation. When it comes to exhilaration, the Babylonian may well take the ticket. But the game of chance shows only at its purest a structure that applies to all kinds of play. And the rule that the gambler pay his debts shows only how far human beings are prepared to go – the price they are, ultimately, willing to pay.

II

If play takes uncertainty and gives it over to human control, doesn't that make it a definitively creative act? Isn't this what creativity is – imposing order on chaos or taking shapeless matter and moulding it into form? From out of a sea of disorder, play creates small islands of design – ear-marked and carefully set apart. It interpolates into a universe that's beyond man's control little worlds of his own devising, and it's this which confers on the player the power of a god. To say this is no exaggeration. For man is prey to all that the natural world can hurl at him in the way of weather or elemental calamity, to all that his treacherous fellow-man can inflict by way of accident or injury, and to the very worst that his own irrational impulses can do to destroy his sanity and equilibrium. That the bare forked animal should take from all this the materials with which to imitate his predicament in play is indeed nothing short of miraculous.

Not only that, it also represents his first giant step towards civilization. For to submit uncertainty to control is already to have seen the world as uncertain, already to have perceived it as a phenomenon, as the object of shrewd observation. Such an objectification of the world marks the first stumbling towards human consciousness, the earliest move in separating from an ambient world. Whatever its superficial resemblances to animal play, this is the point at which human play moves inexorably to a different plane. For, in being able to situate his world as 'out there' – as an environment which can be characterized, understood as risky or unreliable – the human being is no longer in a continuum with Nature, bound blindly to the wheel of biological necessity. He has emerged from this as-yet undifferentiated state, surfaced from the primal depths into light. From the first great step of seeing the world as uncertain and repeating that experience in play, it's a relatively small step to start controlling that world with tools. Out of play come technology, art, and civilization. *Homo ludens* predates *homo faber*.

The fundamentally creative and civilizing power of play is something which writers on play have classically emphasized. Play is the beginning of great things, for sociologist and psychologist alike. The most primordial expressions of play to be found in the ancient past or in the rites of primitive societies reveal civilization in its infant state; the playing child is father to the civilized man. Indeed, archaic play and child's play are often treated as interchangeable, one the emblem for the other. In *Beyond the Pleasure Principle* (1920), for example, Freud famously describes a small boy playing a simple, solitary game. The game involves repeatedly throwing a cotton reel attached to a piece of string within the curtained folds of his crib – 'gone!' – and pulling it out again with a cry of unmistakable satisfaction – 'there!'. The game, muses Freud, represents the boy's mastery of an uncertain world. For it recreates – but this time on the child's own terms – the experience of watching his mother leave him periodically in the routine rounds of domestic life. 'The child cannot possibly have felt his mother's departure as something agreeable or even indifferent', Freud comments, and so he has converted an experience of unpleasing passivity into one of active control. It's now he who commands this whole business of coming and going. And, since the game stages the mother's disappearance and return within a single act, the little boy has, in effect, authored a complete play, simple, yes, but identical in structure and aesthetic principle to the most sophisticated of adult productions. The game represents not only the grounding of civilized adulthood (the boy was Freud's own grandson) but the origin of all human art. For the individual child, as for society as a whole, play marks the first 'great cultural achievement'.

We'll come back to Freud later on. It's with a different writer, however, that I'd like to begin – someone in whom Freud would show much interest and with whom he was to find a great affinity. This was the German poet and playwright, Friedrich Schiller. In *On the Aesthetic Education of Man* – a series of philosophical letters first published in 1795 – Schiller discussed the question of play at length and was perhaps the first writer of the modern age to trace the founding role of play within the history of human art and civilization.

With the distant rumble of the French Revolution in his ears, Schiller was writing during that heavenly dawn when other young poets felt it bliss to be alive – an expectant and breath-catching time when a whole new age of personal freedom and political liberty seemed to be within historical grasp. But when Schiller looked around him what he saw was not a Europe poised ready to grasp this beckoning dream. To his dismay, he found either lethargy or materialism of the most depressing kind. People either thought or felt too much, he decided. Either they so intellectualized things that their passions and enthusiasms remained unengaged, or they gave themselves up to a fine frenzy of feeling which left their intelligence undisturbed. Without a commitment to the political ideals of that time that was both passionate and reasoned, a great historical moment stood in danger of fizzling out, of sinking as untraceably as water into sand – an unthinkable occurrence, an opportunity almost criminally lost. The reason for this state of affairs, in Schiller's mind, was that contemporary man lay caught between two conflicting philosophical positions. On the one hand, there was a bloodless Kantianism which so abstracted human experience as to model the actual world on a world conceivable by the mind. On the other, there was a crude empiricism which brought everything down to the level of the body and which judged experience on the basis of fragmentary sense impressions. Being a man of his time, Schiller expressed the problem in terms of a division – no, as a catastrophic divorce – between reason and feeling. Mind and heart were fatally out of touch with each other, and the result was to leave the citizens of the world patently ill-equipped to realize the glorious future which history seemed to be offering them.

It was no good appealing to the mind alone, reflected Schiller – presenting man with theoretical abstractions of the Good or with reasoned imperatives for moral action. You had to engage his feelings, inflame his soul. A person had to want to do the right thing, had to have an inclination – an inner bent – towards Beauty and Truth, so that, as if by a second nature, duty would come spontaneously from within. To say this was not to propose a rule of feeling. Left to themselves, the passions had a way of being violent and selfish, and led only to destructive anarchy. The point was to reconcile feeling and thought, to bring the two back together in a mutually fulfilling and fruitful alignment – just what Schiller found lacking when he looked so despondently about him. The aim was to arrive at a reasonable, ordered society but one in which the rule of reason and of law was not achieved at the cost of suppressing feeling. For, as Schiller saw it, suppression was what inevitably resulted when a person's heart and mind were out of synch. When thought and feeling were at odds with each other, the intellect could only maintain its autonomy by suppressing the feelings out of existence. In this case, the individual was at war with himself – no better than a victim of his own inner Terror. Instead of harnessing his passions he was wasting precious energy suppressing them. Anticipating something that Freud would later develop in *Civilization and its Discontents* (1930), Schiller suggested that what was true of the in-dividual person would also be true of society at large. Where the individual tyrannized himself, the State would tyrannize the individual; where a person brought parts of himself forcibly into line, trampling resistance underfoot, there too would the State impose on its citizens the full rigour of repressive law. An outer despot would merely mirror the inner. In the ideal State, by contrast, reason and the passions would live amicably together and each person would be a model of flexible self-government and self-regulation. For freedom and liberty to be achieved, then, and for the Revolution to live up to its name, the place to start was not the public sphere. It wasn't a question of dismantling the infrastructure or of embarking on redistribution. For true revo-lutionary potential to be realized, Schiller said, the place to start was within.

Yet you couldn't just stop everything, couldn't hold society up while its citizens underwent this important process of re-education. The State wasn't like a clock which the watchmaker could allow to run down before he set about fixing its parts. It was necessary to find some other way – some form of vivisection with which to heal the rift at society's core while it was still living and breathing. And this was where play came in.

For Schiller, play provided a space, set apart from the world of work and adult responsibility, where rational, civilized man could get back in touch with his feelings. Play represented a median point between the two positions which Schiller saw as fundamentally opposed – pure sensation and abstract thought. Play allowed the thinking person to revert – but under conditions of the strictest control – to the sensuality of his beginnings. To illustrate his case, Schiller referred equally to the savage who – first contemplating the world as object – stood wonderingly outside his hut, and to the child who, in a similar way, emerged from the sheer swirl of the indeterminate into the first glimmerings of perceptual light. It didn't greatly matter to the argument which of these examples he used because, in either case, play was an intermediary – a point of transition – between the inchoate flux of the senses and the incipiently shaping capacities of thought. Sensation was where everything began, the primal grounding for all later conscious existence, and what Schiller was to call the sense-drive would always refer back to this point of origin, tug thought back towards mindlessness and to the ultimate inertia of the inorganic state. But from sensation emerged thought – from this murk would limpidity arise – and the contrasting form-drive would always pull in the opposite direction, onward and upward towards reason and order, starting with the earliest, most tentative steps and leading up to those heights of intellectual sophistication which transformed a playing child into the adult philosopher, or a once-savage tribe into the most technologically advanced of societies. It went without saying that such a development was a triumph of human achievement. But if the intellect kicked the ladder away – if it denied its sensuous heredity and tried to hide that untidiness away – those fatal flaws would inevitably arise which Schiller observed all around him: over-intellectualism and sentimentality.

The play-drive – what Schiller was variously to call the third or middle way – was what brought sense and form back together. It put civilized man back in touch with his sensuous past. It returned him whence he came and did justice to that womb of night. For play established that sense and form were interdependent. Before man determined a point in space and time, neither space nor time existed. But without that pre-emergent experience of absolute space and infinite time he couldn't have come to an awareness of either. In play, man returned to this negative, indeterminate state – what Keats called Negative Capability – and it was this which provided him with the source for all subsequent creativity. Returning to that negative state and putting chaos in the service of form . . . put like this it becomes even clearer that what Schiller was describing was the aesthetic. Play was only a more homely term for something that was, ultimately, sublime – the capacity to create art.

Play was the creative treatment of chaos. In play man reconnected with this primal state of negativity – one fully acknowledged to be beyond thought and logic and therefore outside his control. From this raw material he extracted material and from this material he fashioned form. The random was given shape and structure, the arbitrary was subjected to control. In the particular case of the poet, for example, the 'mind takes a hand as lawgiver' and 'subjects the arbitrary activity of the imagination to its own immutable and eternal unity'. In moral society, more generally, it became a question of 'abstracting from man's physical character its arbitrariness' and making it 'conformable to laws'. The work of art which resulted from this process could just as easily be a cultural artifact – poem or play, sculpture or symphony – as it could be the person himself, the artist who had developed his potentialities to the full. But in neither case were these laws oppressive or restricting. For they were not imposed from without, coercing the sensual while eternally weakened by its resistance. These laws didn't need to be resisted – indeed, they were irresistible – because they took sensuality and worked alongside it in a mutual and creative partnership.

For Schiller, play enabled man to control the contingent, giving him a mastery that was infinitely more powerful than any brittle pretensions of the intellect. With this mastery, furthermore, came freedom. For, once a person had been taught to unite feeling with form, his feelings would be released from their subjection. Where this didn't happen, feeling would remain for ever the prisoner of conscience, leaving individual and society alike the victims of repression. In those places where it did happen, however, man would recover his own freedom from within. It wasn't necessary to shut everything down in order to bring this revolution about. For play and art already had a place in ongoing, everyday life. It was a matter, rather, of education – of teaching people how to play – and this was the aesthetic education which Schiller had set out to describe.

When, as a new-born infant, man first came crying to this great stage of fools, he was pure sensation. When, as a corpse, he left it, he was pure form. In between, if he was to fulfil his creative potential at all, he had to learn to reconcile the two. It was for this reason that, in Schiller's famous phrase, 'man only plays when he is in the fullest sense of the word a human being; and he is only fully a human being when he plays'.

So far-reaching a definition of play may have disconcerted Schiller's readers, but it was to be taken up and endorsed by several twentieth-century writers on play. The Dutch historian, Johan Huizinga, gave play an equally foundational role in human culture in *Homo Ludens*, a book which, first published in 1938, became something of a classic on the subject. In his earlier book, *The Waning of the Middle Ages* (1919), Huizinga had studied the sumptuous and highly mannered court culture of late-medieval Burgundy – a colourful world of tournament, heraldry, and spectacle where life imitated art and where courtiers and knights conducted themselves as if they were characters in an epic or romance. Every aspect of life – conversation, manners, love, or war – was carefully choreographed and staged: structured according to rules laid down by a complex apparatus of courtesy, chivalry, and rank. The effect, for the historian, was so to rarify and codify the ordinary messiness of human existence as to make life itself seem 'regulated like a noble game', and it was this which first suggested to him the intimate connection between culture and play.

In the foreword to *Homo Ludens*, Huizinga describes how, every time he went to deliver a visiting lecture on 'The Play Element of Culture', he found his hosts wanting to change the 'of' to 'in'. But 'of', he says, is exactly what he meant. For he wasn't talking about play as an element or single component within a larger cultural field. For him, as for Schiller, play formed culture's very foundation – and not just inaugurally, as at the dawn of human prehistory, but continuously, right up to the present. Man's drive to play – to control an otherwise chaotic world – was what kept civilization going, what renewed it from one day to the next. Civilization 'does not come *from* play like a babe detaching itself from the womb', Huizinga proposed, but 'arises *in* and *as* play, and never leaves it'.

Wasn't it demeaning, however, to ground the achievements of civilization in play? How could something so frivolous and childish lead to something so solemn and grave? Didn't it belie the dignity of art to bring it down to so unserious a level? Schiller had anticipated this objection when he defended play as the most sublime and serious activity of which human beings were capable. Huizinga, too, would emphasize the distinction, meeting the charge that play was fun-damentally unserious with the claim that play was very serious indeed and capable of arousing in the players a most absorbed and intense concentration. Yet this relation between play and the serious wasn't really the issue. After a while it became pretty easy to take the seriousness of play as read. It was less on this than on the relation between play and reality that Huizinga was to rest his case. For the opposite of play was not so much what was serious but, rather, what was real.

As Huizinga saw it, play was serious precisely because it was opposed to reality. Play was, by definition, an activity which stood outside ordinary life, apart from the unruliness and imperfection of the everyday. The play-world was secluded and distinct – an artificial enclave or special preserve which, because rule-bound and time-bound, was removed from the on-going stream of surrounding events. Play wasn't bound up with the utilitarian or the material – with the bare necessities of scratching an existence, with eating, breeding, and self-defence. For this reason it could transcend such brutish needs and rise above the contingent. Play established a space in which disorder could be disciplined. Here formality and deliberation would obtain and could be exercised – could be practised to perfection – because untrammelled by the exigencies of daily life. 'Inside the play-ground an absolute and peculiar order reigns', Huizinga wrote, play 'creates order, *is* order. Into an imperfect world and into the confusion of life it brings a temporary, a limited perfection. Play demands order absolute and supreme'.

As his earlier study of medieval courtliness had shown him, however, such order needn't be limited to mere games. Play could be a whole way of life. Card games, board games, games of sport and games of chance, could perhaps be seen as ludic interludes, but only if understood literally – as intervals that came between the acts of a larger play. If play's basic characteristic was the imposing of order on chaos, then it could be argued to extend to virtually every aspect of human culture, from language – 'the first and supreme instrument which man shapes' – to any other activity which betrayed man's blessed rage for order. Though it might seem sacrilegious to suggest it, Huizinga said, there was in essence no difference between the hallowed space set aside for the game – the table, board, play-ground, pitch, field, theatre, or stadium – and that sacred spot consecrated to ritual. For – similarly set aside from everyday life, isolated, and performed with hushed solemnity and decorous ceremonial – the ritual act possessed all the characteristics of play. In the same way, the formalities of the tennis court were essentially the same as those of a court of law – another enclosed, contestatory, and rule-bound space. If rules regulated what happened on a sports pitch, the same could be said of the pitched battle where, again, a special place was set apart and the actions performed on it subjected to the rules of war. As a procedure for ordering his experience and for exerting his control over a changeable world, play showed man at his most creative and dignified. And it allowed Huizinga to extend the word's definition to include almost every conceivable aspect of human culture: language, ritual, courtship, poetry, myth, warfare, politics, science, law, and philosophy.

The theme was taken up by the French sociologist, Roger Caillois, who in 1946 reviewed *Homo Ludens* in an appendix to his book, *Man and the Sacred*, and who used this essay as the basis for a longer study, *Man, Play, and Games,* first published in 1958. Although he didn't agree that play could extend as far as the sacred, Caillois was in full accord with Huizinga's basic thesis that play and reality were distinct. Real life was a jungle where a thousand perils lay in wait. From out of this screeching, squawking environment, play carved a special place – a sanctuary, a blessed clearing where harried man could escape and fleet the time carelessly under conditions of his own devising. From this earliest distinction between a world that lay under human control and a surrounding chaos that didn't, there grew – as if by a natural process – a technical mastery over nature's resources which would lead ultimately to civilization, technology, and all the sophistications of city life. For Caillois, as for Huizinga, play represented a milestone in this development.

Caillois took up and developed several of the points Huizinga had made. Anyone who dismissed play as a trivial irrelevance, he argued, was going up the blind alley which tried to distinguish play from the serious. Toys or games which might at first have looked simply recreative – a meaningless sideline to adult life – were instead to be viewed as historical residues, the now-atrophied traces of something that had once been of the utmost importance. The mask, for example – in the modern world, a mere plaything for children – was regarded in less developed societies with a rapture and seriousness that bordered on awe. For Caillois, seeing toys and games as the relics of earlier times proved that play itself evolved. Where Huizinga had suggested that civilization evolved from play, Caillois proposed that play had an evolution of its own – that different kinds of play represented different stages on a scale which extended from the most childish and primitive games at one end to the most complex and sophisticated ones at the other. This meant, Caillois added, that you could tell what kind a society was by the kind of games it played – that you could establish a sociology derived from games.

At the simple end of the scale, Caillois put the generic type he labelled *paidia*. This was play at its most childlike – free, frolicsome, fun, raucous, and improvised. At the other he put *ludus*, where play was, by contrast, regulated, ordered, disciplined, systemized, and, eventually, institutionalized. That Caillois was – like Schiller, Freud, and Huizinga before him – collapsing the ontogenetic and phylogenetic categories into one another is clear from his choice of vocabulary. *Paidia* represented the world of childish things from which both individual and society at large would later develop. *Paidia* and *ludus* were not so much categories of play as ways of playing, and under these two broad headings Caillois was to unfold a whole typology.

Under the looser, freer *paidia* came mimicry – the invention of an imaginary world – and what Caillois called *ilinx* or vertigo – a category which included anything that aroused seizure or giddiness, from childish acts of swinging, twirling, or dashing about to the trance-inducing dance of the whirling dervishes or the orgiastic frenzies of shamanistic or Dionysian cults. Under the more orderly, regulated *ludus* came *alea* – or games of chance – and *agon* – games of sport, contests and competitions. Of the two, the former was the more regressive since it induced in the players a deplorably supine attitude to fate. But the game of chance still came under the heading of *ludus* because it was regulated and calculated. Chance was objectified there in a way that would have been impossible for the animal, savage, or child. For Caillois, however, the highest form of play was without doubt the *agon* – the organized game which took the human competitive spirit and channelled it away from rivalry and internecine strife towards the pursuit of excellence for its own sake. *Agon* was orientated towards success. It replaced man's proneness to chance – even a chance of his own making – with a cult of achievement. It encouraged and rewarded the trials and aspirations of human effort. *Agon* was meritocracy in action.

So it wasn't just that play was fundamentally creative and an important feature of civilized life. More than that, suggested Caillois, play itself had a history and aetiology. Not all play was equally creative. Play represented man's relation to his world but, in its earliest stages, that relation was still unstable and insecure. At that point, man still remained in thrall to magic and illusion. He had yet to bring himself and nature under the sway of reason, and the mastery which his play seemed to grant him was thus a false or a vain one. Individuals or societies which played this kind of game still had a fair way to go. But from this kind of game grew others of greater order and complexity, and to play these was to have made a critical step towards the light. For the essence of *ludus* was that self-mastery and sublimation of the instincts which lay at the heart of the civilizing process. Sometimes it was possible to see this development take place within a single culture. The Greeks, for instance, had moved from the excesses of Dionysian rites to that supreme example of the *agon*, the Olympian games. 'The world *evolution* acquires acceptable meaning', wrote Caillois, 'only if one is aware of the results obtained; that is, ceremonies and temples, the desire for order, harmony, proportion, logic, and science spring from a legendary background haunted by magic bands of dancers and black-smiths, Cyclopes and Curetes, Cabiri and Dactyls or Corybants, turbulent bands of terrifying, masked half-men and half-beasts, such as centaurs'. To move from one to the other was to pass through the narrow door which gave on to civilization, progress, and a future.

In 1971, the British psychoanalyst, Donald Winnicott, brought to-gether and published under the title *Playing and Reality* a number of papers which he'd published elsewhere. The book's theme was the founding role of play in the development of human creativity. Based on his experience as a paediatrician and psychotherapist, Winnicott's work was grounded in the analysis of patients – of babies and young children in particular – but, as he stressed in his introduction, this clinical material formed the basis for a much wider discussion. For the study of play had implications which extended beyond the clinic and the psychological particularities of individual cases to incorporate a whole cultural field, including both the creation and appreciation of works of art. Winnicott didn't refer to Schiller, but his own account of play as a potential space or intermediate area between inner and outer – feeling and form – had much in common with the poet's description of play as a middle state or 'third joyous kingdom' where the child first became a human being and where adult man could learn once again how to make himself whole.

Winnicott's ideas on play grew out of his work on a particular phenomenon that was an everyday occurrence and easy enough to observe – namely, that babies and very young children frequently became attached to, not to say inseparable from, a given object, most often a grubby bear or chewed bit of blanket. Isolating this phenomenon, Winnicott named it the 'transitional object' and, as he noted with a certain degree of satisfaction, in psychoanalytical circles the idea quickly 'caught on'. But what had so unremarkable and indeed unglamorous a feature of nursery life got to do with the higher reaches of art? The answer was that the transitional object occupied a critical place in the child's early development and helped bridge the gap between two different states which for Winnicott, no less than for Schiller, was essential for the subsequent growth of the human creative spirit.

In its earliest weeks, a new-born infant existed in a state of pure indeterminacy. With no sense of a distinction between subject and object or between itself and the world, the child and external reality formed a single, sensuous continuum. The baby subsisted in a symbiotic and dyadic relation with a mother who was still a long way from being recognized as separate. When the breast appeared for the child to suckle, it didn't, from the baby's perspective, come from the outside. Rather, suggested Winnicott, it was hallucinated or magically conjured by the infant itself. The job of the adaptive mother – the famous 'good-enough mother' – was to respond to her child's needs with a degree of sensitivity such that she was able to 'produce' the breast at exactly the point when the baby was ready to 'create' it. This situation would be repeated over and over again, with the child 'creating' the breast for itself countless times. Since the breast was not yet 'out there' but a continuation of the child's inner reality, its appearance seemed, from the child's point of view, to be of its own making and under its own omnipotent control. By fitting in with this, the mother afforded her child an opportunity for experiencing the wondrous illusion that the external world corresponded with its own capacity to create.

Such satisfactory mothering in a child's earliest weeks set up what Winnicott was to call the 'facilitating environment'. Through repetition and continuity, the mother had, all being well, succeeded in assuring her child that its environment was trustworthy and benign. This was important if not essential because it laid the foundations for the infant's ability to deal with the radical disillusionment that was to follow. For that early experience of omnipotent control was, sadly, not to last long. As the child began to swim up out of that primal fog, the dawning sense of a subject/object division brought with it the uncomfortable realization that external reality was a separate thing. Not only was reality no longer under the child's magical control but, worse still, it became a stubborn source of quite unasked-for – not to say undeserved – frustrations. This sudden loss of omnipotence was an experience of 'immense shock' to the child, one which Winnicott did nothing to downplay. The next task awaiting the good-enough mother was to shepherd her child through this period of disillusionment – to teach it that reality was no longer its own to command but something that had to be adapted to.

This fall from grace was neither easy nor quick. The child had to be helped, cajoled into relinquishing that state of bliss, and something had to be brought in to relieve the strain of its tumble into reality. Here the world of play stood ready to ease the transition; and this was the place of the transitional object. For, as Winnicott clarified, it wasn't the object itself that was transitional. Rather, it represented 'the infant's transition from a state of being merged with the mother to a state of being in relation to the mother as something outside and separate'. The qualities of the transitional object were paradoxical. On the one hand, it was most definitely not a hallucination or figment of the child's imagination. It was a separate, concrete object, 'the first 'not-me' possession'. On the other hand, it differed from other objects in the child's world – toys, pets, furniture, parents, or siblings – in that it was endowed with special, even magical qualities and, as a result, was clung to with a quite uncompromising ferocity, and absolutely could not be substituted, mended, or altered in any way – even washed.

The transitional object was so-called because it stood halfway between that illusory world, over which the child had experienced apparently total control, and the real world, over which it hadn't. It occupied a 'potential space' that was neither inside nor outside – neither the child's inner psychic reality nor the external world – but somewhere between the two, on the border between fantasy and fact. Winnicott stressed the paradox. The transitional object was already out there as a concrete object yet at the same time it was also created by the child as if from nothing. It was both taken from the world and given to it – a paradox which recalls Schiller's description of play as a drive which aimed 'so to receive as if it had itself brought forth, and so to bring forth as the intuitive sense aspires to receive'. The transitional object enabled the child to negotiate the difficult passage between illusion and reality. Establishing the child's capacity to create, invent, originate, devise, think and dream up forms, the transitional object marked the beginnings – however humble – not only of that particular child's creativity but ultimately of all human art. The connection between the two was a given. For, like Schiller, it was Winnicott's aim to draw attention to 'a third area, that of play, which expands into creative living and into the whole cultural life of man'.

One way or another, Schiller, Huizinga, Caillois, and Winnicott all stress the creative and civilizing power of play. And, although coming from different disciplines and specializations, it's noticeable how readily, for each of them, the story of play becomes a story of progress. For Schiller and Winnicott, play showed the way out of sickness into health for society and individual alike. Winnicott wanted to develop a therapy in which the patient would learn how to play, for play facilitated personal growth and led to the formation of group relationships. For Schiller, teaching man how to play was the cure for all social ills, and at the end of his *Aesthetic Education* he looked ahead to the utopia of the 'Aesthetic State'. For him, this was society at its optimum – a place where, perfected by play, man would submit not to might or to right but to freedom. This was the only way to make society real, Schiller urged, for it 'consummates the will of the whole through the nature of the individual'. For Caillois, too, *agon* was the highest form of play because the entire social structure depended on it: social progress consisted in developing and improving the conditions for competitive play. And, for Huizinga, play not only formed the basis for civilization but civilization itself was something played. That play was progress was the important thing. This came above everything else and transcended any difference of political persuasion. Whatever a particular writer's preferred image of the perfect state, play was still the way to get there. For Huizinga, with his grounding in medieval courtliness, play was essentially gentlemanlike – a matter of good sport and fair play. For Caillois, by contrast, *agon* epitomized a more democratic ideal where advantages once bestowed by the accident of birth could now be achieved through merit and open competition.

It's true that, with his tendency to see things 'on the wane', Huizinga presented contemporary civilization as in decline. In his view, modern man had forgotten how to play and this was nowhere more evident than in changing attitudes to war. So long as wars had been fought according to recognized conventions – to the underlying code of honour which respected the parties as antagonists with equal rights – warfare could be treated as a form of *agon*. But the modern concept of total war had put paid to that noble ideal. And Huizinga's remark that war left the bounds of civilization once it was waged 'outside the sphere of equals, against groups not recognized as human beings' – written as it was in 1938 – reads now with an ominous poignancy.

But this didn't contradict the basic argument. On the contrary, it only underlined the point that play was creative, civilizing, and progressive. A decline in play meant a decline in civilization, and the degeneration of culture was – for Schiller as much as for Huizinga – only a symptom of man's failure to play. The thesis remained intact. Play imposed order on chaos. It submitted uncertainty to human control and, in separating its own regulated world from a disorderly world outside, it marked the first step towards civilization. It made man the master of his environment. It submitted that environment to rules of man's own making, rules which at first would lead on to and then daily reinforce the principles of order, justice, and law. At its furthest, play showed man at his most dignified and sublime. It was what singled him out from the animals, and what made him proud to be a human being.

III

Where – if allowed to develop unimpeded – might this great march towards progress end? How far could it go? It really seemed the sky was the limit. From the most unpromising of beginnings – a chewed bit of blanket or cotton-reel toy – the most wonderful things would arise: art, drama, culture, technology – in a word, civilization as we know it. In these progressivist accounts, play began when the newborn's illusory control over reality gave way to the child's actual control over his own small world of self-invented objects and self-created roles. From this developed the game – or, rather, an infinite variety of games, all with different degrees of complexity, but in each of which, one way or another, the play-world was controlled – regulated, delimited, and strictly separated off from a chaotic reality outside. From this enclosed world of play, in turn, derived those principles with which man would come to shape and order that outside world – to tame it, civilize it, and bring it under his own control. Where might this great technological advance end up? It had already made huge strides . . . it's even put men on the moon . . . could it make man master of the universe? The newborn's illusion of control seemed capable of becoming a reality.

For Schiller, Huizinga and the others, play was of crucial importance – so trivial a subject worth discussing – precisely because it had implications which went beyond the world of childish things. A game was only a microcosm of something larger. It allowed observers like Caillois or Winnicott to show operating in miniature principles of order or competition which – when put into action in the wider world – would have the most far-reaching of effects. In the history of the individual or of society at large, play may once have been a form of escape – men may have fled from a world they couldn't control into one which they felt they could. But, in the accounts of play we've just looked at, this control of the play-world had a way of extending outwards towards a control of reality. Mastery in play came to confirm mastery of the world. Civilization, as Huizinga put it, was played. It was true that games still invited man to turn his back on the world, to turn his captivated gaze inwards towards the centre of the magic circle he'd made, be it theatre, stadium, or gaming-table. But, as a general principle of order, play also encouraged him to look up and away – outwards towards reality and to a world which, if it really were as subject to his control as the world of play, was indeed a thing of beauty and a source of understandable pride. Play stood at the transitional point (the formula is becoming familiar) between a world of man's own making and the larger world in which he found himself placed. It put his world in relation with the cosmos and invited a comparison between the two.

One way of putting this idea was to say that play put man in relation with the divine. This, at least, was how Plato expressed it, for in book seven of the *Laws* he wrote:

> I mean that we should keep our seriousness for serious things, and not waste it on trifles, and that, while God is the real goal of all beneficent serious endeavour, man, as we said before, has been constructed as a toy for God, and this is, in fact, the finest thing about him. All of us, then, men and women alike, must fall in with our role and spend life in making our *play* as perfect as possible . . . Hence it is peace in which each of us should spend most of his life and spend it best. What, then, is our right course? We should pass our lives in the playing of games – *certain* games, that is, sacrifice, song, and dance – with the result of ability to gain Heaven's grace, and to repel and vanquish an enemy when we have to fight him.

If man saw himself as a plaything of the gods, Plato judged, he would develop a suitably reverential attitude towards the divine. To see life as play – as a play of the gods – was to put things in their proper perspective, to learn to distinguish what was truly serious from what only seemed to be so. People were too easily embroiled in their fraught and busy world, too easily preoccupied with things that only seemed to be of immediate moment or concern. Seeing the world *sub specie ludi*, by contrast, would teach man his proper place as a humble creature in a cosmos ruled by powers that were beyond his control.

Yet for Plato there was also a direct correspondence between man and the gods – an equivalence that was specifically to be expressed in play. Man may have been the gods' mere toy, but play also elevated him to their level. For the philosopher it followed logically that, if the gods played, then man should play too. In his playing, man was god-like. Imitating the gods brought out what was best in him. Play put man in relation with the gods – it humbled him but it also raised him up, it prostrated him but also allowed him to approach the gods with something nearing equality. Moreover, play wasn't only transitional – it could also be transactional. Through play, men could communicate if not negotiate with the gods – an idea that was summed up in the act of propitiation, in the games, sacrifices, singing and dancing which Plato listed as different ways of living life as play. Earlier, in book two of the *Laws*, Plato had suggested that rhythm and harmony were divine gifts bestowed on men by Apollo and Dionysus. Without these gifts, men would have remained like young children or animals, spon-taneously leaping and darting about, uttering unformed cries of joy or fear. But, bequeathed by the gods, rhythm and harmony transformed this disorder into order, converted these uncontrolled movements and sounds into dance and song. The order that resulted was necessarily pleasing and that pleasure could be defined, Plato suggested, as play (*paidia*). In play, men were the humble, chastened recipients of gifts from on high, without which they would have been as mere children. But they were also ennobled and humanized. These gifts allowed them to imitate the gods and to render back to their benefactors – in the form of worthily ordered games, sacrifices, dances, and songs – the very thing that make them god-like. In play, men shadowed the gods. They presented themselves to the gods in the gods' own image and reverently gave back what they took – in the hope, naturally, of receiving more. Propitiation was a reciprocal gesture – which was why it was supposed to work.

Plato made the connection between ritual and play, and Huizinga – who saw himself following in the same tradition – approvingly quoted this passage at least twice in *Homo Ludens*. Not only did it underline

29

the formal similarities between play and ritual – from the beginning Huizinga had described the spot set apart for the game in sacred terms, as consecrated and hallowed. It also endorsed what was perhaps his most contentious claim, namely that play could be extended to include the holy. For Huizinga, ritual was – like play – a humanly created world of order, ceremony, and design. It related man to the wider world – in this case, a world of spirits and gods whose greater powers the ritual act was designed to appease. The order of ritual – which developed into a stickling for exactitude, a need to repeat certain procedures and formulae to the letter – was supposed to invoke a corresponding order in that wider world. Ritual had its origins in play, Huizinga believed, and in it 'man's consciousness that he is embedded in a sacred order of things finds its first, highest, and holiest expression'.

Roger Caillois was unconvinced. Discussing Huizinga's book in *Man and the Sacred*, Caillois agreed that play and ritual were equally serious and that, formally speaking, they were identical – both did indeed presume a special place, rigorously set apart from the ordinary run of events. But, as far as their functions were concerned, play and ritual couldn't have been more different – indeed, they were diametrically opposed. In play, man was carefree and cavorted happily – safe from the dangers and encroachments of real life. The player submitted himself to risk but only to a risk of his own making, one that was carefully controlled in advance and quite different from the unknown perils which lurked in the real world and which were liable to rain down on him from above without warning or any consideration of desert. It was with a sigh of relief that, escaping from reality into play, he left life's myriad uncertainties behind. But in the sacred it was the other way round. Here man came face to face with what terrified him most – with those dark, inexorable forces that overpowered his will and exceeded his understanding. Here the mood wasn't playful but abject – man was supplicant, awe-struck, and entranced. The celebrant didn't flee from reality into ritual but the reverse – he staggered dizzily from the temple back into daylight, relieved to return from the mysteries to the mundane familiarities of ordinary life. If in play man was a creator – in control of his self-made world – in the sacred he was a mere creature, haplessly subject to greater powers that were beyond his control.

Yet, in describing the ritual act, Caillois didn't in fact oppose play and ritual so much as show one to be a microcosm of the other. The differences he described – of purpose or of mood – were differences of degree but not of kind. In play, man protected his own, small, created world – the rule-bound world of the game – from the chaos that was perceived to lie outside. In ritual, he sought to protect his reality – the world in which he found himself – from the larger chaos that was perceived to lie beyond that. But the two weren't opposed: one was only a smaller version of the other. The play-world fitted inside the real world, and the rules of ritual sought to preserve the order of that real world in the same way that the rules of the game sought to preserve the order of play. Play and ritual may not have been the same but a continuity still lay between them. The play-world was knowingly and deliberately fashioned – often with beautiful or ingenious results. The same could not be said of the external world which could be ugly, treacherous, and unreliable. But, through the ritual act, the external world was still conceived of as something at least theoretically order*able* – as either a potential order which could be worked on and altered for the better, or an existent order which could be upset and altered for the worse.

In effect, as Plato had suggested, ritual treated reality *as if* it were play. Admittedly, it was someone else's play – the play of perhaps malevolent gods. But, if treated as such, reality could at least begin to be thought of as modelled on human play – as similarly hedged about, ordered, and protected from uncertainties outside. Play was what made the connection, what brought the gods over to man's side or suggested a point of comparison between the two. It was play that pointed up the wished-for similarity between a self-made world which man did control and an external reality which he didn't but would have liked to. As Huizinga had suggested, play gave rise to ritual. For the whole point of ritual was to establish this connection and to use it as a bargaining counter in brokering deals with the higher powers. As Caillois concluded, in fact, man resorted to ritual to try and exert some kind of control over the future – to bring about victory or avert disaster. Man may have been nothing but a plaything of the gods, but by doing what he did in play – by imposing order on chaos and by turning otherwise formless movements and cries into regulated mimes and chants – man made ritual. And in ritual he mirrored the gods, faced them on their own terms.

Some forms of ritual made this connection between man and god more explicit than others. Plato had listed games, sacrifices, singing and dancing as kinds of play – forms whose beauty and regularity imitated that of the gods. But there were also rituals which would come nearer to our definition of plays – dramatic productions and theatrical shows – in which men didn't simply imitate the orderliness of the gods but went so far as to imitate the gods themselves. In the *City of God,* Saint Augustine described how the Greeks and Romans put on theatrical performances in which they represented the various rivalries and adulteries of the gods in acted narrative. These were no grunting chants but sophisticated, highly crafted, and specifically literary productions which displayed the powers of human creativity at their height. According to Augustine, the pagans believed these shows to have been expressly commanded by their gods who took delight in seeing themselves represented and who threatened displeasure if any part of the spectacle was omitted or under-performed. Since these shows were based on a fundamental identification between god and man, they became the ultimate form of propitiation – the practice had begun in the fourth century BC when dramatic representations of (and to) the gods were made to ward off the effects of a particularly virulent plague. So closely were these plays bound up with ritual that the Greeks revered their actors as profoundly as their priests. And, although the Romans didn't go that far, holding actors in lower esteem, they still admitted these theatrical shows to be an essential element of their religious devotions.

Augustine attacked this kind of play. He frothed venomously against the theatrical rituals he described not only because they openly displayed scenes of abomination and wickedness but because – which was much worse – they represented the gods in the first place. If the gods were capable of being represented, didn't that make them mere representations? Play marked a continuity between man and the divine – it revealed man in the image of the gods. But the mirror reflected both ways, and Augustine was concerned with what happened when he looked in the other direction. From this perspective the gods themselves began to look disturbingly like human beings. If play was able to dignify men – to raise them above the level of animals and children, allow them to imitate the gods and aspire to excellence – there was also another side to the story. For play also threatened to debunk the gods – to bring them down to the level of men, to reduce them to poor, shrunken things, mere imagos of their inventors. As far as Augustine was concerned, this opened the flood-gates on the pagan gods once and for all, for nothing so clearly revealed them to be mere fictions, projections of the human mind. People were still disputing whether or not actors deserved as much honour as priests, given that the ceremonies they performed had been instituted by the gods. 'How is it', asked Augustine, amazed, 'that the inference has not rather been drawn that they themselves are not real gods and are not in the least worthy to be accorded divine honours by the community?'. What Augustine mocked in the ritualistic dramas of late antiquity was the absurdity of men imitating gods who were so patently imitations of themselves. Putting its faith in such false gods, it was scarcely surprising that Roman civilization was falling apart, Augustine thought, its moral fibre weakened and unable to withstand the barbarian hordes in the aftermath of whose decisive sack of Rome he was writing.

For Augustine, play made the connection between man and god too explicit – it put them in perilously close relation. But it wasn't, of course, a question of abolishing that relation altogether. He attacked play because it brought man and god too close together – it suggested a continuity between like and like, an identification between the two which had a way of collapsing one into the other. In such circumstances what people badly needed was a transcendent Deity – one sufficiently elevated that any danger of his being taken for an idol would be removed for good, a supreme Creator who could never again be mistaken for a creation of the human mind. This, he believed, was available in the form of the Christian God who, unlike the classical pantheon of all too recognizably human deities, was mysterious, apart, and One. But, even if Augustine's aim was to set man and God as far apart from each other as he could, it obviously wasn't his aim to sever their relation altogether. He wanted to separate man from God – to put them at opposite poles – but not to divorce them. The Christian was to keep a safe, awed distance from God, to look up at him from a long way off, peer humbly as if through the wrong end of the telescope. But, however far away, God was still an object of veneration and still very much in relation with his creatures. Christianity may not have called it play – and may not have represented God in ritualistic dramas of propitiation – but its acts of worship took this idea of a relation for granted. And, in any case, the Augustinian God – that supreme Author or Architect of the universe whose powers of composition were such that even the most sublime acts of human creativity were but copies of his inimitable perfection – was as closely modelled on man as any. For Augustine, God's architectonic powers were essentially those – only exponentially magnified – of the artist.

However far away you stood from a mirror, in other words, it would still reflect both ways. Man remained in relation with the divine wherever he was placed in the scheme of things – whether humblingly remote or flatteringly close-up. It was a difference of degree not of

33

kind. Play pointed up that connection – it made it possible to look in either direction or in both directions at once. But it was a matter of emphasis and definition, not of wiping play off the map. It was possible to regard play as dangerous – as liable to shrink the divine to unacceptably human proportions – and therefore to downplay it, as Augustine did, by abolishing stagey rituals and refusing to confuse acts of worship with something so intrinsically childish. But it was also possible to be more comfortable with the idea of play, better able or inclined to accommodate the implications of its double vision. It was possible to make explicit what Augustine wanted to conceal, to spell out the connection that play made between man and the divine. Indeed, it was possible to play with the tricks of perspective which this double vision allowed – to make sudden shifts from the over-awed, long-distance view to dramatic fore-shortenings which brought man and God face to face.

The age-old metaphor of life as a play exercised these optical illusions with particular economy, holding in fascinated juxtaposition the two different ways of looking at the world. Either man could be viewed as the mere creature of an alien, mysterious and distant God, a puppet in someone else's play, a pawn in another's game. Or life could be seen as organized according to principles of order and design which, if emulated by human beings, made them god-like and able, potentially, to civilize their world and master their universe. However you looked at God or man, play still stood between the two. The world-as-stage motif tended to put both perspectives together in one dizzying moment of double focus. At one end of the scale, the more remote God was, the more humble were his creatures. But the more perfect God's order was, the more noble was its imitation by humankind. And the greater the achievement of mankind, the likelier it was for man to see himself as god-like. The more possible it was, in fact – by now moving towards the other end of the scale – for man to see himself as God's very inventor, especially when he had cleverly epitomized all this in a single poetic metaphor.

Even when invoked to lament life's absurd defiance of logic or human justice, the play metaphor still offered some residual consolation. Man might be a mere puppet jerking around on an alien stage – the only account of 'this ridiculous world' for Sir Walter Ralegh, writing from prison in 1612. But this play was still presumed to be scripted and plotted in advance. However inaccessible or unintelligible the script, it still postulated a God – 'the Author of all our tragedies', Ralegh called him – an Author whose divine word was, moreover, being imitated by the writer even at the moment of speaking his existential despair. And, at the most nihilistic extreme – where God as an object of imitation or awe had disappeared altogether into an interminably awaited Godot – it was still the play metaphor that came to hand. In the absence of God, the playwright could reproduce in his own dramas a human tragi-comedy which, for all its futility and absurdity, was nonetheless still authored by human beings.

Augustine may have wanted to suppress plays but he couldn't suppress the play metaphor. The image of life as a play had a remit broad enough to make it pretty well indestructible. For it did no more nor less than situate man in the wider world, put him in relation with the cosmos. Exactly where on the scale he might be placed within the overall order of things was a matter for the individual conscience. The play metaphor was flexible enough to stretch from awe down to nihilism – from seeing man as a mere plaything of the gods to seeing him as sole playwright of the universe. The play metaphor made it possible to take up any position between the two, including the paradoxical view that man was both imitating an external order that was divinely ordained, and, at the same time, imposing on nature an order of his own ori-ginating. The image of the world as a stage could accommodate the atheist as well as the saint, for its basic premise was the idea of order and control. Whether that order was attributed to God, to the gods, or to man was, ultimately, neither here nor there.

Take game theory, for example – an account of rational decision-making and strategic planning which was developed in the 1940s by the Hungarian mathematician and physicist, John von Neumann, and the German-born economist, Oskar Morgenstern, whose joint book, *Theory of Games and Economic Behaviour*, was published in 1953. Combining mathematics and economics, they used games as the starting point for a theory of rational behaviour which came to have significant implications for military strategy and financial planning. The theory began with the simplest games – ones which involved the players in a choice between two strictly delimited alternatives: as, for example, when two players each turn over a coin. If the two coins match, the first player wins, if they don't, the second does. What mattered in games such as these was the strategy involved. It was no good the first player playing to win – repeatedly turning up heads, for example – for the second player would quickly catch on and respond accordingly, turning up tails. The point of the game was to keep your opponent in the dark, and the best way to do that in this particular case was to simulate the randomness of chance.

From these simple games the theory moved on and upwards to more complex situations involving many more players and a multiple range of choices – choices which might fall between conflicting if not incommensurable alternatives. Such 'games' were relational – and the decisions taken during them interactive – in that they depended on the behaviour of the other players, behaviour that both could and could not be predicted ahead of time. This, in turn, opened out onto a whole conspiratorial world where winning – or, rather, not losing – became a matter of outwitting one's opponents: of knowing their motives and guessing their intentions, but also of being ready to intercept their deceptions and to counter these with false trails, bluffs, and counter-bluffs of one's own. This was the world of military intelligence and economic forecasting where awareness was the name of the game. Game theory assumed that individuals would operate on a rational basis. Given as much information as possible – information which it was the players' job to garner and decipher – individuals would act rationally, would base their decisions on what they knew and act accordingly. It was true that they had to operate in an imperfect world where not everything was known and not every fact was at everyone's fingertips all of the time. But game theory offered a strategy for rational compromise – for making the best of the situation which the circumstances would allow, for maximizing the chances of success by minimizing the chances of failure. Game theory enabled people to calculate probability and so to manage risk.

The game metaphor suggested itself because to see man as a player – as *homo ludens* – was primarily to see him as a rational animal. Von Neumann and Morgenstern deplored the then-prevalent Keynesian view that emotional and psychological factors necessarily muddied any rigorously mathematical understanding of economics. For them, this was a regressive throw-back to the misty days of intuition and guesswork which had pre-dated the advances of modern science. Game theory, by contrast, postulated a totality of information. Even if it wasn't known by a particular individual at any one time, total information could at least theoretically be known. The facts were out there to be ascertained. Partial information could lead to total information given world enough and time. If the information-gathering were exhaustive or optimally efficient, everything could eventually be brought to light – all the relevant data made available, all the strategies, ruses, and devices of the participants exposed to view. The rational player was part of a rational world, in other words, and game theory – itself a supremely rational system – made the connection between the two, putting men on the progressive road towards full knowledge and promising to change people's lives 'once a fuller understanding of human behaviour has been achieved'. Like chaos theory, game theory implied that there was an order out there if only everything could be known, and that – however difficult to measure or understand, however infinite or complex the chain of causation – there was still, at bottom, a reason for things. Game theory had little to do with the cultural manifestations of play – with drama or ritual. But the play metaphor lent itself so readily because its underlying ideas were order, intelligence, and control. Whether omniscience was attributed to God, man, or a supercomputer in the end made very little difference – at least, not to the idea of play.

The mathematical calculation of probability went back to the seventeenth century. In fact, it began with the question of gambling debts. In the early 1650s, the Chevalier de Méré – a French nobleman, amateur mathematician and philosopher with a passion for gaming – put to the young mathematical prodigy, Blaise Pascal, a brain-teaser that had foxed mathematicians for centuries. If two players – of equal skill – laid equal bets on a game of chance and then proceeded to play but were, for one reason or another, interrupted when one of the players was ahead but not the outright winner, how should the stakes fairly be divided between them? Given that one of the players had a better chance of winning than the other, was it possible to calculate the probability of his doing so exactly, and, if so, to take this into account in awarding him his fair share?

This question had come to be known as the 'problem of the points', and to work it out Pascal entered into a correspondence with one of the greatest mathematicians of the time, Pierre de Fermat. Between them they solved the problem and gave birth to probability calculus. In a letter to Fermat dated 29 July 1654, Pascal began by posing a simple case: suppose two players were playing a game in which either needed three wins to succeed outright, and suppose that each had made a pledge of 32 pistoles (a pistole was a gold coin worth about 16 or 17 English shillings at the time). The game was broken off when the first player – call him A – had won two points, the second, B, one. How should the stakes be distributed? Pascal's answer was as follows: were A to have won the next game, he would have been the outright winner, entitled to sweep the stakes and take all 64 pistoles. Were B to have won it, on the other hand, both players would have been evenly matched with two wins apiece, so the stakes could have been divided equally between them – effectively restoring them to the positions they'd been in at the beginning of the game. At the point of the interruption, then, A was guaranteed at least 32 pistoles – if he lost, he'd be no worse off than when he'd started. But he also had a 50% chance of winning the other 32 pistoles as well. For the stakes to be divided justly, therefore, A should receive 32 + 16 = 48 pistoles, and B the remaining 16 (= 32 – 16). By this means, the probability of an unknown outcome was quantified, and from this simple example Pascal and Fermat went on to elaborate ever more complex cases involving greater numbers of players and an infinite number of games.

In the course of their calculations, however, it never occurred to either mathematician to ask why the gamblers should pay their debts in the first place or what would happen if they didn't – if, for example, A had suddenly made over all his winnings to B in a spontaneous gesture of generosity, or if B, piqued at discovering that A had been sleeping with his wife, seized the whole pile of coins in a fit of morally righteous revenge. That Pascal and Fermat didn't indulge in such imaginative speculations can hardly be a matter for surprise. They were mathematicians, after all, not novelists. The Chevalier would have considered them quite insane had they started musing about the exploits of A and B. For them, it was axiomatic that debts were paid, and A and B were simply abstractions with which to calculate probability. For that was the point: Pascal and Fermat solved the problem of uncertainty by calculating it. Theirs was a breakthrough because they devised a way of quantifying an outcome that was unknown, of submitting uncertainty to measurement and so of putting it under human control. The vagaries of A and B – or B's wife, for that matter – were contingencies that lay outside the field of the calculable. And the not paying of debts lay out there too – as a possibility not thought of or, if it had been, banished as an absurd irrelevance, as one of an infinity of possible occurrences that could neither be calculated nor controlled.

The correspondence between Pascal and Fermat broke off suddenly on 27 October 1654. Shortly afterwards, Pascal underwent a religious conversion, retired from the world, and entered into an ascetic retreat as a lay member of the monastery of Port-Royal in Paris. But, although he gave up the practice of mathematics (in a valedictory letter to Fermat dated 10 August, 1660, he described it as 'useless' and 'only a craft') he nonetheless applied what he'd discovered about probability to his new situation. For it opened out onto questions of decision-making – on how one should act in situations of uncertainty. From Port-Royal, Pascal turned these thoughts to a consider the most profound and consequential case of all. If a person were uncertain as to the existence of God, how should he live his life? The result of Pascal's meditation was the famous 'wager', first published in the collection of fragments known as the *Pensées* in 1670:

> God is, or is not. But towards which side will we lean? Reason cannot decide anything. There is an infinite chaos separating us. At the far end of this infinite distance a game is being played and the coin will come down heads or tails. How will you wager?

Pascal's wager took the form of an imagined dialogue between himself and an intelligent doubter. Pascal didn't attempt to persuade the latter of the existence of God. Instead, he aimed to show the most rational course of action that was open to him, given his state of uncertainty. He presented his case in terms of a ratio between two quantities: one finite – earthly life, and the other infinite – the afterlife. Suppose the doubter chose to live his life as if the infinite did not exist – that is, to live a life of pleasure, hedonism, and excess. If he turned out to be right then nothing would be lost. But if he turned out to be wrong – and the infinite did exist – then he would have lost everything. Worse than that, he would have struck the most terrible bargain, because he would in effect have sacrificed the infinite for the price of what was merely finite – given up the possibility of eternal reward for the few paltry pleasures of earth – the Faustian dilemma. He would, in other words, have paid massively over the odds. Given that the existence of God could not definitively be known one way or the other – that remained a matter for the faith which the doubter was unable or unwilling to muster – then his wisest and most prudential course, Pascal demonstrated, was to bet that God did exist and to act accordingly, by leading an upright life, attending Mass, and so forth. In that case, the most that he could lose, if he turned out to be wrong, was finite – the mere pleasures of an earthly life. But what he stood to gain, in the other eventuality, was infinite – eternal life. In other words, he would have made a very good bargain indeed. The most reasonable course was therefore to behave as if God did exist – to pay a finite price for what, at the worst, would be a finite loss, but what, at the best, would be an infinite gain. Put like that, it seemed pretty persuasive.

It's noticeable that, in transferring his mathematical speculations to the theological sphere, Pascal continued to take it for granted that the gambler would pay his debts. That rule remained as axiomatic for the players in this game – man and God – as it did for A and B. Indeed, the human gambler couldn't not pay his debts, for he was engaged in paying his side of the bargain simply by virtue of being alive. His finite, earthly life, whether good or bad, was what he put into the pot and, whether he lost it for nothing or gained eternal life for it, he still couldn't get it back again at the end. The human partner in this game was not in a position to renege on his debts. But Pascal assumed with equal assurance that God too would honour his word. That God might cheat or back out of the deal didn't enter into the calculations. It went without saying that God would keep his side of the bargain and reward the virtuous man with eternal life. The logic of the wager depended on it. This was the premise from which all followed: either God existed, in which case the doubter's choice of life could affect his chances of eternal reward, or he didn't, in which case it didn't matter anyway. It wasn't a possibility that God might exist but change his mind at the last minute out of spite, delinquency, or sheer fun. For Pascal, this was unthinkable – the equivalent to God not existing at all. Either God paid his debts or he didn't exist. There was no third alternative. A maverick, cheating God wouldn't be God. Like his contemporary, René Descartes, Pascal rested his faith on the fact that a good God would not deceive us.

This good God may have been a long way off, at an infinite distance from human endeavour and understanding – mysterious, baffling, and remote. But he was still assumed to be reasonable. Human reason may have been unable to comprehend him or prove his existence – Pascal didn't even attempt it – but it could at least assume some kind of continuity with him. There were certain things on which God and man were agreed. The paying of debts attached effect to cause: if the gamble paid off, the gambler would win, if it didn't, he would lose. This logic was never open to question, and the fact that it wasn't preserved the binding and absolute nature of the contract. God was bound to keep his Word – indeed, the Word was God.

The gaming metaphor, like the play metaphor, put man in relation with God. It linked the two together as partners in a deal. In this respect, they mirrored each other across the void, no matter how vast the distance was between them. In Pascal's image, they faced each other as slightly wary but, at bottom, basically gentlemanly players tossing coins across an infinite expanse of green baize. The doubter might at this stage have reflected that they looked rather like one another. But, whether it was an eternal rule laid down by God and merely imitated by his humble creatures, or whether an expression of their own control over uncertainty which they then projected out into an eternal godhead, either way, the logic of cause and effect remained paramount. Whether you were a believer, an atheist, or somewhere in between, this rule remained in force – and the play metaphor allowed for all possibilities. Whatever else, the rule that debts made in play must be paid remained sacrosanct – to be held to and respected by cheat, doubter, philosopher, hermit, and saint alike.

Of the Death of God,
Deconstruction, and Play

If there was one person who changed all this, it was someone who could, depending on which way you looked at him, be described as any – or, indeed, as all – of these things: the brilliant young philology professor turned freelance philosopher who, in 1882, took it upon himself to announce to a shocked world – or, to be more accurate, to an unprepared and, at that stage, still relatively inattentive world – the news that God was dead. Not unlike the mythical madman in whose mouth he put his famous pronouncement, Friedrich Nietzsche saw himself as coming too early, as ahead of his time. The scandalized silence, dumb astonishment, or frank indifference which greeted his words in Book Three of *The Gay Science* showed him that the world was not yet ready for them, and not for several years would they be heeded or granted the seriousness with which they would subsequently come to radicalize philosophy and open the way to a post-modern world. To credit Nietzsche with bringing revolution about single-handedly is not entirely a figure of speech. No individual thinker had gone so far before – none had broken so decisively with religion nor so effectively smashed that good old God of former times into a thousand redundant pieces.

Which is not to say that Nietzsche was an enemy to play. Indeed, if anything, his could be seen as the ultimate philosophy of play, its supreme quality that of playfulness. He was writing about play from the beginning – from the opening page of his first book, *The Birth of Tragedy* (1872) – where he suggested that the contest or *agon* in which Apollo and Dionysus confront each other in taut compromise – their respective tendencies towards words and music pulling in opposite directions – in turn gave rise to that other archetypal form of play,

Greek tragedy. There were echoes of Schiller here – the drives towards form and sense locked together in productive combat in a third realm of play and aesthetic creation. In Nietzsche's later works, this struggle came to be internalized within the single individual – the Superman eternally wrestling with competing drives inside himself, forging a dialectic between form and chaos in an unceasing act of creativity and heroic self-mastery. But the model for such embattled productivity was always the sportive *agon* of ancient Greece, and, in 'Homer's Contest' – a fragment written in 1872 though only published posthumously – Nietzsche described the spirit of competition and struggle for superiority which the ancient contest enshrined: a restless, bristling energy, a determination to succeed at all costs and to prove oneself by putting others down. The *agon* was a source of life to the Hellenic state, renewing it, spurring its members on, stimulating them to feats of ever greater excellence and perfection. The superlative individual destroyed the competition for he had no equal, no sparring partner to fight with, and the only place for such a person was *hors de concours* – traditionally either ostracism or exile. For Nietzsche, no further proof was needed that 'the contest is necessary to preserve the health of the state'.

On the face of it, this sounds very like Roger Caillois who, nearly a hundred years later, was to describe *agon* as the highest form of play and as the basis for every civilized society. But, in the course of arriving at his own estimate of play, Nietzsche had pulverized everything that the likes of Caillois stood for. His *agon* was not the open competition and fair play of Caillois' description but a vicious fight to the death powered by all the teeth-gritting energies of rivalry, envy, and hatred. In his hierarchy of play forms, Caillois had ranked *agon* above the frenzied, hypnotic, and orgiastic cults of what he called 'Dionysian societies' – cultures he had no qualm in describing as primitive and the emergence from which was, in his eyes, a prerequisite for the birth of civilization. Caillois didn't describe the latter as Apollonian – nor did he mention Nietzsche – but it's obvious that the opposite of the Dionysian represented everything he considered civilized – order, progress, and stability. For him, *agon* led to civilized life, it was played by civilized societies, and it strengthened civilization by cultivating the very values of reason and rule which constituted civilization itself. The shift from the throbbing paroxysm of the Dionysian rites to the regulated serenity of the competitive game gave rise to a 'new social order' and could be described as progress in so many words.

For Nietzsche, however, such an attitude towards civilization – as prevalent in his own day as it was in that of Caillois – represented the most pernicious smugness and self-satisfaction, the most odious, puffed-up, and misplaced pride. It was to be the object of his lifelong antipathy and of wave after wave of his batteried assaults. It was in *The Birth of Tragedy* that Nietzsche first elaborated the startling reversal that would come to characterize all his writings. Everything that was most valued and esteemed – everything that the word 'civilized' conjured up – everything serene, orderly, advanced, and refined was not, in fact, to be thought of as the glittering culmination of some great march towards improvement and progress but, on the contrary, as the most pathetic and cringing decline. What industrialized, urban society most con-gratulated itself on – its art, science, technology, and education – were not achievements of the spirit but rather symptoms of its over-exhaustion and disease. Instead of seeing the Dionysian as some crude, primaeval regression thankfully left behind for the sunnier climes of an en-lightened, civilized existence, Nietzsche saw it as mysteriously powerful and strong, and the latter as, by contrast, atrophied, effete, lethargic, fussy, and overblown. To the dismay of his academic colleagues, he blew apart their most cherished values – logic, precision, and accuracy – and poured blistering scorn on the scholar and librarian as mole-like, pettifogging creatures who would have been beneath contempt had they – and the values they held most dear – not evidently been so satisfying to grind to a pulp.

As Nietzsche saw it, western civilization had early fallen victim to a perverse and invidious rationalism which had stymied the Dionysian spirit for good and had killed Greek tragedy – then embodied in the works of Aeschylus – in its cradle. It wasn't an overdose of Apollo-nianism that had done it. As Plato had suggested, Apollo and Dionysus were both companions of the dance, between them the bestowers of rhythm and harmony on humankind. The birth of tragedy was the product of their union, and depended on their passionate if stormy relationship. What had finished the Dionysian off was rather a bland and sterile theoreticism which Nietzsche found exemplified first and foremost in the figure of Socrates – the quintessential 'man of theory' whose philosophy of life may have given birth to civilization but only to a 'theoretical culture', an Alexandrian culture of librarians and scholiasts of which the pedant was, in Nietzsche's own day, its best if sorriest representative. Such a civilization put reason above unreason and made knowledge the highest good, banishing the irrational from view and judging the unintelligible to be devoid of meaning. Socratism took over the Apollonian for its own ends, adopted and appropriated its traits of beauty, line, form, lucidity, transparency, and comprehensibility. But these were no longer in dialogue with the dark heartbeat of the Dionysian. That had been surgically removed leaving the Apollonian qualities pristine and uncompromised but, in Nietzsche's view, crippled and only half alive. Nietzsche pictured Socrates in his prison cell wondering – having been ordered by a voice in a dream to start practising the art of music – if there were not, after all, something beyond the limits of his logical universe, some realm of wisdom or of art from which the logician was excluded. Like Schiller, Nietzsche counted the cost of a society which over-intellectualized at the expense of its passions.

Theoretical man prized knowing above all else. Socrates had awarded knowledge the highest honour by claiming, himself, to know nothing whatsoever – for he thus distinguished his own understanding of things from the mere presumption of knowledge which he otherwise found all around him. According to the oracle, Socrates was the wisest of men. In questioning the citizens of Athens, he had demonstrated that everything which they thought with all confidence that they knew was in fact a fragile set of suppostions which could all too easily be refuted and proved to be laughably wrong. The logician's mind separated darkness from light, reduced chaos to order, and differentiated the misty, error-prone regions of the human mind from the radiant clarity of a knowledge that was, at least theoretically, graspable. In the same move towards distinction, moreover, Socratism also took from the Apollonian the virtue of individuation – of marking the individual off from an ambient chaos and so making him a human being. This principle of individuation in turn gave rise to society – not to the swirling mass of Dionysian revellers as they swept past, caught up in the dance and united as if in one body, but to the sober commonwealth of citizens, a collective of monadic unities.

But, while these boundary lines may have made men and society, they were also capable of closing in – of restraining and imprisoning both. Apollonian art had been similarly bordered – staked about with fortifications, its little islands and eddies of order periodically broken up and swept away by the great Dionysian tide. But that glorious conjunction of making and unmaking represented, for Nietzsche, human creativity at its highest. When the rational assumed autonomy, by contrast, and suppressed the irrational from view, the two were no longer operating in fruitful dialogue, and this was why, for Nietzsche no less than for Schiller, theoretical man was so shrivelled and shrunken a creature. Theory brought everything within the narrow circuit of the thinkable. It reduced everything to the feeble confines of the human mind, bound it all within a nutshell. This allowed the human mind to pat itself on the back and to look on the world with a proprietory and self-congratulatory air. It put man in a position to plumb the depths of Nature, to treat the universe as decipherable, as a code to be broken and assimilated. Everything could theoretically be known and this attitude provided the grounds for the scientist's breezy optimism:

> It believes that the world can be corrected through knowledge and that life should be guided by science; that it is actually in a position to confine man within the narrow circle of soluble tasks, where he can say cheerfully to life: 'I want you. You are worth knowing'.

For Nietzsche, the great sin of theoretical man was to prize above all else a quality – knowledge – which he presumed to be, even if only in theory, within his own grasp. All awe, mystery, and engagement with life were lost as this creature complacently looked out at the world from the comfortable terrace of his own mind. Yet this move was made by all those who admiringly held up civilization as an achievement, who isolated its best qualities as being orderly, and who attributed that orderliness to human making. It was such a move which writers like Huizinga, Caillois, and Winnicott were to make, where the order that obtained in the small, enclosed world of play came somehow – as if by a sleight of hand – to be transferred to the wider world: as if control of the one automatically led to control of the other, as if play were necessarily the precursor of civilization, and as if such a development were naturally a cause for celebration. For Nietzsche, any such attitude expressed an intolerable egotism on the part of his fellow man, and anything which set man up as a knower and rewarded him for it, aroused in him an unquenchable ire. Game theory – which was to posit man and his machines as the supreme knowers of everything – would have seemed to Nietzsche the symptom of theoretical culture gone finally mad.

What Nietzsche took exception to was precisely what the proponents of civilization drew most comfort from – the extension of the ordering powers of the human mind out into the wider world. While it might have seemed self-evident that man's civilization of the world represented the high-point of his achievement, for Nietzsche the idea that thought could plumb nature – could fathom it, master it, let alone correct it –

was a monstrosity, a preposterous fantasy – the metaphysical illusion under which western man had been labouring for over two millennia. The human intellect – theoretical man's most prized and precious possession – was, as far as Nietzsche was concerned, barely a blink in the eye of nature. Whole eternities had passed none the worse when it hadn't existed at all, and the sense it bestowed of man's self-importance and centrality to the universe had no more objectivity than that of the mosquito which, sailing through the air, quite naturally regarded itself as the king of infinite space. Any presumption of mastery or control over nature on the part of human beings was utterly vain – an absurd grandiosity based on nothing more substantial than the intellect's own flattering and entirely self-generated estimate of itself. The human mind didn't deliver truth so much as illusions that were structured to look like truths. It surveyed the surface of things and gave the name reality to what was no more that its own particular way of seeing.

For Nietzsche, the glorification of man's cognitive powers rested on a fundamental error. Even the highest reaches of conceptual thought had their origins in the human body – not in the sensory experience that had long been a familiar category to sceptical philosophers, but in a crude, creatural materiality which stretched back to the dawn of evolutionary time. The world looked the way it did because man was the creature that he was – because his eyeballs were where they were, his nostrils and ear-drums of a given sensitivity, his brain of a particular shape and size. Nietzsche's typically iconoclastic move was to trace the genealogy of logic – like the genealogy of morals – back to the most maggotty of beginnings. The strength of a conviction rested not on its degree of truth but on its age. The basic notion of substance, for example – an elementary but indispensable building block for ratio-cinative thought – was less a reality than an accident of species-survival. Those creatures who were less attuned to change, less given to seeing everything in flux and better able to suppress variety, to isolate certain features of experience from others – to see a relation between a wild animal, say, and something edible – stood a better chance of surviving than their more sensitive brethren and, after millions of years of trial and error, bequeathed to the race the founding idea of substantive categories on which logical thought would come to erect its rickety temple. To recognize the category of 'leaf', for instance, was to suppress the infinite variety that existed – in space, time, and structure – between all individual leaves. Other basic components of logic – self-identity, number, space and time, cause and effect – came in for similar treatment, proving, to Nietzsche at least, that logic was a fiction based on what we can't see, don't know, and are unable even to imagine. 'We have arranged for ourselves a world in which we can live', he wrote in *The Gay Science*, 'by positing bodies, lines, planes, causes and effects, motion and rest, form and content; without these articles of faith nobody could endure life. But that does not prove them. Life is no argument. The conditions of life might include error'.

To see the world as out there, laid out for man's inspection – a great playing field on which to act out his fantasies of control – was to forget that what was exposed to view was pure projection, a screen on which man's chains of ideas and structures of thought were simply externalized. If the world looked realistic then this was testimony only to his powers of self-persuasion and to the ease with which he came to naturalize his habits of thought. It was he who attributed order and form to the universe. Even something as apparently objective as the orderliness of the stars – from time immemorial cited as proof of nature's inherent design – testified more to the human eye for order than to anything else. What about those galaxies we couldn't fully see or that looked, like the Milky Way, anything but orderly? For Nietzsche, any appreciation of order depended on a grand forgetting. The human consciousness surveyed the world as existing out there and proceeded to make sense of it according to its own subjective principles of organization. Since what was reflected back conformed to those principles, it quite naturally made sense and seemed to provide objective evidence for the intelligibility which the consciousness had looked to find. This process made a virtue of human competence. It bolstered man's pride, inflated his ego, and gratified his need to make order out of chaos. But it also drew a discreet veil over its own self-fulfilling circularity. This was quietly forgotten and – as Nietzsche wrote in *The Birth of Tragedy* – after Socrates, generation after generation of pushy knowers would spread 'a common net of knowledge' round the world, determined to know all, conquer all, and to 'weave the net absolutely tight'. Yet this net was never more than an illusion, a fragile tissue of lies, a mere web of appearance, a veil of maya – beautiful, perhaps, probably necessary for everyday life, and even rather convenient – but no less an illusion for that.

For man to give himself the airs of a deity was bad enough. But humanity descended to a whole new level of absurdity when it started to credit the universe with a creating, orderly God. This wasn't just forgetting. It was outright self-mystification. That human beings should project out into the heavens a glorified version of themselves was one thing. But to bow down before him, to submit to his will, to run their lives according to his dictates – this was quite another. For Nietzsche it was worse than ludicrous. Cowering apologetically before a bogeyman of his own inventing, the believer exemplified the craven meekness and gutless conformity to which all the inanities of organized religion bore ample witness. Nietzsche's particular disgust was reserved for Christianity, for no other religion had developed so elaborate and demanding a system of ethics. Blocking, not to say forbidding original thought, Christianity fettered the otherwise free spirit in a self-induced bondage and bestowed the mightiest-sounding of titles on the most trivial of things. 'Acquired habituation to spiritual principles without reasons is called faith', Nietzsche commented in *Human, All Too Human* (1878). 'Morality trains the individual to be a function of the herd', exploded *The Gay Science*, and was no more than 'a mere fabrication for the purpose of gulling', according to the 1886 Preface to *The Birth of Tragedy*, 'at best, an artistic fiction; at worst an outrageous imposture'. Similar examples could be drawn from across Nietzsche's writings. To say that Christianity tried his patience was to put it on the mild side.

God was the biggest fiction of all. He had never been anything other than a stop-gap, a supposition with which to endow the world with a meaning it didn't have, as Zarathustra was remorselessly to hammer home. Even a vindictive, avenging God was a palliative, a source of solace, in that he allowed men to impute a reason and purpose to an otherwise blank, unresponsive universe. The fact that men wanted – even needed – to attribute meaning to the world didn't in the least make it meaningful. Beneath the polite fiction that the world basically made sense lay the brute reality of a world that was utterly contingent and indifferent – quite beyond the compass of human reason or control, and impervious to human suffering or existence. At bottom, there was only the echoing chasm of a godless void, the inexplicable and un-accountable emptiness which preceded all man's created orders and upon which his fragile structures stood pathetically superimposed. God was dead and there was no order in the world. To think otherwise was to give in to delusion. 'The total character of the world', Nietzsche wrote in *The Gay Science*, 'is in all eternity chaos – in the sense not of a lack of necessity but of a lack of order, arrangement, form, beauty, wisdom, and whatever other names there are for our anthropomor-phisms'.

An anthropomorphism was what God was at best, a poetic metaphor shaped in man's own image. How could anyone in their right mind seriously believe in so obvious a fabrication? 'A god who begets children on a mortal woman . . . someone who bids his disciples drink his blood; prayers for miraculous interventions; sin perpetrated against a god atoned for by a god', mused Nietzsche wonderingly, in *Human, All Too Human*, 'Can one believe that things of this sort are still believed in?'. Nietzsche mocked the Christian God with the same indignation that Augustine had turned on the pagan deities, and for the same reason. To Nietzsche, this God was as patently empty an idol as the pagan gods had been to Augustine. But the two thinkers didn't resolve the problem in the same way. If Augustine's solution had been to replace the pagan gods – now mere relics, a heap of broken toys – with a bigger, better God, for Nietzsche that only perpetuated the illusion. It was much the same thing as giving man a bigger, better toy. Transcendence – the Christian God's saving grace – was just an idea, a strategy for catapulting him out into the stratosphere that was all too easy to see through. Nietzsche was loth to cast man as so sorry a dupe. For him, it wasn't a question of finding a replacement god – who could never be more than a placebo anyway – but of recognizing man's tendency to console himself with such toys and to obliterate that tendency in a single blinding flash of truth.

It's curious how differently Nietzsche and Augustine approached the question of play. Augustine had fulminated against it. Stage plays brought man and the gods into too close an alignment, making disillusionment with the latter an accident only waiting to happen. His remedy was to ridicule play, to suppress it. Play had no part in a good Christian life. Nietzsche's reaction, however, was the reverse. For him there was no point in trying to put truth – even a transcendent one – back behind the illusion, because the accident of disillusionment would always be waiting to happen. You could never counter illusion because you could never step outside the illusionistic, fiction-making, tale-spinning machine that was the human mind. Since you couldn't avoid illusion – everything was illusion: logic, reality, and God – Nietzsche's remedy was to make a virtue of it. If you couldn't beat illusion, you could join it, and Nietzsche embraced it like a long-lost friend. Life was illusion. It had never been anything more nor less. Its was all semblance – 'error, deception, simulation, delusion, self-delusion', as he wrote in *The Gay Science*.

This gave rise to a whole new metaphysic – or, more accurately, to a metaphysic with the 'meta' taken out. It was no longer a case of casting about for some more transcendent content lying behind or beyond the physical world. That was a lost and thoroughly discredited cause. It was rather a matter of glorying in form. In an empty world, surface was all anything ever came down to. Illusions were the only truth. And illusions were the province of the one creature for whom Nietzsche had any time – the artist. So long as he recognized his illusions for what they were and refused to be seduced into forgetfulness or faith, the artist redeemed himself, saved himself from the sins of folly, error, and superstition. Illusion was 'the only possible mode of redemption', Nietzsche wrote in the 1886 Preface to *The Birth of Tragedy*. 'Art, nothing but art!', he cried in a fragment published after his death in *The Will to Power*. Art alone could rescue man from nihilism, and redeem the man of knowledge, the man of action, and the man of suffering alike.

Since illusion – from *in ludere* – literally means 'in play', Nietzsche didn't banish play, as Augustine had tried to do, but rather made it the sole principle of the universe – the one abiding feature of the known and the knowable world. In *Human, All Too Human*, he approvingly cited Simonides – the Greek poet who died the year before Socrates was born – advising his compatriots to treat life as if it were a game. Life was a play, especially for the heroic individual who had trawled his way through the dark night of nihilism to emerge on disillusion's other side, ready to take up his role in what the Preface to *The Genealogy of Morals* (1887) called 'the Dionysiac drama of man's destiny'. By this, however, Nietzsche most definitely did not mean that life was like a play – that it resembled the orderliness of a stage-play or of an organized game. Order didn't come into it. It was a symptom of his impatient contempt for such rule-bound play that, in *The Birth of Tragedy,* he scorned the New Comedy – tragedy's sorry successor – as 'chess-like'. The play he had in mind was not in the least like chess. It wasn't governed or stately. It wasn't a shaping or an ordering but a Dionysian shattering – a making and breaking of form. In this, Nietzsche went further than Schiller. Schiller had looked to improve society – to give substance to the great social upheaval that was happening all around him and to make liberty and equality mean something real. Nietzsche's utopia, by contrast, looked distinctly anti-social. It unfolded itself in the glorious self-assertion of the artist – a figure with whom Nietzsche identified in his own impassioned writings. Schiller's Aesthetic State – that third joyous kingdom of play – could perhaps momentarily be glimpsed in Presocratic Greece where men had once 'managed a classically pure third mode of existence', the loss of which *The Birth of Tragedy* never ceased to mourn. But Nietzsche's vision of towering artist-figures thrashing out their lives in embattled, internalized play seemed rather different from the social democracy which Schiller had in mind.

But Nietzsche's play didn't end in tears. On the contrary, it ended in laughter – in the metaphysical exhilaration of Zarathustra, the most high-spirited of Nietzsche's creations, who bequeathed laughter to those who would listen: 'Laughter I declare to be blessed; you who aspire to greatness, learn how to laugh!'. It led back to the 'Homeric laughter' described in *Human, All Too Human* which, untrammelled by the killing spirit of Socratism, recognized the true emptiness of things. Man as player became a child again, and such was the condition of the artist. It was his glory never to have grown out of the games of childhood and youth, never to have 'matured' into the linear contractions of logical thought. Bearing the wisdom of both savage and child, the artist was to make men childlike again and to bring them his message from the primal depths, even if – as the untimely reminder of an ancient past – he was, like the prophet, and not unlike Nietzsche himself, all too often rejected by his tribe.

The first part of *Thus Spoke Zarathustra* (1883) began with a fable of three metamorphoses. The spirit had to pass through a camel and a lion in order finally to become a playing child – 'a new beginning, a sport, a self-propelling wheel, a first motion, a sacred Yes', a holy affirmation that gave rise to 'the sport of creation'. For the unthinking, playing child – who brought things into being unmediated by reflection – was the ultimate creator, and his play the image of creation itself. If – as a celebrated fragment from *The Will To Power* put it – the world was 'a work of art that gives birth to itself', then any creator was quintessentially childlike – *'pais paizon'*, a child at play. And, at the end of *The Birth of Tragedy,* Nietzsche found the metaphor of the creative spirit – forever making, and destroying what it's made – summed up best by the Presocratic philosopher, Heraclitus. Heraclitus had described a child on the beach who was building a sandcastle – eternally knocking down what he'd built in order to start all over again.

II

Nietzsche's image of the dabbling child gives a measure of how far removed his idea of play was from that of the other writers considered up to now. For them, the most important ingredient of play was order. Play was ordered if it was nothing else. Order was the common denominator of play in all its forms, including the apparently formless excesses of what Caillois called *ilinx* or vertigo – wheeling about, making oneself giddy – for even these were carefully separated off from reality – in fairgrounds, rituals, or games – and thus depended on a primary sense of boundary. Play carved a space out of chaos – a clearing in the forest – and this formed the first step in a quickening march towards progress. The clearing developed into a city, the playing child into the adult man, the primitive tribe into advanced society. Play was the ultimate metaphor because it suggested order and rule, from the loosest convention which separated the play-world from reality to the most complex elaborations of rule, code, and tactical manoeuvre. It was the orderliness of play which put man in a special relation with his world and which first made him postulate his gods. It was order that made him potentially god-like in his own mastery of that world, or which posited a transcendent God who – although as far away from humanity as it was possible to be – was still recognizable in his orderliness and in his fundamental willingness to play by the rules. Even where the outcome of events seemed baffling or absurd, God could still be thought of as playing by rules – they just happened to be hidden or obscured from human view. The play metaphor covered all eventualities.

For Nietzsche, however, order was pure illusion, and any cheery optimism that was based on it – any sense of mastery or control – no more than a ludicrous imposture. Order wasn't a matter for self-congratulation. Rather, it was 'the pretentious lie of civilization', as he put it in *The Birth of Tragedy*, a flimsy if pretty veil which hid from man the ghastly pointlessness of his existence. While the likes of Caillois were to see play as the origin of man's later conquest of the world – the order of the one being a testing-ground for the control of the other – Nietzsche, characteristically, saw things the other way round. For him, any conception of mastery was a childish delusion. Mistaking illusion for reality, man neither saw the truth – there was no underlying truth to be seen – nor engaged with the real world. Instead, as he wrote in the essay 'On Truth and Lie in an Extra-Moral Sense' (1873), he did no more than play 'a game of blindman's bluff on the backs of things'. Game-playing that would have spelled civilization, order, and control to Huizinga and the others, for Nietzsche exposed the utter infantilism of such an idea. For him, being taken in was the most unacceptable error – being gullible enough to confuse reality for fictions which merely called themselves truths. But to recognize illusion for what it was, to grasp the absurd truth that surface and falsity was all everything came down to and to create illusions over and over again – to play ceaselessly and carelessly like the child in sand – that was the supreme activity of the artist. For Nietzsche, the sandcastle wasn't the starting-point for grander, ever more complex structures. It had no ulterior goal. It was only ever a sandcastle – fragile, trivial, and pointless – eternally knocked down to be built up again and eternally built up to be knocked down. That the play metaphor could stretch from an image of the utmost orderliness to that of orderlessness *par excellence* testifies to its customary elasticity.

It was Nietzsche's typically uncompromising attitude which allowed him so ruthlessly to de-idealize, to strip away any vestigial traces of what might have been hopeful or comforting – how nice to think that a sandcastle would turn into a cathedral! – and to see the sandcastle for what it was, not as a symbol for something else. Indeed, the tendency to look for meaning behind an image was, for Nietzsche, the very symptom of man's disease. Human beings had projected their patterns of thought out onto the world and called those patterns reality. Since they were standing behind those patterns all the time, this process naturally gave rise to what had been perhaps the most enduring feature of western metaphysics since Plato, namely the notion that there was always something behind the surface – a more authentic, more 'real' world somehow lying behind or beyond the physical world of experience and perception, eternally grounding the latter and verifying it. This was the metaphysic which postulated an Idea behind a Form, an essence behind phenomena, a reality behind appearance, a cause behind effect.

The most subtle, sophisticated, and comprehensive ordering system which human beings had yet come up with was language, and, before Nietzsche, philosophies of language had generally assumed that a world of things ultimately lay – however obscurely or inaccessibly – behind the world of words. Perhaps the most elaborate version of this philosophy was the Judaeo-Christian theology of the Word – what Jacques Derrida has called 'logocentrism' – which put behind language the biggest thing that human beings could think of. It was on this supposition – that words had meaning and that God was their ultimate guarantee – that Pascal could logically enter into his contract with him. God and man were speaking the same language. They were united in a common cause – that of logic – and committed to upholding one of logic's major premises – the binding of cause to effect. Pascal chose the image of the gambler who pays his debts in order to tie the smallest conceivable cause – a wager – to the greatest possible effect: in this case, eternal life or eternal damnation. God as *logos* was necessarily a good, Cartesian God who could be relied on to play fair and not to cheat. If he existed – and if a man lived a good life – then it followed that he would reward that man with heavenly bliss. If not, not. Pascal's wager had less to do with the good life or eternal salvation than with clinching the deal – with establishing a logical God who would underwrite the logic of the bet. An *a priori* logical God would preserve the force of the syllogism and stand behind every other contract that human beings ever made. He would make the wager absolutely water-tight. To a believer, the circularity of this argument was its ultimate proof.

For Nietzsche, however, language was no less an illusion than anything else. Indeed, it was probably the greatest illusion of all. In *Human, All Too Human*, he wrote:

> The significance of language for the evolution of culture lies in this, that mankind set up in language a separate world beside the other world, a place it took to be so firmly set that, standing upon it, it could lift the rest of the world off its hinges and make itself master of it. To the extent that man has for long ages believed in the concepts and names of things as in *aeternae veritates* he has ap-propriated to himself that pride by which he raised himself above the animal: he really thought that in language he possessed knowledge of the world.

From man's ensuing belief that he had discovered the truth, Nietzsche continued, 'the mightiest sources of energy have flowed. A great deal later – only now – it dawns on men that in their belief in language they have propagated a tremendous error'.

The error was that language postulated a truth lying behind the suppositions it made when supposition was all there ever was. 'What, then, is truth?', Nietzsche famously asked in 'On Truth and Lie in an Extra-Moral Sense', but 'a mobile army of metaphors, metonyms, and anthropomorphisms – in short, a sum of human relations, which have been enhanced, transposed, and embellished poetically and rhetorically, and which after long use seem firm, canonical, and obligatory to a people: truths are illusions about which one has forgotten that this is what they are'. To believe in truth – to believe that there was a meaning to be found behind words – was as erroneous, not to say as neurotic, as to believe in God, although it was perhaps more difficult to avoid. After all, even the atheist tended to mean what he said. But Nietzsche's drive towards extremity was a symptom of his tendency to take things as far as they would go, and, if he looked ahead to the isolated, anti-social, non-communicating, illusion-loving, tormented creative artist (not so different, perhaps, from what Nietzsche, in his final madness, would become), then his radical philosophy inaugurated a revolution that would, in time, come to have the widest repercussions. For Nietzsche's idea of language as pure surface – as a shimmering play of empty signs – would become the new gospel of the postmodern. Nietzsche was ahead of his time. The dawning sun which he sensed approaching 'only now' in 1878 would take several more decades to reach the position it's risen to since.

Nietzsche's philosophy heralded a whole new way of looking at things. What looked real turned out to be a myth. Most consequentially, what looked so real that it was simply taken for granted – barely given a second glance – was also a myth. It wasn't just this religious belief or that social custom but the most basic categories of thought, the most elementary of founding perceptions that were up for grabs, waiting to be exploded as the groundless foundations on which whole social, ethical, and political structures were built. The cathedral had only ever been a sandcastle, never anything more. The process of identifying such structures as myths and bringing them tumbling down is, appropriately enough, what's known as deconstruction. To describe Nietzsche as the father of deconstruction is only in part a rhetorical gesture. There have been other great prophets of demystification, but it was Nietzsche who specifically philosophized this vision. And, of all the harbingers of post-modernity, it was he who first took disillusionment to its logical – or perhaps one should say alogical – conclusion. Order was no longer humanity's grandest and most self-justifying achievement. It was the most embarrassingly grandiose of illusions.

Indeed, it was more sinister than that. Order wasn't just an illusion. It was a delusion – a deliberate mystification. It could induce a blind conformity – the most servile submission to certain codes of practice. For Nietzsche, Christian morality was perhaps the most insidious example of this. If order was a mythology – an ideology – then deconstructing it had political implications. For the power to construct a reality – to impose it or get it accepted as such – was the most effective form of political power. It could – as religion proved – subjugate whole populations for generations on end. Seen like this, order wasn't so great an achievement after all. Rather, it was a giant hoodwinking which depended on misrecognition – on the all too human tendency not to ask questions but to go sheepishly along with things just because that was what everybody else was doing. It was the job of the deconstructionist to redeem mankind from this wholesale spiritual slaughter and to save society from the frauds of its own inventing. Since then, the cathedrals haven't stopped toppling down.

In the mid 1950s, Roland Barthes wrote a series of essays which he published in 1957 as *Mythologies*. His aim, as the Preface spelled out, was to scrutinize the 'decorative display of *what-goes-without-saying*' so as to make out the 'ideological abuse' that was actually paraded there. The most ordinary aspects of life – soap powder, hair-styles, steak and chips – were treated as sign-systems to be read and decoded, revealed for what they really were and their pretensions to universal truth unmasked once and for all. Because his theme was the explicitly banal, Barthes chose his examples from among the trivia of everyday life – magazine articles, news stories, advertising slogans, photographs – the detritus of a culture which, because mass produced, imposed on the population its version of reality with a particularly inescapable and invidious totality. For Barthes, the whole of France lay dreaming or half-awake beneath a common veil – an anonymized humanist culture decked out to look like reality. Everything – from the press to the cinema, theatre, fiction, rituals, table-manners, conversation, and clothes – was naturalized and normalized, handed down as the ineffable and self-evident way of the world. This was good form, just the way things were done. There was no end to the subtle ruses bourgeois ideology could come up with to perfect its subliminal advertising for itself. One of its most cunning devices was to stage certain moments of subversion (the avant-garde, say) or even to draw attention to the weaknesses of its most Establishment institutions – to the pettiness of the Army, to the worldliness of the Church – so that it could re-affirm its over-arching order in spite of everything and bolster its mores all the more. Diversity was flattened out and denied. The most culture-specific of customs and codes were passed off as a natural order in the name of an essential, common humanity, a sunny 'family of man'. This, Barthes felt, was the 'very principle of myth: it transforms history into nature'. Barthes saw it as his duty to defamiliarize the lowliest, homeliest habits of thought and to lift the lid on the creeping bourgeois ideology they exemplified.

The first essay in *Mythologies* was, as it happens, about play – about that supreme form of *agon*: wrestling. It was typical of Barthes' wry de-idealizing that he should choose a popular sport – one more at home in squalid halls or on the back-streets – rather than the rule-bound elegance of, say, judo or boxing, games more likely to have been selected by civilization's defenders as exemplars of the orderly fight. The contest in wrestling was brutal and gladatorial, as cruelly, unremittingly theatrical as the Greek drama, Roman triumph, or Spanish bull-fight. Here everything was simplified, reduced to the barest essentials. The point of wrestling was to act out and visualize a situation which, in normal circumstances, remained private – the struggle between strong and weak, or, when moralized, between good and evil, noble and base, or beautiful and ugly. In good Nietzschean fashion, wrestling traced the genealogy of morals back to the sweaty exertions of two human combatants. Like the Punch and Judy show, it presented a mime of suffering – an exhibition of conquest and defeat – in its barest, most satisfying form, satisfying because it tied cause firmly and unequivocally to effect. Here suffering – graphically displayed in the greased bodies, whether writhing or prone – was assigned an immediately intelligible cause – namely, being beaten, kicked, bruised, pummelled, punched, or thrown down by another human being. Wrestling made sense of human suffering it by inserting it – as if by way of explanation – into the simplest story of justice imaginable: the weak are beaten and deservedly punished, the strong conquer all. This was the justice of the play-ground, justice made easy, justice without tears – for the spectators, that is, who remained captivated by a spectacle that was stunning and almost beautiful in its sheer simplicity. The spectators imbibed from this spectacle a grandiloquence which was 'nothing but the popular and age-old image of the perfect intelligibility of reality'. What wrestling portrayed was 'an ideal understanding of things . . . in which signs at last correspond to causes, without obstacle, without evasion, without contradiction'. But play didn't augur civilization, didn't grant an op-portunity to praise it. On the contrary, wrestling gave Barthes a chance to bury it – to be the prize fighter himself who brought civilization down to its knees, exposing its codes of honour and justice in their stark physicality for all the world to see.

If the reality that was turned to the human gaze was nothing but a mythological construction – a mere fiction or tissue of lies – then its illusion of 'depth' and claims to naturalness were the greatest con-tricks of all. Surface value was all there was – the sum-total of everything –

and this was why Barthes found himself particularly drawn to the more superficial media of advertising and photography. The current fad for ornamental cookery, for example, took the brute reality of food – and the still more brute reality of being able to pay for it – and subsumed both beneath an oleaginous glaze of creamy jellies and lucent syrups which became a metonym for ideology's own soothing function. Looking and cooking collapsed into one another when *Elle* magazine photographed this smooth, pink food from afar as if it were a work of art, a feast for the eyes rather than the taste-buds – eyes that were themselves being invited to glaze over with the insistent repetition of ideology's most insinuating and self-disguising theme.

Those tissues of lies which most effectively seduced were those which induced a sense of inertia and calm, a reluctance to quibble, and a willingness to sink back into the comfortable solace of recognition. Language was the greatest seductress of all, and as Barthes was later to recall in *The Pleasure of the Text* (1973), a text was – from *texere*, to weave – quite literally a fabric or tissue of lies. Hierarchized with all those subordinate clauses, governed by grammatical rules, its sentences end-stopped and purposive, language was the instrument best designed to lull human beings into thinking that the world was orderly and made sense. The most consoling texts were those which pandered to this and so reassured, the 'readerly' text or 'text of pleasure' which – whether a general system of signs or a specific bourgeois novel – allowed the reader's sense of reality to chime in harmoniously with the reality that lay all around him, one an extension of the other. Such was the cosy, non-threatening text which promoted a comfortable reading practice – a Montaignean ideal of house, countryside, reading lamp, and decent distance from mealtimes and noisy family – but one which, at the same time, was also capable of revealing bourgeois reality for the fiction that it was. Either way, whether aware of the illusoriness of language or whether ensnared in all its tempting refinements, playing with words was all it boiled down to in the end, for Barthes no less than for anyone else:

> The pleasure of the sentence is to a high degree cultural. The artifact created by rhetors, grammarians, linguists, teachers, writers, parents – this artifact is mimicked in a more or less ludic manner; we are playing with an exceptional object, whose paradox has been articulated by linguistics: immutably structured and yet infinitely renewable: something like chess.

In his *Outline of a Theory of Practice* (1972), the sociologist, Pierre Bourdieu, also looked at those discourses which went to make up the envelope of perceptions and prejudices within which people lived, worked, and made sense of their world. Like Barthes, Bourdieu too was interested in what 'goes without saying because it comes without saying'. Ideological systems were fictions, Barthes suggested in *The Pleasure of the Text*, supported by a jargon or sociolect – a set of concepts, attitudes, beliefs, and opinions – which handed down the authorized version of reality. As Nietzsche had insisted, truth was nothing but the solidification of old metaphors passed on as stereotypes which, because no longer recognized as such, endowed this particular version of reality with a sense of inherent rightness. In the same way, Bourdieu saw that this set of opinions was a projection, and that the closer the fit between an objective order and the subjective principles of organization which built it, the more natural and self-evident the social world would appear. This experience he defined as *doxa* – to be distinguished from orthodoxy (straight, or more properly, straightened opinion) and heterodoxy (the possibility of alternative modes of belief). *Doxa* was not a set of consciously held or articulated opinions but rather what *wasn't* thought – what went without saying, what was taken for granted – the consensus which gave rise to actions that were either spontaneous or automatic. *Doxa* was the neutral background, as given and unremarked upon as the air we breathe, 'the universe of that which is undiscussed, unnamed, admitted without argument or scrutiny'. *Doxa* was less a world-view than the precondition for a world-view, a set of assumptions so basic as to be beyond need of demonstration – 'the sum total of all the theses tacitly posited on the hither side of all inquiry'.

Doxa formed the surround, the environment, the soup in which society swam. It was inescapable – taken in and absorbed as if by osmosis at every moment of every day. It was imbibed with mother's milk and inculcated thereafter in upbringing, schooling, and general experience. *Doxa* internalized opinions until they were no longer opinions as such but mere presuppositions made all the more lasting and durable precisely for becoming second nature. The world which *doxa* presented was the starting point for whole structures of thought and organization, and for the individual's own set of habits and personal views. But the initial process of that world's construction was hidden, dismissed as irrelevant, or simply never thought about – a premise which could be taken as read. For Bourdieu, *doxa* gave rise to the habitus which, like Barthes' myth, was similarly 'history turned into nature, that is, denied as such'. The habitus represented the totality of norms, customs, and expectations which endowed a given culture's world with the appearance of necessity. It made up the ordinary, commonsensical world, the blanket acceptance of which caused 'practices and works to be immediately intelligible and foreseeable'. The habitus made the world seem familiar. It left man at home in a world that he knew and which he had made thoroughly homely for himself. It showed the world in its orderly aspect and reassured him that he was justified in regarding it as knowable and orderable, as within the compass of his own cognition and control. Soothing and palliating, the habitus granted man the certitudes that he craved and for that reason it cheered and contented him. The solace it produced was not ecstasy or *jouissance* – the experience of disequilibrium, of 'shock, disturbance, even loss' which would follow the dismantling of his presuppositions. Rather, as Barthes differentiated it, it produced *plaisir* – the experience of 'euphoria, fulfilment, comfort (the feeling of repletion when culture penetrates freely)' – the experience, that is, of having those presuppositions quietly, consolingly affirmed.

The point of the habitus was to forget it. Like Barthes' myth or Nietzsche's reality, the habitus depended on collective amnesia. It was this which made society work – enabled it to rattle happily along on its predestined lines and boringly to get on with things. Life, after all, went on. The habitus gave unity and regularity to the entire set of practices which made up a society, orchestrated them without a conductor. These practices were not conscious, voluntary actions. They were not – except under the most inefficient of repressive régimes – a matter of knowingly obeying specific or observable rules. Rather, the habitus brought things down to the level of gut, purveyed its wisdom as common knowledge and common sense. People did things because it felt right – sensible, reasonable, expected. Even if they did things that were stupid, irrational, or subversive, it was because these were contained within the basic framework of presuppositions on which everyone was – at bottom – agreed.

For Bourdieu, this necessarily revolutionized the practice of sociology. Human agents were evidently not the all-knowing, calculating creatures which social science had made them out to be – understanding all their actions in the round and operating in the full knowledge of their consequences and repercussions. A practice such as gift-exchange, for example, consisted for Bourdieu of a 'sincere fiction of disinterested exchange'. Cycles of reciprocity, indebtedness, and obligation were euphemized, masked, and pushed decorously out of sight. In sociological and anthropological theory, gift-exchange took place in the full light of rational day. Like the scientists who were looking at them, everybody knew exactly what they were doing. But in practice, Bourdieu argued, human beings cultivated vagueness. You didn't make a return gesture the minute you received a gift – didn't return it back again (an insult), didn't write your thank-you letter there and then. You allowed a polite interval to elapse so as to make your own act of giving seem spontaneous and sincere – a 'genuine' gift and not some predetermined event in a series of interlocking actions. The objectivism of social science was itself the product of subjective principles of organization. The process by which objective analysis would, say, designate certain sub-systems within a sociological field-study was itself 'nothing other than the habitus'. Thought's self-reflecting circularity covered everything, including sociology itself. It was Bourdieu's advance to see the fiction of objectivity for what it was and to recognize that neither he nor his own text were exempt.

Bourdieu was clear that the habitus was a political instrument and that the 'power to impose the principles of the construction of reality – in particular, social reality – is a major dimension of political power'. Set up to reproduce and reduplicate itself, the habitus caused society to remain trapped within the particular version of reality it had made for itself. More to the point, a section of society could be made unwittingly to go along with that version of things – however disadvantageous to itself – only because it was incapable of or discouraged from thinking anything different. This was a most effective form of oppression – when one section of society was made to oppress itself without knowing why. In *The Pleasure of the Text*, Barthes objected to the phrase 'dominant ideology' on the grounds that, as an overarching structure of practices and thoughts, dominant was what ideology was. But it was correct to speak of the 'ideology of the dominant class' – the set of assumptions and received ideas which presented a world hierarchically organized so as to advantage some over others, and which the former self-interestedly passed off as the natural order of things. For Bourdieu, likewise, while the dominant class had good reason to preserve *doxa* and to protect it, the dominated class, by contrast, would benefit from stripping it away and exposing it for the fiction that it was. Only when the dominated had 'the material and symbolic means of rejecting the definition of the real that is imposed on them' and when 'the arbitrary principles of the prevailing classification can appear as such' could revolution occur and real social change finally begin to happen.

The passage quoted earlier in which Barthes compared the use of sentences with playing a game of chess was followed by a wicked afterthought: 'unless for some perverts the sentence is a *body*'. What this deliciously enticing thought suggested to Barthes was the 'text of bliss' – not the comfortable, content-filled bourgeois novel, the dumpy 'text of pleasure', but a meretriciously empty text, a playful text of pure erogenous surface. In seeking out this text of delectation – and in experimenting with it in his own discontinuous and designedly non-academic prose – Barthes was following Nietzsche in his flight away from the clanging thoughtfulness of the metaphysical towards the irreducible physicality of the body. He wanted to get away from the sentence as artefact, as the solemn object of linguistics or criticism, as 'a logical, closed measure'. What he wanted to savour – with an eroticized 'textual body' – was a bliss that wasn't structured according to the grammatical constraints of subject and predicate, an ecstasy that couldn't be spoken but only moaned. He wanted words to be a whore but not a wife, that's to say, and it was in much the same spirit that the American psychoanalytic critic, Leo Bersani, wrote his book *The Freudian Body* (1986). For here too the text – principally the Freudian corpus (the 'body' of the title) but also the bourgeois novel (Henry James) – was treated as a body, the relation between its teasing surface and its supposedly sober content being carefully examined, probed, operated upon, and eventually submitted to invasive surgery.

Both theory and fiction presented myths – ordered, intelligible narratives of sexuality, in the case of Freud, and of human character, in the case of James – which, like mythologies or the habitus, were deceptive and self-serving fictions. In the case of *The Portrait of a Lady*, for example, the 'ordered significances of realistic fiction are presented as immanent to society, whereas they are in fact the mythical denial of that society's destructively fragmented nature'. Both psycho-analysis and the bourgeois novel mythologized the human being as readable, and in both this was a 'fundamental political strategy' making assumptions, as it did, about what the self was and positing an absolute relation between inner and outer. But the very attempts of Freud and James to render their myths intelligible – to create theoretical and narrative coherence – were themselves embarrassed, disturbed by unlooked-for counter-forces which threatened to confuse, contradict and finally to collapse them. Freud's tireless efforts to clarify and explain, to bring psychoanalysis to the widest possible audience, for instance, frequently served as a strategy to undo any explanation whatsoever, psychoanalysis being a peculiarly paradoxical attempt to theorize 'precisely those forces which obstruct, undermine, play havoc with theoretical accounts themselves'. To pay attention to such moments of textual distress was in itself a political gesture, for being alert to the 'confrontation between the intelligible and the unintelligible' revealed those mythologies for what they were. Freud and James may have resisted – Freud straining all the harder to make himself understood, and James 'redeeming' content by demonizing the empty superficiality of a character like Madame Merle. But the critic – that stripper away of veils – was able to reveal the failures of such resistance, to explode content as a falsification, and to promote the ticklish, titillating, skin-deep sensation of a reading that was 'most resolutely superficial'.

Bersani was to pursue this theme in *The Culture of Redemption* (1990), for the culture to which he referred – and which was the target of his pointed attack – was one which, against all the odds, continued to resist: persisted, that is, in denying the true emptiness of things and still tried vainly to put content back behind form and to restore meaning where it didn't exist. It was a feature of this culture that art should be understood primarily as redemptive – recuperative or compensatory. If human experience was fragmentary and incomplete, art came along and rectified things, filling the gaps, gathering parts into wholes, and welding the fragments together into encyclopaedic totalities. As such, art was glorified DIY, a salvage operation on life. This tendency to make something better out of what was already there appeared nowhere more strikingly than in that favourite fall-back of civilized culture – the idea of sublimation. Sublimation took the lowly dregs of human experience – sex, passions, feelings, dreams – and transmuted them into something higher. From what was partial and scattered came something universal and whole. Out of infantile passions came adult rationality, out of unreined sexual desire came brotherly love, out of hatred came noble competition. This was the basic shaping spirit which fashioned order and led on to art and civilization. According to this metaphysic, art was sublime because it rehabilitated fallen experience. Indeed, to continue the theological metaphor, it 'redeemed' that experience. In a way that's by now familiar, art flattered man with pleasingly god-like powers by allowing him to think that he'd mastered and controlled the raw material of experience. If art was an improvement on nature, then it was likely to be improving, and this was the origin of the notion that art was morally uplifting – an idea which allowed critics as well as artists to feel so good about themselves.

Needless to say, Bersani's aim was to deconstruct such deludedly smug self-satisfaction. His material, again, was psychoanalysis and literature, and the ways in which monuments of – and to – order in fact gave themselves away at every turn. Attempts to construct a theory or narrative inevitably betrayed signs of their own destruction. Efforts to put substance back behind form and to invite the interpreter to extract meaning triumphantly from it like a plum from a pie could be shown to dissolve into helpless self-contradiction. The Freudian account of sublimation, for example – including its elaboration in the work of Melanie Klein – turned out not to be a story of heroic self-sacrifice but the exact opposite. 'Far from being a transcendence of self-interest', Bersani wrote, 'sublimations are the elaborated forms of self-enjoyment'. What looked like self-discipline was actually an exquisitely savoured state of masochistic self-annihilation. The move to gather the ego together and gird its loins in preparation for higher things was, as it turned out, a merely temporary consolidation on the way to an orgasmically repeated self-shattering into bliss.

It was Bersani's aim to scupper redemption once and for all – to reveal it to be a false and falsifying illusion which belittled art and patronized human beings by fobbing them off with so obvious a lie. In direction and motive he was following Nietzsche's lead. Yet 'redemption' in the sense that Bersani was using it was not the same as the 'redemption' that Nietzsche meant. Indeed, Nietzsche meant redemption (as he meant play) in sense totally opposed to that of everyone else. The 'culture of redemption' which Bersani was criticizing used the word in the normal theological sense. This was a godly world, it said, in which the ego was 'redeemed' – corrected, improved upon, sublimated – and made god-like in its aspirations to creativity, civilization, and order. God was in his heaven and all was well in the world. Nietzsche, by contrast, used redemption in a radically atheistical sense. This was a godless world, he said, in which there was no content, no transcendently meaningful Word but only surface. It was not a redemption of the ego but a redemption *from* the ego which art brought about. Greek tragedy exploded the illusion of individuality, broke down ego boundaries, dissolved any pretensions to knowing, and merged mind and body into the pure surface which was the sum total of all that there ever was. If all was a lie, then not to lie about the lie was the only solution, which was why, for Nietzsche, 'illusion is the only possible mode of redemption'.

It was to clear up this confusion and to explore the implications it had for his own argument that, at the mid-point and 'conceptual centre' of his book, Bersani turned to *The Birth of Tragedy* as a 'philosophical condensation' of everything he'd been saying. For Nietzsche, the tragic hero or artist regressed to the state of primal oneness or non-differentiation which was the Dionysian. Thus, Oedipus' incest was not primarily a violation of order 'but – more literally, more corporeally – a dissolving of the boundaries of his distinct being in this fusion with the (m)other'. In his reading of Nietzsche, Bersani traced the paradox of how tragedy – an art form and therefore necessarily Apollonian – nonetheless managed to move backwards towards the pre-verbal formlessness of the non-differentiated, annihilated, or shattered self. How could tragedy formulate that formlessness, speak what, by definition, could not be spoken? By way of answer, he suggested that it was this paradox itself which made tragedy redemptive. Tragedy redeemed precisely by *not* providing a moral but, instead, by making possible a return to this jouissant absence of being. It was the paradox of 'Dionysian art' – the conundrum of 'a *figure dissolving its own figured state*' – which alone was capable of bringing this about.

In Nietzsche's terms, the Dionysian 'needed' the Apollonian in order to accomplish this. It needed form – even the wordless form of music – in order to take shape. Tragedy wasn't nothing – it had a definite form, after all. But – and here Bersani took further and clarified Nietzsche's theme – the Apollonian was, in any case, nothing but form. The Apollonian wasn't content dressed up to look beautiful but just pure, empty surface. This new-look, post-modern Apollo had no inner content or core meaning. He incarnated emptiness and, as such, began to look rather like his Dionysian brother in his radical destabilization of logical category. As a paradoxical 'Dionysian art', which combined pure surface with inarticulable formlessness, Greek tragedy opened the way to the unconscious. What it 'redeemed' was not the ego or the differentiated, individuated self but rather its opposite – egolessness. Tragedy wasn't an ethical, exemplary, improving, gap-filling, fetishizing art which put something where it didn't exist. Rather, it was a paradoxical, self-contradictory, self-shattering, formally form-destroying art which made a virtue out of a hole.

In sum, the tension between Apollo and Dionysus was, as Bersani saw it, Nietzsche's way of allegorizing the non-productive but endlessly repeated movements of being. The ego didn't leave the blissful, non-differentiated state of babyhood behind in order to stride purposefully forwards towards some mythical sublimity, on the way to civilization and progress. On the contrary, it sought to return to that state of primal darkness – a kind of pre-forgetting – over and over again. Indeed, the ego constituted itself *in order* to break itself apart. Its aim wasn't order – the order of civilization was at best only a side-effect. Its aim was an anarchy which pre-existed all order and blew that order apart as a mystifying fiction. Dionysian art endlessly repeated this to-and-fro between an individuated self, on the one hand, and a pleasurably shattered self on the other, alternately shaping and dissolving the boundaries of the self like some manically indecisive potter. 'Art plays with these boundaries', wrote Bersani, 'to the point even of reflecting upon that play in its moves along the boundaries between the bounded and the unbounded'. This coming together in order to fall apart – this interminable rising and falling – could be seen, perhaps, as Bersani's own version, only here explicitly sexualized, of Nietzsche's sandcastle, which was for ever going up and coming down. And, since it was *de rigueur* for the deconstructionist to include himself and his own writing in this whole out-rubbing exercise, it was only appropriate that Bersani should dismiss his own work on sublimation – anticipated in the last paragraph of *The Freudian Body* – as nothing but a species of play:

> let us frankly express our relief at having found in Freud himself (and in spite of Freud himself) convincing grounds for dismissing our own thoughts about sublimation as nothing more – and nothing less – than the play of a consciousness resolutely attached to the always ambiguous pleasures of its own vibrations.

III

We've come a long way from where we started. We began at the gaming tables, where the gambler who'd lost at play was scraping back his chair and looking round at his fellow players, stunned at the scale of his loss. But, unless they've a mind to relent or to treat him as a special case – and there's no reason why they should – what he finds reflected in their eyes is a stern and immutable law: 'thou shalt pay thy debts'. Yet, whatever he stands to lose – no matter the disrepute, the financial embarrassment, the pain he's about to inflict on his family and on himself

– the gambler always submits to his fate. By entering into the game he's willingly laid himself open to this, consentingly made himself hostage to such misfortune. The possibility of material loss is the price he's paid for a psychological gain – a gain the pleasure of which so outweighs even the most acute displeasure that it makes the bargain worthwhile every time. For the rule that the loser pay his debts binds cause to effect. It attaches material consequences to a cause of human making. While life may throw its worst at him and surprise him with the most unpleasant of reversals, here at least his fate, good or bad, is under human control – to be decided by the flick of a ball, the throw of a die, or the turning over of a fatal card. This brings with it a sense of control – a sense of a power over destiny – which, as pleasures go, is as good as it gets. It's not surprising he finds it addictive.

This sense of control over an uncertain world is, one way or another, the basic component of human play in all its forms from jigsaws to drama. Gambling is an exemplary case only because it shows that control operating with an illustratively stark simplicity. For here the whole thing is completely man-made. No attempt is made to distract or to prettify, to disguise the situation's patent artificiality. The cause on which so much is made to hang is pointedly – gratuitously – symbolic, a mere number which, whether on a lottery ticket, roulette wheel, die, or playing card, is in itself wholly empty. The fact that there's no limit on what a player can stake and lose, moreover, shows how much human beings value this sense of control – the price they're willing to pay for it. Clearly, it exceeds all measure. The gambler is free to stake anything he likes – everything, if necessary. However much it is, no price can be too high. The point of gambling – what makes it such a good bargain and therefore so compulsive – is that the player pays a finite amount – no matter how large that is – to buy what is effectively an infinite gain: the assurance that he's living in a logical world where cause is attached to effect. The loser pays his debts not only because he's contracted to do so but because this rule underwrites every other contractual agreement ever made. It affirms the syllogistic logic that 'if' will be followed by 'then', and reassures him that he's part of a principled, orderly universe where things can be guaranteed to make sense. This is a source of profound consolation and makes life worth living. If it costs a fortune, it's still cheap at the price. People wouldn't gamble otherwise. Play situates man in a world that's laid out to his cheered and unblinking eye to be comprehended, mastered, and controlled. Even if its complications and mysteries elude him at any one time, that world is still theoretically knowable, and, as Socratic man, he has – or he has awarded to himself – the power to know it.

This construction of a logical world in play marks the first step on the road to human creativity. The classic writers on play say so, and this earliest move – whether made by an individual child or by an infant society – leads on, in its turn, to art, technology, and civilization in a story that's cheerfully progressive. The little world of play – set apart, ringed about, internally ordered and rule-bound – puts itself in relation to the wider world in the hope that order will be found to be the underlying principle of that too. Play puts man in touch with the divine, and, as ritual, it makes explicit the relation between a play-world that's under human control and the real world that is under the gods'. Whether the real world is ultimately man's own to understand – as in the giddy heights of game theory – or whether it's perceived to be the creation of an ineffable God before whom he prostrates himself as an unworthy imitator, doesn't in the long run make much difference. However remote that God is, he's still in relation with his creatures and still recognizably playing the game. This idea of a logical world – made comprehensible to the human mind and reflected back to it by a logical God – finds its culmination in Pascal's wager, where God and man face one another across the gaming table and cordially agree to play by the rules.

So much for the cheery narrative of progress. It took us up to the summit of the mountain and bid us look down on the prospect below – a sunny panorama of sparkling cities, triumphs of design, and other monuments to human ingenuity. But, for all its tempting conclusion, the story didn't end there. The tale contained a fatal flaw, and the same circularity which shored up its confidence would in turn be what brought it down. The self-validating logic of the Wager wasn't equally persuasive to everybody. Philosophically, it was first and most rigorously blown apart by Nietzsche, who pointed out that the assumption of a logical world was in itself a logical manoeuvre, no more than a presupposition. Within the circuit of that logical world, God – if he exists – is good and there's every reason to play. But outside it things look very different. Take that presupposition away and the whole edifice crumbles, leaving nothing but a pile of sand. Whole world orders – philosophical systems, ethical régimes, social and political structures – are based on foundations no more substantial, and any accompanying sense of complacency or pride is grounded on even less.

The deconstruction of the last few decades has brought everything crashing down. It doesn't replace a bad order with a better one. It pulls down everything – even its own claims to theoretical coherence – in a veritable implosion of forms. Not a stone still stands. The most cherished achievements of human civilization – language, politics, science, law – have been revealed to be sacred cows, mere idols of the mind. Any order is a delusion, nothing more than a fictitious figment projected out onto a meaningless world. All is surface and illusion – trivial, pointless, and lacking in substance. To misrecognize this – to insist, against all the odds, on putting meaning back where it doesn't belong – is only a childish game. Worse than that, it's a deliberate self-mystification for which the deluded deserve everything they get. To rest one's faith in a logical world shows not the best but the worst – the least human – attribute of humanity, for it reduces men to trotting sheep in their meek conformity. To persist in this belief is a disease of the mind, nothing less than an organized neurosis.

So that seems to be that. We're back at the beginning with nothing to show for it and nowhere to go – back at the bottom of the mountain, since the mountain itself has disappeared, gone up in a cloud of unknowing or shrunk down to a mere handful of sand. So where do we go from here? We seem doomed to go round in circles either way, whether we choose the self-validating logic of the wager or the self-cancelling rhetoric of deconstruction. It might look like a complete impasse, the total end of everything. But it isn't, in fact, the end of play. People are still playing games, still creating orders for themselves. Deconstruction hasn't put an end to that. Order might be illusory and the scramble for it frankly neurotic but that doesn't mean people want it any the less. And that's true not only of those who remain mystified but of those who count themselves enlightened as well. They too are still submitting to the mythical pleasures of logical thought no matter how fictitious they know those pleasures to be. There's no reason why they shouldn't. The fact that a pleasure is illusory doesn't necessarily make it any less pleasant – if anything, it probably makes it rather more so. But, even if they wanted to renounce that pleasure, those who've been enlightened wouldn't be able to. Not even deconstructionists can escape it. They may aspire to a state that's beyond the illusionistic, mystifying practices of the human mind but – as they are the first to point out – this idea is itself a product of that mind. Even thinking about deconstructing the mind is still an idea which has a logical coherence of its own. They can't get beyond that point. And, since they couldn't even if they wanted to, they calculate that they might as well enjoy illusion for what it's worth – an entirely pragmatic move. Enforced pleasure, however illusory, perhaps isn't so bad after all. That's why, for all the collapse of order, people still come back to it – continue to opt for its deceiving wiles – and there's no greater proof of this than the fact that they're still writing.

Puppies chasing their tails may be the paradigm of existential pointlessness. But they don't write about it. The same could be said of Nietzsche's sand-playing child. The one thing he's not doing is writing about his experience – he epitomizes the joyous thoughtlessness of play. But Nietzsche is writing. Not only that, in choosing this particular image, he's borrowed a highly literary metaphor – one that derives from a philosophical tradition that stretches all the way back to Heraclitus. This image brings its own pleasure with it, in other words. It is formal, literary, and traditional. It makes sense. It allows Nietzsche paradoxically to figure what can't be figured. But it doesn't – it can't – actually enact the mindlessness that Nietzsche is driving at. It might look as if his argument culminates in the ideal idea-less-ness of the child. But what it actually ends up with is the philosopher's *image* of that child. There's no going beyond that. Language – that bewitching veil of illusions – invariably interposes itself between the thinker and his desired state of thoughtlessness, and, for all its lies, it brings with it a residual pleasure of its own. The experience of mindlessness – of being ejected from language, of having all one's presuppositions taken apart – would be more akin to going mad, having an epileptic fit, or being knocked unconscious. It wouldn't be remotely pleasurable. Not even Nietzsche could 'do' *jouissance* – at least not on the page. There, the best that he – or anyone else – could do is to point to it, to signal it by such stylistic gestures as freeing up punctuation, being 'poetic', or departing from the more obvious norms of academic prose. But this is only ever *jouissance* by default – only ever an approximation, a *jouissance manquée* – which might as well, after all that, be pleasure anyway. *Jouissance* may be the ideal but it's one that can't be delivered, and, as an unavoidable second-best, *plaisir* (as Barthes differentiated it) continues to hold out an irresistible appeal. Otherwise, Nietzsche and everyone else would have stopped writing long ago. Pleasure might be illusory and neurotic. It might offer the most tasteless bourgeois satisfactions of a cultural tradition that's recognizable, quotable, and comfortably accommodated under the educated belt. But no one's renounced it yet.

So what we're left with after deconstruction is not mindlessness so much as a kind of hyper-awareness. In a deconstructed and disillusioned world, a person may know very well that everything's an illusion, but still go along with it. Post-modern man may understand all too clearly that he's prone to mystification at every turn. But he still chooses to exist in a state of paradoxically enlightened mystification. Indeed, he has very little choice in the matter. Even if he's thoroughly convinced that reality is a colossal joke, that all man-made orders are mere myths designed to dupe – even when he's been properly demystified and hasn't an illusion left standing – in realizing that, whether he likes it or not, he still remains a thinking, ordering, and image-making creature. There's no getting round it. The most dedicated deconstructionist knows what he's doing – is still, after everything, left with himself. The best he can do is to set up ever more distant frames of ironic detachment, raise himself up on platforms from which to survey everything – including his own act of surveying – as pointless, empty, and absurd. But, so long as he's doing this, he's still got his feet firmly on the scaffolding. He's not fallen off into unconsciousness, not taken that impossible leap into the dark. There's no escape from the mind, from its wheedlingly pleasing cogitations, its promises to understand and control. Its pleasure might be utterly false – the order it peddles a pack of lies, the consolation it offers a warping disease. But every neurotic illness has a gain – and this particular one proves impossible to renounce.

The deconstruction of logical thought doesn't mark the end of things. It doesn't in fact change a great deal. People are still playing, still ordering their experience, still continuing to write about it. They may know what they're doing or they may not. They may believe or they may doubt. They may be mystified or thoroughly enlightened. But they're still doing it all the same, and, since they haven't much choice anyway, they're probably enjoying it just as much in either case. Perhaps the mystified are better off in the long run. With less to worry their heads about they just get on with things as they'd have had to do anyway – and this has universally been thought of as wisdom. But those who see themselves as enlightened are hostage to their knowledge. They can't help what they know. And, since – barring accidents – they can't go back, they might as well make a virtue of what they know. Ratio-cinative thought, deceptive as it is, still allows them to see and to arti-culate more clearly than anything else does the tragi-comic paradox of their situation. At the far end of disillusionment, there's the jadedly playful cynicism of Slavoj Žižek, the Slovenian critic who reckons, in *The Sublime Object of Ideology* (1989), that even 'cynical distance, laughter, irony, are, so to speak, part of the game'. Knowing full well that what you're doing is ideologically conditioned doesn't stop you from doing it. Knowledge doesn't distinguish you from the crowd, doesn't make you one of the elect. It doesn't prevent you from doing what everyone else is doing, doesn't redeem you from ideology. You wouldn't want it to in any case since that would mean going mad. Knowing all this and being ironically self-aware about it doesn't change anything, doesn't make you particularly superior. But it does at least have one small advantage, however dubious and paltry the consolation. It does leave you with the words to say it.

That's why, in the pages that follow, it'll be words that I'll mainly be talking about. The writers mentioned in this chapter have, between them, considered every aspect of play – have run the whole gamut, from sandplay to chess, from ritual to wrestling. But what this book will be most concerned with is words about play – with how play gets to be written and written about. To write about play is itself a kind of play. It bears all the hallmarks. Language is the most basic shaping, forming medium. It takes a mass of unformed and uncertain thoughts and imposes on them an order and design. It fits ideas into a logical sequence and makes them obey at least a minimal set of grammatical rules. A text makes a contract between writer and reader who agree for a period to play the same game, however pointless or empty it may be in itself. This could, of course, be said of all writing, not just writing about play. As Huizinga found, if you define play as 'an activity which proceeds within certain limits of time and space, in a visible order, according to rules freely accepted, and outside the sphere of necessity or material utility', you end up with a definition of poetry. If the definition of play is broad enough it can cover just about anything. But, even if it represented only the tiniest sample of all that play could be said to cover, writing about play still has one thing to be said for it. It's self-reflexive. If nothing else, this should grant the satisfactions of economy – of allowing us to see how play works at the same time as it's being talked about. To write about play – whether in theory or in literature – is to isolate it, to set it aside and earmark it as a distinct category and subject. It's a continuation of the move which brackets off a rule-bound space and time for the playing of a game. Writing about play is playing. You don't have to be particularly knowing or self-conscious about it. You don't have to be arch, precious, or self-deprecating, don't have to draw attention to the fact that your own text is a species of game-playing.

You needn't admit that or even know it. But if you want to – or just can't avoid it – at least you've got the words to say it.

The writers we started out with were perhaps the most happily unconcerned or unaware that their own writing was a form of play. They had good reason to stop short of ironic self-reflection and to save being troubled by that particular hall of mirrors. Roger Caillois' fourfold schema of *ilinx*, mimicry, *alea*, and *agon*, for example, expressed nothing so clearly as a bid to order, a theory which offered the comprehensiveness of an over-arching design. But – for all his sensitivity to the dangers of setting up 'some kind of pedantic, totally meaningless mythology' – his system was, all the same, a beautiful example of what he was writing about – the imposing of order on chaos. And, like those other great fourfold systems – Northrop Frye's classification of all world literature under the seasonal archetypes of comedy (spring), romance (summer), tragedy (autumn), and satire (winter) in his *Anatomy of Criticism* (1957), or Kenneth Burke's treatment of the four master tropes of metaphor, metonymy, synecdoche, and irony as the gateway to 'the discovery and description of "the truth"' in *A Grammar of Motives* (1945) – Caillois' global theory of play, published in 1958, had as much to do with the reconstruction of a world recently shattered by war as with anything else. For him, the self-evidence of a logical world needed to be re-affirmed at that point, not taken apart.

Winnicott, too, had a professional interest in steering clear of some of the more dispiriting disillusionments of ironic self-detachment. In *Playing and Reality*, he cited the case of a patient – a middle-aged woman – who didn't know how to play creatively and who wasted her time in the compulsive and empty playing of solitary games like patience. These games, as Winnicott observed to her, went nowhere – they were dead-ends, they had no creativity, no poetry in them. There was nothing he could do with them. But had she done something different – had she, for instance, *dreamt* that she was playing patience – he could have done something with it: 'I could make an interpretation. I could say: "You are struggling with God or fate, sometimes winning and sometimes losing"'. Had she done this, she would, in other words, have been playing his game, his game being – like the proper play that he was theorizing – to interpret things, to order them, to analyze them: in a word, to impose order on chaos. The patient would then have entered into the mutual play that was Winnicott's whole therapeutic aim and procedure. Winnicott was the first to admit that this order had to come from the patient herself and that the clever analyst who tried to impose his own brilliant interpretations did no good to anyone. But, although unacknowledged, it remained implicit throughout his writing that the analyst's own work – in sorting material and making sense of it – represented a model kind of play, a model which was to be gratifyingly reflected back at him in the play that would lead ultimately to the patient's cure. Winnicott's belief in the cure was unshakable – his reputation as a theorist and as a therapist depended on it.

It was the writers we came to later on who applied a greater degree of self-consciousness to what they were doing, and who exploded the serenity of a Winnicott as the sorry mystification of theoretical man. It was Nietzsche and those who followed him who pointed out that a self-validating theory was an empty one. If you started out by pre-supposing a logical world, then obviously a child's first moves towards that world were going to look like a positive step. They marked the beginning of a process the writing about which represented a grand culmination. Those happily constructive theories of play naturally lent themselves to the story of progress because they situated the theorist at the far – that is to say, at the cured, healthy, creative, and civilized – end. No wonder they were so cheerful. The more deconstructive writers, however, saw this circularity as unacceptable, as distastefully self-serving. They were the first to deny themselves the hollow satisfactions of its optimism. For them, logical argument was an illusion designed to boost the morale of logical man. They didn't shrink from spelling out the implications this had for their own arguments nor from de-mythologizing themselves. All language, including their own, was the father of lies, the sinister origin of ideology's whole bamboozling exercise. But, since there was no getting away from it – since illusion was all that there was – it left them free to play. It didn't deliver them into *jouissance*, the mindless play of the happy sand boy, but it gave them the next best thing: pleasure – a knowing, ironic, mindful play whose paradoxes could go on being spoken and written about.

Play has two sides to it. It erects structures, effects boundaries, and establishes rules which, although potentially beautiful and complex, are fictitious and have no basis in fact. The orders that it makes are both creative and illusory, in other words. The writers we began with emphasized only the first of these. For them, play was creative – Creative, even. It made worlds. It constructed and built. It made man god-like, master of his theories and of his universe. But these versions of play had too obvious an investment in themselves. They went round in circles. The writers we looked at later on emphasized play's other side. For them, play wasn't constructive but compulsive. To submit to illusions was pathological – it was neurotic and repetitive. To set up order as the principle of the universe was to peddle a myth and to theorize was only to perpetuate the lie. But these later accounts weren't purely destructive. The most compelling, at least, were able to show play in both its aspects – as creative as well as neurotic. They suggested that enlightenment didn't necessarily mean the end of play but a sophistication of it. They showed that you could know what you were doing – and know that it was illusory – but still do something creative and pleasurable with it all the same. You could still make words and worlds, still fashion images, still write texts, still weave together the threads of the veil. The most interesting writers on play are those who emphasize both its functions – who are able to show that play is both creative and illusory and who manage to do so without getting stuck in the sterile circularity of an argument that either validates or cancels itself. In what follows, there are two writers I'd like to look at who, I think, do this in particularly interesting ways – William Shakespeare and Sigmund Freud.

The playwright and the psychoanalyst don't have much in common with one another. They belong to epochs that were historically remote and governed by quite different cultural and material conditions. Although Freud frequently referred to Shakespeare, and wrote an essay on 'Creative Writers and Day-dreaming' (1908) which suggested that imaginative writing was the paradigm of all play, it won't be Freud's discussions of Shakespeare nor psychoanalytic readings of fiction that I'll be considering here. What I'm interested in are the ways, both subtle and stated, in which each writer meditates on play – the ways in which each approaches and treats the issues of order and illusion for which play is both a metaphor and an example. The kinds of texts they wrote couldn't have been more different. Freud was writing analytical, propositional prose. Shakespeare was writing drama which, with its absence of a controlling narrator, is possibly the least propositional kind of writing there is. Nor did either of them put play at the centre of things. Shakespeare didn't write irritatingly tongue-in-cheek plays about play. Freud didn't build his theory around it. For both, play as such – specific pastimes, sports, or games – was a relatively marginal subject, something they picked up and referred to only in passing. Yet, in both cases, the issues of order and illusion – which play gathers up and speaks to – can be seen to be central to their whole undertaking.

It's with Freud that I begin, and the next chapter starts by looking at his book, *Jokes and Their Relation to the Unconscious*, first published in 1905. For Freud, jokes are adult play – the nearest we get in adult life to experiencing again the joys of childhood. Jokes allow a person to revert to pleasures that were last enjoyed in infancy before all the pressures and constraints of civilized adult life began to set in. Jokes are a licensed return to freedoms long since forbidden. Smutty or sarcastic jokes, for example, satisfy sexual and aggressive urges that have been repressed but not forgotten. Jokes offer a rebellion, a fleeting but blissful escape from the constraints of morality and law. That's what makes them so enjoyable. The joke book belongs alongside those other texts written at the founding stage of Freud's career – *The Interpretation of Dreams* (1900) and *The Psychopathology of Everyday Life* (1901) – for jokes, like dreams and slips of the tongue, bear witness to the unconscious, the haunt of those repressed but irrepressible desires which succeed, in spite of everything, in circumventing the censor of adult consciousness and having their wicked way.

It's not at first obvious to Freud that his own book is a joke, that his theoretical presentation itself shores up the same civilized and repressive constraints – above all, the intellectual constraints of reason and logic – from which he argues jokes to be a longed-for liberation and blessed relief. This paradox isn't made explicit, perhaps because at this stage there was too much at stake – his reputation as a scientist and status as a serious thinker. It's passed over altogether by the psychologist, Ernst Kris, and the art historian, E. H. Gombrich, who between them found a whole theory of creativity on what Freud has to say about humour and jokes. But the paradox still registers itself. It makes itself evident in the ambivalences of Freud's text – in the ambiguity of a metaphor or the illogicality of a rhetorical turn. Freud seems to have been uncomfortable with this text. It's one of the few he didn't obsessively return to, update and revise. But the paradox that troubles it reappears later in *Civilization and its Discontents* (1930) where Freud reflects more openly on the embarrassing paradox that his own theories – organized and coherent as they've aimed to be – have been written in the name of those same illusory values of order and self-control which are capable of making the individual unhappy if not of driving him mad.

What really clinched the problem was the question of wordplay. In the joke book, Freud had suggested that nonsense jokes and plays on words thankfully released a person from the tiresome requirement of having to make sense all the time, returning him to the joyous mode of childhood when he was allowed to experiment with gurgles, rhythms, and sounds with no regard for logical sense. Needless to say, this is a pleasure Freud forgoes in the course of theorizing about it. As a theoretical man, he imposes on himself the stern duty of making as much sense as he can. But it's a duty, all the same, that brings with it a pleasure of its own – the dubious satisfactions of coherence. The neurotic allure of illusory orders continues to hold out its appeal, even to the father of psychoanalysis, and the next chapter pursues this theme by looking at what happens when people talk about wordplay – above all, when they talk about puns, puns being the prototype for all later games with words.

Puns exemplify the problem for they show language to be both meaningful and meaningless at the same time. On the one hand, what makes a pun different from mere babble is that it has a point. The ideas it brings together will cause hilarity or embarrassment only if the ensuing clash makes some kind of sense. You've got to get the joke – it isn't wordplay otherwise. To get a pun is to redeem meaning, to find a sense underlying the apparent nonsense – a satirical connection, say – and so to shore up the priority of logical thought. It is to bring a word over from meaninglessness and restore it to meaning, to set up a dividing line between the two, and to situate yourself, naturally, on the meaningful side. But puns also pull in the opposite direction – towards linguistic disorder and chaos – and nothing so clearly betrays the illusoriness of logical thought and its claims to coherence and clarity. Puns show language to be mobile and friable, and not just sporadically – in isolated spots of trouble – but, potentially, all of the time. Given the chance, language is liable to go off in unwarranted and arbitrary directions, to break down into a quagmire of mere sounds. The distinction between what puns and what doesn't – between, for example, a dream and a dream analysis – is a useful working hypothesis, but no more than that. The analyst's orderly prose is no less prone to wordplay than anything else. What shows that distinction up for the fiction that it is are not so much the 'good' puns – which make sense and, so redeemed, can raise a laugh – but the 'bad' ones: those stupid, pointless, gratuitous puns which make no sense at all and raise only a groan. They raise a groan because they show language in its real state and kiss goodbye to the serenity of logical coherence for good. When bad puns appear in Shakespeare they unsettle confidence and disorientate interpretation. And, although Freud strives to maintain the distinction and to differentiate the puns of jokes and dreams from 'our everyday, sober method of expression', the pointlessness of this exercise is made evident and is taken up by his follower, Jacques Lacan, who goes further than most in his mission to demolish the difference and to expose logical order as a fraud.

Lacan, however, still writes – even if there are some who, confronted with his deliberate obscurity, not to say incomprehensibility, would dispute this. The final chapter of this book looks more closely at pleasure – at that consolation prize of being left to think and write. A strange kind of consolation, this, since it's both creative and illusory – irresistible and neurotic at the same time. It begins with Freud's account of the cotton-reel game in *Beyond the Pleasure Principle* (1920). The little boy who throws his bobbin inside his curtained cot and pulls it out again – 'gone! there!' – is staging the disappearance and return of his mother in a one-act play. His game – a drama in miniature – consoles him because it's repeatable. The play takes actions out of time. It end-stops the uncertainty and open-endedness of existence and puts it under the child's control. A mere twitch on the thread and lo! his mother is restored to him. In adult drama, too, the scripted repeatability of a stage-play transmutes the irreversibility of actions which, in the real world, are bound by consequence and contingency. In life, we can't undo things once they're done, but in play we can repeat them – fall in love, die, or whatever – over and over again.

Perhaps, as Nietzsche believed, tragedy offers the deepest, or strangest consolation of all. For tragedy doesn't enact just any kind of loss or uncertainty. It enacts the very worst kind – death. Tragedy rehearses the most consoling illusion of all – that death itself can be repeated, played, and played again. Naturally, everyone knows it's a fiction – what could be more fantastical? Yet the satisfaction that undeniably remains is the peculiar pleasure of enjoying what's an obvious fib. This last chapter looks at the playing of death in four of Shakespeare's plays – *Julius Caesar* (c.1599), *Hamlet* (c.1600), *Antony and Cleopatra* (1606-7), and *The Winter's Tale* (1610-11). It considers how Shakespeare and his characters articulate the conflict between the shattering finality of a unique and unrepeatable event – the assassination of Caesar, for example – and its subsequent repetition in play – 'How many times shall Caesar bleed in sport?'. In each of these plays, as his characters play – and play with – death, Shakespeare explores and promotes the paradoxical pleasure that tragedy affords. He leaves us asking, in the end, whether play isn't all that there is. Play may be a consoling illusion, its reiteration a neurotic compulsion to repeat. But that didn't stop Shakespeare writing plays. People are still watching and reading them. They are still playing, still writing plays of their own. Illusory the pleasure may be, but could anything be more creative than that?

**

Between 1739 and 1740, the young Scottish philosopher, David Hume, published his *Treatise of Human Nature* – an exercise in scepticism which went further in exposing the illusoriness of the mind's cherished orders than anyone had gone before. In terms of temperament, Hume was as different from Nietzsche as it was possible to be – his urbane and crystalline prose a million miles from Nietzsche's raging torrents. But Hume anticipated by a century and a half the collapse of order which Nietzsche and those who followed him carried through. For Hume, too, all was surface, pure appearance. There was no underlying truth, no inherent certainty – even in logical presuppostions which, on the face of it, looked as obvious and indisputable as the relation of cause to effect. What bound these two together – a flame and the heat it gave off, say – wasn't truth so much as belief, the product of habitual observation. It wasn't that the flame really was hot but that repeated experience had set us up to believe that – and to have that belief confirmed – only because we couldn't see the point or the necessity of thinking anything else.

It was from custom alone that people inferred things, even such basic things as causality, identity, and existence. These were mental impressions – forcible, maybe – but not more objective for being so. Even those classic exemplars of logical purity – geometry and mathematics – fell short of perfect precision and exactitude for they, too, were derived from mere appearances: from mental pictures of line, point, number, and relation. The degree of certainty accorded to such demonstrations had more to do with the strength of the feeling that they were correct than with anything else – with that satisfying sense of things being right, of falling into place. There were no truths as such, only degrees of belief. Things seemed more or less convincing according to how vividly they impressed themselves upon the mind. Certainty was only a feeling of certainty, nothing more. Even reasoning was only a 'species of sensation', leaving Hume with a wholly aesthetic philosophy in which it's 'not solely in poetry and music, we must follow our taste and sentiment, but likewise in philosophy. When I am convinc'd of any principle, 'tis only an idea, which strikes more strongly upon me'. The mind was an illusion-spinning instrument, a theatre in which perceptions passed, re-passed, and glided away. Man could never leave the theatre because there was nothing whatever outside it. The mind was the necessarily solipsistic origin of all it was pleased to call truth. Reality was nothing more than a truth-effect of the mind's own conjuration, our reason 'a kind of cause, of which truth is the natural effect'.

As a consequence, knowledge dissolved into doubt, certainties into mere probability. You might feel more assured of something after you'd seen a growing number of demonstrations of it. But truth wasn't cumulative. You were only piling up suppositions, adding more probabilities to one another. Besides, probability itself was only 'an idea'. The sense that something was more likely to happen because there were a greater number of chances of its doing so rested, ultimately, on the feeling – again, secured only by habit – that there was a difference between a large and a small number. But difference in magnitude was just a way the mind had of conceiving number, just a trick of the imagination. At bottom, it had no more objective validity than the feeling that derived from imagining the difference between two guineas and a pile of a thousand. In order to comprehend this – 'one of the most curious operations of the understanding' – Hume imagined to himself a single die: one on which four sides were marked with a particular number of dots, and the remaining two sides with a different number. Common sense would dictate that the first was more likely to come up. Even if you couldn't be sure which it would be, you could – according to the mathematical laws of probability – at least be certain that the first had a higher chance of doing so. Yet even this, it turned out, was a myth. It depended on ideas of superiority and inferiority in number – on the notion that four times was greater than twice – that were, again, only habits of mind. In the same way, the relation – apparently so obvious – between the throwing of the die (cause) and a given side coming to lie face up (effect) was in fact only the result of the mind's inability or reluctance to stop short along the way – as if in a kind of freeze-frame – and to form some other, quite different idea: such as, for example, the die's molecular collapse.

Concluding Book I of the *Treatise*, Hume surveyed the ruins of thought and considered the situation he was left in after he'd applied his sceptical arguments to everything, including himself. His own reasoning deconstructed itself, of course, leaving him totally alone, with a non-existent world outside and ignorance and doubt within. He found himself faced with an unenviable choice 'betwixt a false reason and none at all', between a mad lie or a mad truth – the mad lie that reality was real and that there was an intrinsic order to things, or the mad (and maddening) truth that reality didn't exist at all and there was no order to things whatsoever. You could resolve the dilemma by doing what everyone else did – by trying to forget all about it. But you couldn't stop thinking. And, in the end, Hume opted for a kind of to-and-fro – into his library to think, and out of it again to live. Having tortured his brain with contemplations of nothingness, he'd throw it all up and return to the human world of conversation, friendship, and ordinary life. But, once tired with amusement or refreshed by a solitary walk along the river-side, he'd return to his contemplations. And so it went on. He wouldn't take his doubts too seriously . . . yet this course was, in itself, to take them most seriously of all. He wouldn't become an earnest, tub-thumping zealot. That wouldn't be true to his nature. Instead he would become a dabbler and a dilettante – and perhaps the most playful philosopher of them all:

> The conduct of a man, who studies philosophy in this careless manner, is more truly sceptical than that of one, who feeling in himself an inclination to it, is yet so over-whelm'd with doubts and scruples, as totally to reject it. A true sceptic will be diffident of his philosophical doubts, as well as of his philosophical conviction; and will never refuse any innocent satisfaction, which offers itself, upon account of either of them.

One of the things Hume would do, on leaving the solitary cogitations of his study, was to dine, converse, and make merry – to go off and play backgammon with his friends. One wonders how – after all his thoughts on probability – he would have regarded the throw of the dice. How would he have played the game? Would he have gambled on it at all? Would he have risked laying a bet on the outcome? It would be interesting to know if he had . . . Would he, of all people, have paid his debts?

Joking and its Discontents

At the beginning of 1905, two manuscripts lay side by side on adjoining tables in Freud's study. According to his biographer, Ernest Jones, Freud had worked on the two simultaneously, moving from one to the other as the mood took him – the only time he'd ever combined the writing of two essays so closely together. They were published at more or less the same time, later that year. One of them – to which Freud was frequently to return, making additions and revisions that would change it out of all recognition – went through numerous editions, to become one of the most canonical of the Freudian texts: the *Three Essays on the Theory of Sexuality*. The other – to which Freud made a few small changes in its second edition of 1912, but to which he never again returned – remains perhaps the least well-known and least read of all his writings: the book on *Jokes and Their Relation to the Unconscious*.

In the *Three Essays*, Freud addressed the question of human sexuality. Where did it come from? What was the origin of all its bewildering – not to say bizarre – variations? What was it that disposed people towards the opposite sex, the same sex, or both? What caused them to be aroused not only by youth and beauty but by ugliness and old age? Why were some people turned on not by other human beings but by fetishistic objects, animals, faeces, even dead bodies, or by certain practices like self-exposure or torture? It was popularly assumed that a person's sexuality was innate – that their masculinity, femininity, or whatever grew as naturally as a plant from a pod. But this, Freud believed, was mistaken. As he saw it, a child was born with a powerful sexual instinct – that much, at least, was innate – but the aim and direction of that instinct was completely unformed. At that stage, sexuality was pure energy – as yet unchannelled, unshaped. The new-born child was a sort of desiring blob, its sexuality all over the place and directed at anything and everything that was likely to give it pleasure. In the first instance, this was usually the suckled breast. But that energy was soon directed at other things, above all at its own body – an endless source of excitation and satisfaction in thumbsucking, excretion, the stroking of its various erotogenic zones – but also at other people in the child's immediate environment – its parents, nurses, siblings. In Freud's technical vocabulary, the new-born infant was 'polymorphously perverse'. With no inherent aim, its sexuality tended in all directions at once, independent of its objects and indiscriminate in its choices, having at that stage only one aim in view – the uninterrupted pursuit of pleasure for its own sake.

In the course of time, however, this sexual energy was to be subjected to a series of inhibitory and repressive forces, both from within and without. This began with the restraints of morality, disgust, shame, and the incest taboo – at first externally imposed by family and society but soon internalized and lastingly transformed into self-constraints. Later, the physical changes brought on by puberty prepared the body – if not the mind – to subordinate its other pleasures to the genital zone, reproduction being sexuality's new biological and socially justified aim. Freud figured these various restraining forces as acting on sexuality like so many barriers or brakes. In his favourite image, sexuality was a river or stream – impelled forwards by a natural energy but its channels and tributaries successively blocked or dammed up, forcing its natural flow into one direction or another. Like water, sexuality was fluid, amorphous. It wasn't a single whole but a collection of component parts innately various and uncombined – independent of one another. It was only very gradually that these diverse elements were brought together and amalgamated. But the process was slow and subject to infinite vicissitude – and the adult sexuality that resulted from such a history wouldn't necessarily be consolidated or unified. The chances were that a person's sexuality would be mixed and hybrid – that it would shift and change in the course of a lifetime and develop in more than one direction at once.

Powerful as it was, this sexual energy was also highly delicate and liable to be arrested or fixated at any point or points along the way. The results were of the kind that Freud saw about him every day, and not only in his consulting room. There was the sexuality that was or remained in an unrestrained and undeveloped state: as in the young child who still had no shame about its body, or in the women (a curiously 'immense number') who were – or had an aptitude to be – prostitutes, willing and able to perform any number of sexual acts for the purposes of their profession. There was the sexuality that had been pushed around by the various encroaching forces of repression but which had succeeded in circumventing them in more or less satisfactory ways. This resulted in the perversions, from the mildest lingering over a caress that was preparatory to the sexual act to the wilder shores of exhibitionism, fetishism, sado-masochism, and necrophilia. There was the sexuality that had been so blocked off and beaten down as to have been repressed out of all existence – or, rather, to have come out in the hysteria and neuroses of which Freud was to make his life's work. And, finally, there was the so-called 'normal' sexuality – even though it was perhaps the least likely to survive this developmental assault-course intact – heterosexual monogamy whose sole aim and pleasure was avowedly limited to the altruistic necessities of biological reproduction.

In the joke book, the picture was the same. There, too, early childhood was presented as a blissful state – not of innocence but of freedom. In that still protean state, the child could pleasure itself and play, his instincts and desires still unformed, unshaped – unfettered by the constraints that were all too soon to descend. The infant could babble and drool to its heart's content, experiment with words and sounds with supreme disregard for meaning or sense. He could desire and enjoy – indulge erotic and aggressive fantasies unhindered by punishment or prohibition. This was a state akin to what, in a letter of 1818, Keats had called the 'Chamber of Maiden-Thought'. In his allegory of human life as a mansion of many apartments, it was this which followed on from the very first 'infant or thoughtless Chamber' where the baby was still merged with its mother and not yet introduced to the elementary separations which first inaugurated thought. Emerging into thought but not yet hemmed in or hedged about by intellectual constraints or moral laws, the child – in what were definitely to be the best days of his life – cavorted joyfully in this second chamber, which was intoxicating in its light and atmosphere and not yet darkened by knowledge or experience.

In that glorious state, the child remained free from the pressures that would in time come to contain and enclose him. He wasn't yet prey to those barriers which he'd one day have not only to accept but actively to erect and maintain himself – a process that was figured by Freud as one of relentless work and on-going effort: a permanent outlay of energy or spending of what he called 'psychical expenditure'. In due course, that state of freedom would be lost for good, sacrificed to the prevailing state of repression. The civilization into which the child was born – and to which he was required to conform – represented a series of forces and agencies which acted on him as it acted on his sexuality, controlling his impulses and regulating his desires. His former liberty became a thing of the past, and, in adult life, he endured in a state of unremitting infringement, trespassed upon by the excessive demands of his social and moral world. Prone to colossal downward-tending forces, the civilized adult emerged as a creature monitored, measured, immured, and the object of unrelenting surveillance.

It was from this insufferable prison-house, Freud suggested, that jokes offered a sought-after release – a temporary respite from the otherwise unceasing demands of civilized life. Jokes began as play, and, in the course of their development and sophistication – from the simplest jests to the most abstruse of witticisms – they always harked back to that period when a child enjoyed the free use of its words, thoughts, and desires. Jokes formed a window on the chamber of maiden thought, allowing again a brief access to its heady and scintillating delights. They rebelled against authority, liberated from law, and threw off the onerous burdens of a complex and rule-bound existence. Jokes relieved a person from the overbearing pressure to conform and to submit to the dictates of moral or logical order. They interrupted the smooth surface of orderly life, especially when the mood was cheerful and relaxed, inhibitions lowered through alcohol or good company. A licensed rebellion, jokes allowed a person to indulge once more in pleasures long since forbidden – nonsense, wordplay, sexual and aggressive desires – free from criticism or reproach. Reason, critical judgement, and suppression were the forces the joke fought in succession. Re-establishing the freedoms of childhood and setting aside the constraints of moral and intellectual upbringing, jokes permitted the civilized adult to be infantile again. Jokes were 'developed play'.

Verbal jokes, for example – a huge category, and the place where Freud started his analysis – referred back to the child's earliest and freest experience of words. As the child gradually acquired language, his early pleasure in nonsense, repetition, and sound-play came to be subjected to the myriad laws governing sense. The constraint of having to make sense meant that he had to learn to abide by the rules of grammatical permissability, and, as babble gave way to meaning, more and more utterances were disallowed him. The infant was increasingly obliged to hold back from the laziness and play of idle prattle, even though, as Freud remarked, 'it cannot be doubted that it is easier and more convenient to diverge from a line of thought we have embarked on than to keep to it, to jumble up things that are different rather than to contrast them – and, indeed, that it is *specially* convenient to admit as valid methods of inference that are rejected by logic and, lastly, to put words or thoughts together without regard to the condition that they ought also to make sense'. Freud envisaged the child's development of language skills as a gradual encroachment – an imperceptible darkening of the infant chamber – as, little by little, lazy thinking, digression, faulty reasoning, and moments of distraction or illogicality came to be curtailed. Jokes promised a return glimpse of that ancient time – a snatched enjoyment of childhood's intellectually idle state, long since denied to the rational adult. A dispensation from the need for logical coherence, the verbal joke, nonsense joke, the pun, or play on words became a pleasure which could be repeated and explicitly enjoyed as a 'rebellion against the compulsion of logic and reality'.

As well as 'innocent' jokes – jests which played with words but which didn't necessarily have any underlying irony or piquancy – there were what Freud styled 'tendentious' jokes – jokes which had a definite aim. The object of jokes such as these was to ridicule a person or type by exposing them to satirical or bawdy humour. Smutty and sarcastic jokes came into this category – and they referred back to those early days of childhood when feelings of sexual desire or overpowering rage could seize the child in all their primary force, as yet unmodified and unmuted by repression. Obscene jokes, for example – whether lavatorial humour or sexual innuendo – gave vent to childish exhibitionism, to the fascination with sexual organs, the desire to touch and to see. Such jokes satisfied the suppressed desire for unlimited sexual conquest and promiscuity. They even served as a kind of surrogate for these, so that a person who laughed at a dirty joke was effectively laughing as if 'he were the spectator of an act of sexual aggression'. In a similar way, jokes with an aggressive tendency – invective, satire, caricature, lampoon – made good the repressed desire to attack, destroy, seize, bite, and penetrate one's fellow human beings. Tendentious jokes thus licensed those urges – sexual and aggressive – that had been progressively reined in since childhood. The opportunity to indulge a forbidden impulse, moreover, yielded a different pleasure – possibly an enhanced one – from the original impulse itself. A joke's pleasure wasn't simply that of mastery or a sexual caress. It was the satisfaction of breaking a taboo, of going out of bounds. It had the pleasure of the forbidden – rebellious, titillating, and furtive.

The pleasure which a joke afforded existed on two different levels. First, there was the purely formal satisfaction of the excellent joke that did the rounds – cleverly constructed, well-timed, and to the point. This formal satisfaction made up the joke's 'fore-pleasure', which led, in turn, to the lifting of inhibitions and to the indulgence of primal desires, and which – because they tapped into deeper psychical sources – yielded a still greater degree of satisfaction. The same thing happened, incidentally, with the writing or reading of imaginative literature. This activity, Freud suggested in his essay on 'Creative Writers and Day-dreaming' (1908), also had its origins in childhood play, and the aesthetic pleasure that was to be found in enjoying works of fiction was, again, a 'fore-pleasure' – a preliminary to the deeper solace of having one's fantasies acted out in literary or narrative form. While there was no doubting the thrills of reading or writing, however, jokes definitely had the edge. For in jokes the pleasure of relaxed inhibitions was most commonly expressed in laughter. The release from tension brought discharge, and a footnote referring to the joke book in the *Three Essays* made the analogy with the sexual act explicit. A joke, it suggested, was fore-play. It aroused a small pleasure in order to liberate a far greater one which would then ejaculate in an explosion of laughter. The notion that jokes provided release appealed to the intuitive sense that laughter does, after all, relieve tension. The healthy guffaw shakes the sides and relieves the body, and, in states of uncontrollable hilarity, the muscles literally relax and tears and urine flow. In its catharsis, laughter has a well-recognized therapeutic function. And, of the altered state that follows discharge and satisfaction, images come readily to mind of the body pleasured, eased, and consoled.

For Freud, jokes subverted order. Directly or indirectly, they spoke on behalf of 'the voice within us that rebels against the demands of morality', confronting and challenging civilization's excessive demands. Jokes represented a constant bridling against that order, a means – sometimes sophisticated, sometimes crude – of getting round the ever-present censor and evading its thwarting obstacles. They worked to counter authority, to get round its strictures, and to compensate the individual for civilization's heavy taxation on pleasure. They delivered the individual from the constant checks, renunciations, and post-ponements which civilization demanded, and – under the licence of social acceptability – allowed for the joyous exercise of those earlier states of thoughtlessness, unimpaired aggression, and sexual gratification that were early childhood. *Jokes and Their Relation to the Unconscious* ended on a note of nostalgia:

> For the euphoria which we endeavour to reach by these means is nothing other than the mood of a period of life in which we were accustomed to deal with our psychical work in general with a small expenditure of energy – the mood of our childhood, when we were ignorant of the comic, when we were incapable of jokes and when we had no need of humour to make us feel happy in our life.

II

Freud's account of jokes was persuasive. It appealed to common sense in evoking laughter as a universally shared phenomenon – and, in this respect, it seemed as compelling in its affirmation of popular wisdom as a joke itself did in militating against analysis and in creating a cabal or group of companiably sociable laughers. That pleasure should follow on from the lifting of inhibitions and relaxing of effort was obvious. It seemed self-evident that feelings of pleasure should accompany a release from pressure, that laughter accompanied jokes, and that laughter was pleasurable. Freud's view also appealed to his libertarian instincts. As he saw it, the person who laughed was rebelling against the constraints of culture and its institutions and, as he put it simply, 'we count rebellion against authority as a merit'. Freud's theory offered the best of all worlds. It suggested that, in jokes, a person reverted to childish mischief but with the added delight of having been *successfully* disobedient. Jokes allowed him to get away with it. A joke ensured the frisson of fulfilling a forbidden wish while avoiding the recriminations that might have been meted out on the real child. You couldn't lose.

All, however, was not entirely well. For the theory of release, logical and self-evident as it seemed, was to run into difficulties that would emerge in the course of the joke book and come increasingly to disrupt the flow of its arguments. Freud was the first to admit, for example, that jokes offered only a limited, contained rebellion. They might disrupt but they didn't destroy the ongoing pattern of civilized life. That remained in place, with all its attendant trials and tribulations intact. Jokes didn't – like the pied piper – lure a person into the magic mountain for good. They offered only a brief foray, a temporary diversion. Jokes ruptured restraint and fleetingly freed a person from the need to hold himself back. But they operated as a safety-valve for the venting of passions and releasing of pressures which – if left unchecked – might cause him to malfunction. The final aim of jokes, in fact, was the smooth running of the overall machine, not the smashing of its engine. This put a somewhat different gloss on Freud's model of jokes as rebelling against authority and on the common-sense view – which it seemed to corroborate – of 'comic relief' as a force for good, a healthy energy welling up from below, a liberating corrective to the overbearing pressures that beset us all.

A person wasn't, after all, granted one laugh in a lifetime – a single, irreversible, once-and-for-all liberation from the constraints imposed by civilized life. Laughter wasn't the decisive escape, a crossing of the final frontier. Clearly, it was something that could be repeated. If a joke lifted inhibitions, presumably those inhibitions would – somewhere along the line – be restored so that the pleasure of lifting them again could be re-experienced with the next giggle, grunt, or guffaw. Laughter wasn't so much a release from prison as a wrested and short-lived parole. Nor did it offer a gradual liberation. It wasn't that a certain quota of laughter would finally succeed in throwing off the shackles of a repressive society, nor that even the tiniest quantities – if repeated often enough – would cure the Freudian subject. Jokes might relieve the pain but they didn't heal the patient, didn't get to the root of civilized man's discontent. Every laugh – no matter how intensely it was appreciated – in effect returned the laugher to the same state of repression he'd been in before. The situation of the Freudian subject was chronic rather than acute. Laughter salved but it didn't cure. It left the patient exactly where he was.

Jokes formed a breach, a rupture. They punctured authority and indulged rebellious fantasies of every kind. But the breach unfailingly closed over again, no matter how often it was made. Like the parting of the waters, the joke was only a temporary, if expedient, miracle. A joke was a bounded moment on the far side of which lay a sea of ordinariness. This formed the backdrop from which the joke's ticklish moments – fun, diverting, scandalous – emerged, but to which, by the same token, the laugher had no choice but to return. The joke ushered him into a play-space of borrowed time only to deposit him back, afterwards, into what – by virtue of this manoeuvre – was set up as being the 'real', that is the normal world. Far from subverting civilized values, jokes were one of the mechanisms by which society naturalized those values and ensured that the prevailing state of repression stayed in place. Recognized as brief interruptions, jokes shored up the priority of those values. Whatever or whoever a particular joke made fun of, the presiding order from which the joke marked itself out as different was tacitly restored every time, and the *status quo* was thus affirmed as the neutral, unremarked background which simply represented the way things were.

The ultimately conservative force and function of joking was nothing new. But the drift from rebelliousness towards order – from the subverting to the supporting of civilized mores – wasn't openly acknowledged by Freud. He seems to have been uncomfortable with it and to have wanted to hold on as long as he could to the model of release, attractive as it was in its appeal to both his libertarian instincts and to common sense. The reluctant shift to the opposite view – that laughter didn't in fact rebel but actually bolstered and reinforced the very repressions that troubled civilized man and threatened to drive him to neurosis – becomes evident more in the overall shape of Freud's book than in any open confrontation. For it's only in the final section – the chapter on 'jokes and the species of the comic' – that Freud turned his mind to this alternative and less happy scenario.

Freud had spent three quarters of the joke book arguing that jokes provided an escape from civilization's incessant demands. In joking, a person became a child again, briefly returned to the former freedoms of play. The joke indulged rebelliousness and provided a belated space for the fulfilment of infantile desires. But when Freud went on to discuss the comic in this final section, the apparent seamlessness of his argument belied an unsettling refutation of everything that had gone before. In the comic, it appeared, there was no such identification with the child but rather the reverse – a distancing or estrangement from him. We find comical, Freud argued, exaggerated movements or facial expressions, evidence of mental feebleness, an imperfect control over the body and especially over its excretory functions. Why? Because these all characterized the condition of childhood. Projecting them onto someone else like a clown or buffoon assured the laugher of his own adult state and proved that he had, thankfully, long since outgrown the distresses and embarrassments of infancy. 'A person appears comic to us', Freud wrote, 'if, in comparison with ourselves, he makes too great an expenditure on his bodily functions and too little on his mental ones; and it cannot be denied that in both these cases our laughter expresses a pleasurable sense of the superiority which we feel in relation to him'.

If the relations were reversed and a person's physical expenditure proved to be less than our own or his intellectual expenditure greater, it wouldn't be remotely comical. A super-sophisticated person like this would inspire admiration and awe rather than laughter. To perceive someone else as awkward, inadequate, or childlike, however, was to establish the superior standard which – by virtue of the comparison – the laugher understood himself to have achieved, and against which he gratifyingly contrasted the other's failure. Provoking laughter at what was childish, the comic served to bolster and enliven all those critical forces which – up until this point – Freud had habituated his readers into thinking of as repressive, inhibitory, and potentially maddening – logical thought, bodily propriety, and self-control. Yet here we find that the comic is on the side of the adult within us and that it re-establishes the latter's authority over the child. Laughter would always 'apply to the comparison between the adult's ego and the child's ego'. We find comical 'embarrassments, in which we rediscover the child's helplessness . . . incomplete control over his bodily functions . . . peculiar lack of a sense of proportion'. 'Those things are comic which are not proper for an adult'.

The standard set up by the comic, in other words, was that of the repressed, controlled, civilized adult – exactly what jokes were supposed to subvert. The comic established a principle of exactitude, of measured expenditure – just the right amount, neither too much nor too little. Our sensitivity to the slightest deviation – registered in caricature or mimicry – suggested with what finesse this principle had been assimilated. As Freud remarked, civilization was marked by the higher priority it gave to the mind over the body, to the rational and intellectual faculties over the physical. The more civilized a person or society, the more the body and the physical world were controlled by the mind and its inventions – evidence for which Freud found in the progressive mechanization of his society. 'A restriction of our muscular work and an increase of our intellectual work fit in with the course of our personal development towards a higher level of civilization', he suggested. 'By raising our intellectual expenditure we can achieve the same result with a diminished expenditure on our movements. Evidence of this cultural success is provided by our machines'. In an interesting departure from Henri Bergson, who had argued in his essay on *Laughter* (1900) that people laughed at clumsiness or actions of clockwork-like regularity because these seemed inhumanly mechanistic, Freud appeared to be suggesting that it was machines that made men like gods. For him, the comic seemed less to grant a rebellion against civilization than to privilege civilization and its self-awarded achievements – progress, order, and industrialization.

If the first and most substantial part of the joke book had proposed that jokes freed a person from unwelcome constraints, the last part suggested that the comic put those constraints back again and secured them for good. If in jokes we'd laughed *as* a child, in the comic, we laughed *at* the child. It all hinged on there being a difference between the two – something that was difficult to maintain because jokes and the comic had so much in common. They were both funny, and there were many occasions when Freud admitted that he couldn't really decide whether a particular story was one or the other. The chief distinguishing mark, as he saw it, was that 'a joke is made, the comic is found'. A joke had to be told. It required a minimal theatre of three: A told B about C. The hearer – B – observably laughed more heartily than the teller – A – because, in addition to having his psychical inhibitions temporarily lifted by the joke, he was also spared the effort of making the joke itself: re-calling it, re-telling it, timing the punchline correctly (A's job). He enjoyed a release from the labour of maintaining a civilized self virtually for free. The comic, by contrast, was not made but found. It required no telling and no audience, but was content with two persons and could occur simply when one person saw or registered something that was comical in someone else. Yet Freud's distinction was in danger of faltering. For he spent a good part of this section on the comic describing how you could make yourself or another person comical at will. You could intentionally be comical, for example, by means of mimicry, self-parody, or caricature – all forms which so closely resembled jokes as to make the distinction between the two pretty meaningless.

When, much later on, Freud came to reformulate the structure of the psyche, this differentiation between the laugher and the laughed at – already strained in the joke book – was to collapse altogether. With the psyche divided up into ego, id, and superego, what had once looked like an identification with the child in jokes became instead the indulgence of one part of the psyche by another. The new anatomy of the mind – first broached in *The Ego and The Id* (1923) – effectively internalized the whole process. Neither identification with the rebellious ego/child – as in jokes – nor with the controlling superego/adult – as in the comic – needed to involve an object, an audience, or a teller at all. A, B, and C were all to be found within. Jokes and the comic could be played out endlessly within the conflictual, embattled arena of the individual psyche. Now, empathizing, identifying, and laughing along with the child was only another way of laughing at him, by including his weaknesses within the larger, more crowded scenario of the psyche as a whole. Laughing 'with' might seem to be generous and magnanimous – a sharing of the experience of human foibles with one's fellow man. But in fact it was no more than a laughing 'at' the weak and feeble part of the self – the ego – either as it was acknowledged or as it was denied and projected out onto someone else. However gentle it might have seemed, this kind of laughter was at bottom mocking, derisive, and superior, for it proceeded from the vantage-point of the adult. And, however noble an attribute, the ability to laugh at oneself testified only to a split in the psyche – with one part, the superego, making mock of another, the ego.

The tidal drift of the joke book away from childhood play and towards adult work was finalized when, in 1927, Freud briefly returned to the subject for the first and only time. In the essay on 'Humour' published that year Freud took up the discussion which he'd embarked on in the closing pages of *Jokes* where he'd suggested that, if a joke required at least three people and the comic two, then humour could be contained within the single individual. Here, any distinction between jokes that were made and the comic that was found finally disappeared. Humour wasn't like telling a joke or laughing at a comic situation. It was an attitude. It was a way of making light of things that might otherwise have caused anxiety or distress, like the criminal being led to the gallows on a Monday morning who commented that the week was beginning nicely. The humorist put things in perspective, refusing to get ruffled or het up about them. He assumed the role of the adult towards a childishness which he found in other people or, most often, in himself. He 'is treating himself like a child and is at the same time playing the part of a superior adult towards that child'. The humorous attitude issued, that is, from the superego – from whose perspective the ego looked 'tiny and all its interests trivial'.

By this stage, Freud's thinking on play, jokes, the comic, and humour seemed finally to relinquish the attractions of subversiveness and to throw its weight behind the forces of civilization and control for good. Having presented those forces over the years as variously repressive, distorting, and painful, Freud, at this stage in his career, seemed to admit his allegiance with them unabashed. Here, humour was philosophical, intelligent, rueful, and wry. It ensured a properly mature and adult way of looking out on the world – accepting all its uncertainties and instabilities with an amused equanimity. Humour was praised as being the highest form of wit, miraculously offering the best of all worlds in that it had both 'something liberating about it' and 'something of grandeur and elevation'. Humour was a rare and precious gift, by no means bestowed on everybody. And, unlike jokes or the comic, it was dignified. By the end of the essay, the superego had not only been rescued but had undergone a remarkable transformation. Instead of the harsh, controlling, mocking, parental tyrant who had mercilessly scoffed at the ego's childishness – as in the final section of *Jokes* – there emerged an indulgent, smiling, forgiving, rather grandmotherly presence who gave the ego space and time to play.

The superego had mellowed a good deal. As Freud's editors put it, this was the first time the superego had appeared in such an amiable mood. In humour, it appeared, the superego did the most uncharacteristic things – like speaking 'kindly words of comfort' to the ego, and downplaying the real dangers of life and so 'actually repudiating reality and serving an illusion'. Freud confessed to some perplexity on this account. Although the pleasure afforded by humour was less intense than the joke's explosive laughter, he nonetheless believed – 'without rightly knowing why' – that we valued it more highly and found it specially liberating and elevating. The reason for this final vindication of the superego and all its pomps was – as we'll explore further below – that ultimately it stabilized and justified Freud's role as a thinker and theorist. In the end, if only to maintain itself and its claims to rational argument and intellectual coherence, theory was going to opt for order – no matter how repressive or soul-destroying that order had been shown to be along the way. Objective and scientific as it aimed to be, Freud's analysis of humour and jokes was ultimately going to move in the direction of the civilized values in which such an analysis had a place. The superego was always to be found at the end of the line.

This gradual triumph of the forces of control over rebellion – which emerged in the overall shape of the joke book and in its sequel in the essay on humour – also came out in the trope which served as the joke book's presiding metaphor: the idea of economy. Freud's notions of exchange, surplus, and equilibrium were grounded in late nineteenth-century physics and, in particular, in the laws of thermodynamics which stated that, however much was exchanged, energy could neither be created nor destroyed. Energy might circulate but the quantities would always balance out in the end. This economic model – which assumed that the energy required for some things had to be borrowed or re-directed from others – remained the basic prototype for Freud's whole theory of psychodynamics, above all his notion that sexual energy that was repressed came to be sublimated and re-used in the development of art, science, and all the achievements of human civilization. This principle of economy appeared throughout Freud's writings, but nowhere more explicitly nor structurally than in the book on jokes – the entire argument of which devolved around the themes of saving and frugality and which could be summed up in Hamlet's famous words: 'Thrift, thrift, Horatio!'

A good many of the jokes in Freud's book are 'economic' in the sense that they're sarcastic jibes or quips of some sort about money. The book opens, for example, with a joke that had already been analysed and discussed by other authorities on wit and humour. Hirsch-Hyacinth – a down-trodden lottery agent and comic creation of the poet, Heinrich Heine – boasts of an encounter with the legendarily wealthy Baron Rothschild who, to his immense pride, had treated him 'quite as his equal – quite famillionairely'. Later, Freud tells an anecdote about a man who went into a pastry-cook's shop and ordered a cake only to bring it back and ask for a liqueur instead. Having drunk it, he was about to leave without paying when the proprietor detained him. 'You've not paid for the liqueur'. – 'But I gave you the cake in exchange for it'. – 'You didn't pay for that either'. – 'But I hadn't eaten it'. A few pages further on, Freud relates an American joke about two shady businessmen who, having amassed a huge fortune, sought to buy their way into respectability by having their portraits painted by the best artist in the city. Displaying the canvases side by side at a lavish evening reception, they asked a leading art critic and influential connoisseur for his opinion of them. After studying the pictures for some time, he turned and – pointing to the gap between them – asked, 'But where's the Saviour?'.

All three of these are tendentious jokes in that they poke fun at individuals or types whose accumulation of wealth is perceived to be less than squeaky clean. The first joke exposes the condescension of the millionaire and deflates his pretensions to aristocratic largesse, for he reveals himself to be not so different from – in fact, as rather familiar with – the entrepreneurial shenanigans of a lottery agent. The other jokes laugh at the sharp practice which makes the capitalist exchange of goods look more like the theft which – according to some influential nineteenth-century economists – it was. And dubious business practices evidently couldn't be all that easily disguised, for the two businessmen – with their tell-tale ignorance of religious iconography and the art-historical tradition – had unwittingly revealed themselves to be the thieves they really were. Underlying all this was a bourgeois business ethic which – by singling out sharp practice and shady dealing for satirical attack – sought to distinguish and so to justify itself. Jokes like these belonged with the moralizing mentality explored by Max Weber in his classic work, *The Protestant Ethic and the Spirit of Capitalism* – like Freud's book on jokes, also published in 1905 – where *arrivistes* were argued to justify their new-found wealth by promoting an ethic of industriousness, self-betterment, and austerity. These jokes were nothing less than a collective salving – or laundering – of the bad conscience of an ambitious bourgeoisie.

Where Freud was most effectively to give away his bourgeois credentials, however, wasn't in his telling of such jokes so much as in the theory he proceeded to erect upon them – a theory that was, from the beginning, presented in terms of saving. The economies which Freud had in mind weren't strictly those of condensing two words into a single pun: familiar + millionaire = famillionaire. Nor were they the result of allusiveness – the appeal to common knowledge and a shared cultural tradition which could be left unsaid and on which getting a joke wholly depended. These amounted to a joke's formal or aesthetic excellence – its fore-pleasure – and were small economies which reminded Freud of 'the way in which some housewives economize when they spend time and money on a journey to a distant market because vegetables are to be had there a few farthings cheaper'. Such savings were not, for all that, to be dismissed out of hand, for the least successful or 'cheapest' jokes were those which – like some puns – barely afforded even this slight satisfaction. Brevity, after all, was the soul of wit. But the economy towards which, after several chapters of discussion and analysis, Freud was heading was one that was altogether more substantial – namely, an economy in 'psychical expenditure'.

Psychical expenditure was the price people paid for civilized adulthood – the constant work of remaining a reasonable human being and not reverting to the selfishness, savagery, and hedonism from which they'd come. It wasn't easy, and Freud presented this work in terms of a ceaseless and ongoing labour. As he saw it, a person was for ever working, constantly laying out an expenditure of effort in order to repress his desires, hold back his aggression, and submit to the requirements

97

of logic and sense – 'both for erecting and for maintaining a psychical inhibition some 'psychical expenditure' is required'. A person was engaged in paying out this daily premium which mortgaged him until death – or at least until second childhood in senility. Psychical expenditure was less an investment than a form of taxation, since a person spent a great deal for very little return – the bare maintenance of a civilized self. It was a high price – too high for the neurotic, who paid out far too much to repress his desires and so bankrupted himself into illness. But the model which lay behind the joke book wasn't the neurotic. Rather, it was the person who got the balance right: the good and sober bourgeois, the law-abiding and tax-paying citizen whose economic success – the result of careful management and putting-by – was well-earned and (so the implication went) wholly deserved.

The overall shift in the joke book – from the apparent subversiveness of jokes to the conservative power of the comic – reappeared, in other words, in the book's controlling metaphor of economy. We end up back with that sad product of civilization – the put-upon, over-controlled, repressed, and potentially neurotic bourgeois adult. Satirical jokes punctured pretension and deflated authority. They relieved a person from the necessity for self-restraint. They meant he need no longer hold back from criticism out of politeness or respect but could let rip and mock figures of authority, eminence, wealth, or success by bringing them down to size and exposing them as cheats and liars. But what seemed, in the jokes themselves, to be a debunking and belittling gesture – rebellious and anti-establishment – was in turn to be recouped by Freud's theory. For what made jokes enjoyable – that little thrill of disobedience – was figured entirely in the good, clean, respectable terms of caution, saving, and thrift. Rebellion was cast in the most virtuous of terms. In laughing at a joke, a person was no longer paying over the odds but cutting a deal and, in effect, making an excellent transaction. He was briefly relieved from an otherwise unstinting outlay of energy – a respite which Freud presented again and again as an efficiency or retrenchment. A good joke might expose capitalist exploitation for the theft that it was; but to laugh at it made – in psychic terms – the best business sense. Freud's model was explicitly that of a business enterprise, the civilized adult being for all the world like a large, complex corporation in which economies of any size would eagerly be seized. Business practices that were disparaged by the jokes themselves would be rescued – saved and defended – by Freud's theory about why they were funny. For the principle of saving or thrift around which he structured his theory of jokes upheld the bourgeois principles of order and restraint against which jokes were supposed to be fighting. Perhaps it was a losing battle, after all.

There was a sense in which this pull towards order in the joke book was inevitable. For Freud was engaged in making a theory – in imposing order on particularly intractable material, hoping to move beyond what had previously been written on jokes by combining those '*disjecta membra*' into a new 'organic whole'. As in everything he wrote, Freud had ambitions towards coherence and clarity and it was these that came out in the final validation of the adult over the child in the discussions on the comic and on humour, and in the underlying endorsement of bourgeois economics. In some ways, the fight was always going to be unequal. However Freud may have deplored the forces of repression – longed to stop work and gone off to play – so long as he was wielding a pen, he remained committed to the values of self-control, logic, and order. Whatever else he was, Freud was a theoretician, a practitioner dedicated to the pursuit of knowledge, however arcane, and to the furtherance of expertise, however experimental. He was a humble servant of civilization, and his lectures, books, and clinical practice all testified to the deep seriousness with which he devoted himself to it. There was no doubt of his commitment to explication, of his untiring efforts to seek out cause and effect. Indeed, it was his lifelong ambition to explain not just any phenomena but precisely those which had been characterized hitherto by their baffling *in*explicability – madness, humour, and dreams. His work in the joke book – as in what were perhaps its closest siblings, *The Interpretation of Dreams* (1900) and *The Psychopathology of Everyday Life* (1901) – was part of his whole-sale attempt to bring the dark, absurd, zany, and bizarre into the clear light of rational day.

The job of rendering the unintelligible intelligible was the self-validating aim of Freud's whole project, and against all this the argument that jokes relieved a person from the work constantly demanded by civilization and delivered him into a mindless, childish state bordering on bliss didn't stand much of a chance. For it was always destined to end up contained and rationalized within the logical constructions of the Herr Professor. Freud made the state of childhood look more attractive in the joke book than anywhere else, sentimalizing it as a long-lost, fondly remembered eden of freedom and play. But, for all the sense of resignation and regret for times past, there was no question of Freud reverting to that state himself. Jokes were only temporary rebellions, after all. The theory of release, attractive as it was, didn't have the courage of Freud's convictions – at least, not of all of them. The image of man struggling heroically to throw off the shackles of civilized life could never ring entirely true: 'what these jokes whisper may be said aloud: that the wishes and desires of men have a right to make themselves acceptable alongside of exacting and ruthless morality. And in our days it has been said in forceful and stirring sentences that this morality is only a selfish regulation laid down by the few who are rich and powerful'. This revolutionary call to arms was bound to sound rather hollow so long as Freud stayed theorizing and remained committed to the values of logic and order which would enable him to write and to be read.

III

For all the logic and appeal of the release theory – and for all the pleasures that were undoubtedly to be found in the relaxation of effort and relief from pressure – Freud seemed unable to arrest the slide of his book in the opposite direction, towards the forces of repression and control. In the course of his reflections, these forces came not only to be theoretically justified – in the form of bourgeois economics – but made to look positively benign, not to say serene – in the form of humour's superior, smiling wisdom. Behind the bids for irresponsibility and freedom stood the theorist who – whether he liked it or not – was already predisposed towards order and rule, and whose own unstinting effort to organize and control his material was bound to militate against the model of play, no matter how appealing that model had, in the course of the argument, been made out to be. It's as if in the end Freud couldn't help coming round to the view that jokes – which he saw as adult play – were ultimately restorative rather than rebellious, creative rather than destructive.

Put like this, Freud's book on jokes would seem to belong with those accounts of play considered in the first chapter – with Schiller, Huizinga, Caillois, and Winnicott, for whom the writer's own logical coherence and orderly prose vindicated the civilized values towards which play was argued to be the first step. For them, play was a creative act from the beginning, to be corroboratingly reflected in their own work on the subject. Freud seemed to arrive at the same point by a more circuitous route. He didn't begin by saying that play was creative – quite the opposite, in the first three quarters of the joke book play was regressive. But he did end up by saying that. So long as writing about play was a creative act – fashioning and perfecting a theory, gathering up the *disjecta membra* and re-assembling them into a new whole – play was destined to be theorized as creative. Since theoretical orderliness underpinned the whole rationale of the Freudian enterprise, then for him finally to acknowledge this – to admit that for him, as for Nietzsche's theoretical man, 'the one noble and truly human occupation was that of laying bare the workings of nature, of separating true knowledge from illusion and error' – was, perhaps, only to be honest.

Yet – in spite of all this – Freud couldn't quite share the cheerfulness and optimism of the theoretical men without qualm. For, unlike them, he remained very much in two minds about the intrinsic benefits of order and its overall value for humankind. Although he couldn't avoid it in his own writing, Freud retained a lurking suspicion that the compulsion towards logic and reason belonged to the same system of values and habits of mind which also had the power to repress the individual, to alienate him from his earliest memories and deepest desires, and ultimately to drive him mad. From the beginning, Freud's understanding of sexuality and the psyche had been dominated by one idea – that of repression. Energies raw and naked in the as-yet un-socialized child were suppressed – subject to forces which bore down on them and violently, if gradually, knocked them into shape. But these forces of repression aroused in Freud famously mixed and ambivalent feelings. On the one hand, they trained the child to adapt to reality and prepared him for all the rigours of adult life. They formed the mainstay of civilization, the highest achievements of which were culture, science, and technology, and the highest accolades of which went to rewarding intellectual endeavour and rational effort. On the other, they mercilessly repressed the child and curtailed his freedoms for good – cooped him up, harassed him, ordered him about – so that it wasn't only the hysterical patients who came to see Freud but every thinking, speaking person who was, to some degree or other, neurotic. As is well known, Freud never resolved this dilemma and came to see the human condition as one of enduring conflict between the forces of freedom and control. In his case, moreover, the dilemma was peculiarly irresolvable. For his theories – which, like any, were a validation of some kind of order – had themselves grown out of his suspicion that the order of civilized society was precisely what could madden and harm.

The theoretical men remained untroubled by this dilemma. They didn't allow themselves to be disturbed by it but ignored it or rose above it – by taking it for granted that order was a good thing, its achievement a success and cause for unequivocal celebration. They chose an account of play which would shore up their own theoretical position – a narrative of progress which saw play as the beginning of creativity and a will to order that was reassuringly reflected back at them in their own logical prose. The triumph of order was taken as read, proving not only the rightness of the argument but their own claims to theoretical eminence as well. Theoretical man's confidence in his own powers, however, was blown apart by Nietzsche who, like those who followed him, dismissed order as a vain illusion and rejected the argument for progress on the grounds that it was all too obviously circular and self-fulfilling. Although these writers couldn't get out of the vicious circle altogether – they were writing too, after all – they could at least see the vicious circle for what it was, indicate that they were inside it, and find jokey strategies for letting everyone else know.

Freud is poised interestingly between the two. He neither ignored the problem – the sense that he was working in the name of a civilization which also made people miserable was always there to haunt him. Nor did he confront it full on – we don't find in Freud the arch wit or self-conscious playfulness of the deconstructionist. Instead, his habitual ambivalence towards civilization – at once man's highest achievement and the very thing that made him unhappy – appeared in all its irresolution, whether he wanted it to or not. The conflict emerged willy nilly in the asymmetries and illogicalities of his texts. As many others have shown, this uncertainty about the benefits of order and civilization came out in virtually everything Freud wrote. It appeared in the rhetorical twists and turns of an argument that half sensed when it was heading towards a contradiction or going round in circles and turned aside – leaving the situation fascinatingly open-ended and unresolved. In recent years, there's scarcely been one Freudian text that hasn't been given the treatment – put on the couch, analyzed, and examined, its internal contradictions – more telling, in every case, than the arguments it ostensibly parades – being teased out and brought out into the light of day.

Another way of looking at the overall shift of the joke book towards order, for example, would be to see it less as re-asserting conservative moral and economic values and the rights of the stern adult/superego, than as proposing what is, in fact, nothing less than a doctrine of pure pleasure. Jokes and the comic might arouse different kinds of pleasure but, in effect, Freud's argument allowed him to suggest that a person was in a state of pleasure *all the time*. If there was pleasure to be found in rebelling against authority, there was also pleasure to be found in restoring that authority. Laughing as a child, in sarcastic or smutty jokes, released tension and relieved a person from effort. But laughing at childishness, whether in oneself or in someone else, brought with it the undeniable pleasures of superiority. Freud's discussions of the comic and of humour may have ended up by putting the superego back in charge of things, but they didn't open out onto a vista of unrelieved suffering as a result. The hard work and effort of the superego were redeemed by their successes – the serene sublimations of the civilized adult – granting a person every right to congratulate himself and to enjoy all the satisfactions of a personal triumph. And, even if there was a contradiction in Freud's account – if pleasure turned out to be derived as much from making rules as from breaking them – he was still able to hold his theoretical head up high. For, while the release theory may have appealed to the commonsensical view of jokes as bursting through fussy convention and kicking against the pricks, the idea of comic superiority also had a venerable pedigree – going back to Plato – as one of the oldest explanations for why laughter pleased. To invite a person to see stupidity and turpitude from an implicitly superior position was to elicit the 'sudden glory' of laughter which, as the seventeenth-century philosopher Thomas Hobbes classically put it, arose from the 'conception of some eminency in ourselves, by comparison with the infirmity of others, or with our own formerly'.

We can begin to see, perhaps, why the superego had to undergo so magical a transformation in the 'Humour' essay – in order to preserve pleasure, of all things. For – rather economically, as it turned out – this transformation came to serve a number of different purposes. Emerging as a serene, unruffled presence possessed of a philosophically ironic outlook on the world, the humorous superego allowed Freud the satisfaction of allying himself with a respectable tradition of theories on the comic. At the same time, it also justified and redeemed that satisfaction by theorizing itself as a source of pleasure – the happiness of making sense and of having a sound cultural tradition to fall back on. In this best of all possible worlds, theoretical man – whether the civilized adult, sober bourgeois, or serious theorist – was not only vindicated but also allowed to enjoy what he did, his efforts being explicitly described as pleasurable. It was, as Freud virtually admits, almost too good to be true. Humour wasn't resigned, it was rebellious – 'like jokes and the comic, humour has something liberating about it' – so the pleasure of rebelling against authority was kept intact. But it also had about it 'something of grandeur and elevation' which was lacking in the other two – the satisfactions of moral and intellectual superiority – so the pleasure of restoring authority was kept too. And all this while Freud could show off his cultivated credentials by allying himself with an ancient philosophical tradition. That was the icing on the cake.

The fact that pleasure was to be derived from such contradictory if not mutually exclusive sources was registered only, perhaps, in Freud's momentary hesitation about this wonder drug that could liberate and elevate at the same time without him 'rightly knowing why'. Having changed the superego out of all recognition into an illusion-loving, pleasure-seeking hedonist, Freud confessed to some confusion: 'we still have a great deal to learn about the nature of the superego'. But, so long as he remained in a state of tactical unknowing, Freud's doubt had a distinct gain – for it covered a multitude of sins. It was able to smooth over contradictions in the argument and to leave him at the end – not unlike the polymorphously perverse infant – able to derive pleasure from as many different sources as were available, and, what was more (in this respect, unlike the infant), able to come up with a theoretical justification for doing so and to derive pleasure from that as well.

So the drift towards order wasn't without its compensations. And, although the theorist was bound, in the nature of things, to have the last word, the ups and downs of his argument ended up by telling a different story – one which threatened to compromise Freud's claims to coherence if not to credibility. As one might expect, a similar contradiction also emerged in the joke book's overriding metaphor of economy. It's true that behind the metaphor there lurked the sensible bourgeois who handled his money matters well. But the balance between repression and laughter that was achieved in humour – without Freud quite knowing why – proved in the metaphor of economy to be even harder to sustain. That too threatened, in spite of itself, to go off in unwarranted directions of its own. And, although Freud had dismissed as 'incomprehensible' the view expressed by other writers on the comic that its pleasure arose from 'the oscillation of attention backwards and forwards between contrasting ideas', just such a comical oscillation appeared – of all places – in the precious metaphor of economy itself.

It came out most clearly in what the outcome of all that saving was supposed to be. A person who laughed at a joke was spared the payment of psychical expenditure, was temporarily excused from his habitual, dreary payments. But the analogy with financial expenditure at this point began to show signs of strain. For to save money was to hoard it – to keep it in the bank or under the mattress. It meant stashing money away – storing it, investing it, allowing it to accumulate – which was the opposite of spending it. But the good citizen who saved on his psychical expenditure didn't then lay those savings aside for a rainy day, didn't re-invest them somewhere else. Instead, like an irresponsible child with his first pocket money, he went off and spent it straight away. The saving of psychical expenditure was, in effect, exactly the same as spending. Energies formerly tied up with the repressing of desires and monitoring of inhibitions were suddenly released to be discharged through laughter – a luxury item if ever there was one. The saver of psychical expenditure didn't exchange what he'd saved for some useful product but spent it immediately on something as useless and wasteful – if enjoyable – as having a good laugh. Unlike the saving of money, the saving of energy was equivalent to spending – for energy, like passion, was something spent. Saving money meant retention – not release – and involved no discharge comparable to what followed saving psychical expenditure. If saving money meant holding something in, saving the latter meant letting it all hang out. As with the triumph of the superego, it all came down to pleasure in the end.

Taken literally, the metaphor of economy on which Freud based his whole theory of jokes would require the laugher to preserve his capital, to hold himself in, and not to spend a penny more. Instead of an explosion into laughter, a literal reading of the metaphor would present an image of the laugher as pent-up, thrifty, and parsimonious, inviting a comparison between the stingy, miserly body – saved from monetary expenditure – on the one hand, and the laughing, liberated body – saved from psychical expenditure – on the other. Freud's theoretical model tended inevitably towards the first of these. Behind the scenes, it sought to sustain the principles of effort and hard work, to uphold the ethics of good housekeeping and sound budget management – the theorist's interests in order and logical coherence depended on it. But the temptations of the alternative proved difficult to resist and had to be fought against all the way. The pleasures of excess and irresponsibility may have been destined to lose out in the end – but not without a struggle. And one could perhaps see that what made the saving metaphor so compelling for Freud was precisely its built-in contradiction. In effect, by blurring the difference between the two commodities that were to be 'saved' – money, on the one hand, and psychical energy, on the other – the metaphor allowed him to have his cake and eat it (icing and all) – which is always the best position to be in. For the saving metaphor in fact presented man's permanent condition to be one of spending. A person was spending something or other all of the time – spending psychical expenditure as a matter of routine, and spending energy in intermittently laughing at jokes. By means of psychical expenditure, the spending of sordid cash was transmuted into the more respectable expenditure by which the honest citizen paid his debt to civilization. But under cover of that bourgeois respectability lay something rather different. For even the thrifty, law-abiding person maintained that state only by means of a constant outlay.

So, after all that, there wasn't any saving at all. It was all spend, spend, spend. On the other side of the thrifty bourgeois – or even a self-caricature of the usurious Jew – lay a fantasy of unrestrained prodigality. The saving metaphor – like the argument of the joke book as a whole – turned out to be highly unstable. If, on the surface, *Jokes* had seemed to be heading in the direction of the rebellious child, then behind that lay the affirmation of civilized adult values in the form of the theorist's superego. But behind that, in turn, lay the superego in holiday humour – a pleasure-seeking epicure. A similar layering appeared in the metaphor of economy. Behind the would-be spendthrift – who rebelled against the establishment by laughing at jokes – stood the sober bourgeois who restored those values by theorizing about jokes. But behind him again stood a figure whose ceaseless and wholly unproductive spending resembled that of the squandering, conspicuously consuming aristocrat more than anyone else – a financially incontinent libertine. As these figures stood – sodomitically – behind one another laughter began to take on something of the character of a perversion. No longer the hygienic overflow of pressure or excess energy – a mechanism by which to regulate the neurotic bourgeois body and keep it healthy – laughter appeared more like a kind of masochistically enjoyed masturbation. Like sexuality that was neither subordinated to the reproductive, genital aim, nor sublimated in favour of higher things, laughter came to be enjoyed for its own gloriously wasteful sake. The instability of the saving metaphor allowed Freud to oscillate wildly between the different positions – the incontinent child, the regular citizen, the anally retentive theorist, and the orgiastically sadistic marquis – doing nothing for the coherence either of the metaphor or of the joke book as a whole except, perhaps, to make both a lot more interesting.

It was always as the theorist that Freud was going to end up. He couldn't help reverting to type, and it was to this point that his books would inevitably return him, if only because it was there that he was thinking and writing – organizing his material and trying to fashion it from '*disjecta membra*' into an 'organic whole'. His arguments would always be contained by this overall aim. Short of abandoning work altogether, there was no getting round it. But in this, as in other such readings of the Freudian corpus, the superego hardly emerged unscathed. The theorist's bids to order were more than embarrassed by an argument that rebelled against itself and erupted – as if in rip-roaringly irreverent jokes at its own expense – into fantasies of perversion and prodigality. Though Freud tried hard to hold on to the serenity of theoretical man, the illusoriness and hopelessness of the task gave itself away at every turn. And, although the superego did its best to hold things together and keep a tight grip on unruly material, it would turn out to be a less than successful taskmaster – more like a dithering and over-sensitive commanding officer than a brutish sergeant major. Though destined – in the theorist's writings, at least – to have the last word, this would prove to be a pyrrhic victory when the superego's claims to authority were capable of being so severely undermined along the way.

The instability of his arguments compromised not only Freud the theorist but Freud the doctor as well. For the practice of psychoanalysis – at least as it was formulated in *The Interpretation of Dreams* and in the early writings on hysteria – was to bring things out from the darkness of the unconscious and into the light of day. By interpreting a patient's dreams, symptoms, and slips of the tongue, the psychoanalyst aimed to drag things up from the inaccessible murk of the repressed and to confront the patient with those repudiated desires – invariably sexual – which his flight into neurotic illness had, until then, successfully concealed. Cure – or a relief from symptoms, at any rate – was predicated on discovery and realization: on bringing about a change from a state of not knowing – repudiation and denial – to one of knowing – acknowledgement and acceptance. Instead of compulsively but unknowingly repeating the traumatic incident that had triggered his disease, the patient would remember it, and, in so doing, break the spell. The therapeutic justification of psychoanalysis rested on the assumption of theoretical

PLAY IN A GODLESS WORLD

man that mysteries could be clarified – that nature could be plumbed, investigated, and corrected – and Freud had some spectacular successes. Yet, confidence in that assumption was no less prone to vicissitude in *The Interpretation of Dreams* than in anything else he wrote, and it was to be particularly shaken in that part of the book where he sought to distinguish between different kinds of ordering thought – namely, in the discussion of 'secondary revision'.

Secondary revision was the unconscious editing process which enhanced some details of a dream and suppressed others so as to shape the whole into a tellable narrative. 'As a result of its efforts', Freud wrote, 'the dream loses its appearance of absurdity and disconnectedness and approximates to the model of an intelligible experience'. Secondary revision removed the dream-content – the actions and characters that were actually dreamt about – one step further away from the dream-thoughts – the underlying but forbidden wishes and desires. It was therefore one of the many distorting agencies or primary processes which Freud identified – including condensation, displacement, representation by the opposite, and so forth – which made the unacceptable acceptable by distorting the unconscious dream-thoughts and obscuring the dream's real message from view. Dreams which seemed relatively coherent on waking had more than likely been subjected to secondary revision and were described as having been 'already interpreted once, before being submitted to waking interpretation'. Secondary revision was one of the most tricky of the distorting agencies precisely because it appealed to the desire for coherence. But this appearance of order was a blind and the analyst was not to be taken in. The more intelligible a dream appeared, the more energetically the analyst had to counter and deconstruct that false intelligibility in order to arrive at the true dream-thoughts lying underneath. 'For the purposes of *our* interpretation', Freud insisted, 'it remains an essential rule invariably to leave out of account the ostensible continuity of a dream as being of suspect origin, and to follow the same path back to the material of the dream-thoughts, no matter whether the dream itself is clear or confused'.

Freud did his best to distinguish what secondary revision did to a dream from what the psychoanalyst did to a dream. The distinction was, he thought, quite clear. If secondary revision endeavoured to make the dream-*content* more coherent, analysis endeavoured to make the dream-*thoughts* more coherent. Secondary revision was part of the censoring, distorting process – it re-arranged the elements of the dream into a coherent narrative sequence so as to distract the consciousness from the forbidden thoughts lying underneath. Analysis, by contrast, was part of the elucidatory, curative process – it interpreted the elements of the dream, in all their incoherence, in order to arrive at the forbidden thoughts lying underneath. Secondary revision was part of the unconscious processes, analysis of the conscious processes, and the person who interpreted his own dreams – as Freud did on many occasions in the dream book – had to distinguish quite clearly between those unconscious forces that had moulded the dream into a coherent form and those conscious forces that sought, in deconstructing and analyzing these, to render the meaning of the dream in coherent form.

All the same, there was a sense in which the two didn't look all that different. They bordered very closely on one another. Secondary revision was a distinctly grey area where the primary processes and the operations of ordinary waking thought merged into one another. Secondary revision and ordinary waking thought, in fact, behaved 'in just the same way'. It was as if, Freud had said, a coherent dream had already been interpreted once, had already been subjected to 'a first interpretation'. Secondary revision was a preliminary, pseudo-interpretation which threatened to lead the analyst further away from his own 'proper' interpretation – but it was, nevertheless, very like the latter. The overall tendency – to render unintelligible material intelligible – was exactly the same, even if the nature of that material – dream-thoughts or dream-content – was different in each case. And, although Freud warned against the lures of coherence when analyzing dream material – 'it is only with the greatest difficulty that the beginner in the business of interpreting dreams can be persuaded that his task is not at an end when he has a complete interpretation in his hands – an interpretation that makes sense, is coherent and throws light upon every element of the dream's content' – he didn't altogether resist those lures himself. For, in practice, virtually every dream in the book was presented in terms of a mystery triumphantly and conclusively solved.

It wasn't an accident that the first metaphor that came to Freud's mind when describing secondary revision was that of psychoanalysis itself. But a disturbing doubt threatened to emerge. Was there really an appreciable difference between the two? Couldn't analysis be a type of 'tertiary revision' which submitted the dream to a similar desire for coherence that actually threatened to falsify? Though it did this in the name of truth and psychic health, couldn't it, in fact, obscure and distort the dream-thoughts still further? How did you know that a coherent dream interpretation wasn't the result of a deceptive bid for order, just as a coherent dream had been? Freud badly needed to distinguish between the two types of ordering thought: the kind that obscured, in secondary revision, and the kind that illuminated, in psychoanalysis. The argument hinged on differentiating the bad operations of ordering thought – secondary revision – from the good ones – analysis. Yet they bore an uncanny resemblance to each other, just as, in *Jokes*, the all-important difference between a joke that was made and the comic that was found collapsed when it transpired that what was found could also be made. It was as if everything was destined to turn into a joke in the end.

The theoretical thinking which enabled the analyst to interpret dreams, cure his patients, and write an account of both, turned out to be less easy to differentiate from the illogicalities and falsifications that were his subject, after all. The light into which the patient emerged was less than clear. If the good economic theorist of *Jokes* had managed his account competently only to have it come back at him in the form of a dirty laugh, so the analyst of *Dreams* held out for the goal of enlightenment only to be lured deeper and deeper into darkness – into more dreaming, even. Here as elsewhere, Freud's ambivalence towards the values of order and coherence couldn't be repressed but returned to cast doubt on the beneficial aspects not only of elucidatory scientific inquiry but of psychoanalysis as well. In secondary revision, the pull towards order and intelligibility – in every other respect, so worthy of imitation and praise – was admitted to be dubious, indeed, to be a particularly devious bluffing device to be treated with the utmost suspicion. As a clinical practice which promised to deliver its patients from delusion and mystification, psychoanalysis deposited them into a state of clear-sightedness or understanding which couldn't be sustained because it had, as Freud himself had half suspected, been illusory all along. Indeed, it was civilization's suppositions about what was orderly and intelligible which, in limiting and inhibiting the patient's desires, had made him ill in the first place and might very well make him ill again. Not knowing may have been dangerous, but knowing had its dangers too. Elucidation might not always elucidate and might not always be a good thing if it did. Perhaps it was all a bad joke, after all.

It was bad enough for the interpreter of dreams to find his own analytical discourse merging into that of his dreamy subject-matter. It was worse still for the writer on jokes. It had been the similarities between dreams and jokes which had first led Freud to writing the joke book. Reading through the proofs of *The Interpretation of Dreams* in the autumn of 1899, Freud's friend Wilhelm Fliess had complained that the dreamer was insufferably witty – 'ingenious and amusing', as Freud was to quote in a footnote to the dream book. The comment spurred Freud into making a theoretical study of jokes – into gathering together and putting to good use the store of anecdotes, witticisms, and puns that he'd been collecting over the years with a view to finding out how jokes, like dreams, were also products of the unconscious. Dreams subjected unconscious thoughts to a series of processes which distorted and disguised those thoughts and so gave the dream its well-known appearance of impossibility and absurdity. These primary processes – all part of what Freud called the 'dream-work' – included the condensation of two or more words and ideas into one; the displacement of one thought onto another; the representation of something by its opposite; and the representation of something by analogy. The same processes appeared over and over again in jokes – indeed, they formed the staple of joking humour, in the form of puns, absurdity, faulty reasoning, or witty analogies. Such patent similarities between dreams and jokes led Freud to the view that they 'must, at least in some essential respect, be identical'.

Yet it wasn't their similarities with dreams but their differences from them that were to make jokes potentially the riskiest, most dangerous saboteurs of the Freudian project as a whole. In the penultimate chapter – one of the densest and most closely argued sections of the joke book – Freud considered what it was that made jokes different from dreams. In the first place, a dream was a totally asocial product, occurring entirely in the mind of the individual dreamer and having nothing to communicate to anyone else. Jokes, by contrast, were quintessentially sociable, as Freud's detailed scrutiny of the joke-telling situation – A telling B about C – had earlier borne out. 'No one can be content with having made a joke for himself alone', Freud suggested. 'An urge to tell the joke to someone is inextricably bound up with the joke-work'. In the second place, a dream not only set no store by intelligibility but positively had to avoid it. The purpose of the dream-work was to make otherwise unacceptable thoughts acceptable by distorting them out of all recognition. But a joke couldn't be unintelligible. What made a joke different from mere nonsense was that it had to make some kind of sense. The better the sense, the better the joke, as Freud's hierarchy of play/jest/joke had suggested. A totally meaningless combination of words approximated to play or infantile babble; a combination that played with sound but not with sense (like a bad pun) was a jest; but a combination which put two words apparently nonsensically together in order to reveal an underlying connection after all – be it satirical or smutty – was a joke. You had to get a joke – it wasn't a joke otherwise – and the condition of intelligibility was therefore 'binding on it'.

Lastly, dreams were wholly involuntary. The dream-work was the result of processes over which the conscious mind had no control. Jokes, too, had an involuntary side. They weren't the result of laboured reflection – an allusion might bring two ideas together and reveal an underlying similarity, but it wasn't a joke. Jokes just happened. They occurred to you spontaneously. You didn't go round 'making' jokes but rather sensed or intuited that a joke was going to jump into your mind by means of an 'indefinable feeling' which Freud could only compare with what – intriguingly using the French word – he called *'absence'*. All of a sudden, unasked for, the joke was there. Yet for all their miraculous appearance – rather like divine grace – jokes also had a more workmanlike side and this was one of the important ways in which they differed from dreams. For jokes weren't entirely passive. The joking techniques – condensation, and so forth – were as unconscious as they were in dreams. But they were also capable of being grasped, recognized, and understood by the consciousness which then had an urge to communicate them. Part of the process was passive and involuntary, but another part involved work – the work (which admittedly existed in differing degrees) of making, telling, and getting the joke. Jokes were both found *and* made. Confronting the contradiction that jokes could both arise automatically and be made intentionally, Freud suggested that a person could knowingly 'plunge' into the unconscious without knowing what he was going to find there.

Jokes occupied a curiously half-way position between what was found and what was made, in other words. The distinction was showing signs of strain even before the discussion of the comic where it would finally collapse altogether. And, although Freud tried to stress the two-sided nature of the joke, there were other places in the joke book where what he emphasized was its made quality. As well as being involuntary, jokes were also produced, performed, improved upon, perfected, and accomplished with what Freud called 'effort' – the hearer of a joke didn't have to 'make an effort' as the joker did. Making jokes involved spending psychical expenditure, of all things. Freud wrote of the displacement technique which was 'part of the work which has created the joke'. Jokes were an improvement on jests because they added 'substance and value', bringing words and ideas together in a witty juxtaposition which 'can certainly not, we must suppose, have come about unintentionally', and Freud's aim was to 'discover the intention underlying the construction of the joke'. By the time he came to discuss the comic in the final section – presumably to substantiate the claim that the comic was most definitely *found* and not made – he was stating categorically that a joke 'never happens of its own accord but is invariably *made*'.

Like dreams, jokes were involuntary. But, unlike dreams, jokes were also invented, constructed, and made – with quite a lot of mental effort, as it turned out. They had to be intelligible. They had to have substance and value – a meaning and a point. They had to be communicated, and they required a third person who responded, judged, and validated their meaning, giving it an 'objective certainty'. The obvious inference was becoming too close for comfort. Writing about jokes brought Freud even closer to the unaskable question than writing about secondary revision had done – how did all this differ from his own theoretical writing? For it to be dreamlike was bad enough . . . but for it to be a joke? Jokes posed the question more pointedly – more squirmingly – than dreams because, like Freud's theoretical writings, they could be made in a way that dreams simply couldn't. It was perhaps to evade or forestall this question that Freud hurried forwards to the final section of his book in order to discuss the comic – which, to his relief, was found not made – in order to get away from the sneaking suspicion that anything that was made threatened to look too much like the effort he was making himself. Though even there the pretence was difficult to maintain, and it wasn't long before the comic began to show signs of being made as well. As in any crisis of faith, what had once been found – an object of belief – had this dispiriting way of turning out to be man-made after all. A miracle of divine grace turned out to be a dirty trick in the same disillusioning way that God turned out to be an idol.

It was for the same reason, no doubt, that – of all the unconscious processes which jokes shared with dreams (condensation, displacement, and so forth) – the one which Freud insisted was 'not relevant for our present purposes' was, wait for it, secondary revision. A comparison with secondary revision (about which Freud was already expressing some doubt as having been 'perhaps too shortly considered' in the dream book) would have brought him up against the possibility that a clear dividing line between conscious and unconscious thoughts, between analysis and dreams, between what was made and what was found, and between what was serious and what was a joke proved so hard to maintain because it didn't, in fact, exist. Instead, rather as in the 'Humour' essay, Freud took refuge in tentativeness and uncertainty, confessing to the 'incompleteness' of his theory and figuring himself, as he did so often, as the intrepid explorer of a dark continent whose more complete knowledge and mapping of the territory still lay some way off.

Freud's chronic ambivalence towards civilization – towards order and, by extension, his own role as a thinker and theorist – returned to haunt him in the form of logical and rhetorical liabilities which destabilized and undermined his arguments, and nowhere more embarrassingly, perhaps, than in the book on jokes. For jokes were unlike any of the other unconscious products that Freud had studied over the years – dreams, symptoms, slips of the tongue – in that they could be made, and, as a result, they couldn't help betraying an unsettling similarity with Freud's own theoretical project itself. In the joke book, Freud swung uncertainly between alternative positions. On the one hand, there was his theoretical will to order (its cleanliness and parsimony both hallmarks of the 'anal character') which staked a claim to coherence and aimed to produce a unified theory, an ambition which – since without it there'd have been no joke book – can't be underestimated. On the other hand, this ambition to unity had a way of dissolving, in spite of itself, into its component parts. The anal character theorized retention to be as pleasurable as release, and the values of virtue and thrift came to be transformed into a fantasy of pleasure, perversion, and prodigality, watched over by an unrecognizably consenting, relenting superego.

It was in *Civilization and its Discontents*, first published in 1930, that Freud came the closest he would ever come to admitting this state of ambivalence. For it was in that essay that he addressed the 'astonishing' contention that civilization – man's greatest achievement – was also what rent his soul and drove him to discontented distraction. Civilization curbed man's natural aggressiveness in order to produce a functioning, well-integrated society. It depended on the individual repressing and renouncing his aggression, but, in so doing, civilization also infringed his freedom. It obtained 'mastery over the individual's dangerous desire for aggression by weakening and disarming it and by setting up an agency within him to watch over it, like a garrison in a conquered city'. This was the superego. Civilization created society –

which was good – but, in ruthlessly repressing primal energies and desires, it tended to produce a neurotic one – which was bad. More concentratedly than anywhere else, Freud focussed on the ensuing 'ambivalence' of the situation, finally coming to define civilization not as the pinnacle of human achievement but rather as an eternal and unwinnable fight between 'the instinct of life and the instinct of destruction' – a struggle that was perpetuated and refereed by guilt.

Civilization and its Discontents took up where *The Future of an Illusion* – published three years earlier – had left off. Like the latter, it too exposed religion as a childish toy, a mass delusion 'so patently infantile, so foreign to reality, that to anyone with a friendly attitude to humanity it is painful to think that the great majority of mortals will never be able to rise above this view of life'. Religion distorted 'the picture of the real world in a delusional manner – which presupposes an intimidation of the intelligence'. The implication of the essay was that – when not mystified by a mass of wish-fulfilments and projections – the intelligence was capable of laying bare illusions and of stripping away the primitive credulousness that counted as religion. Freud emphatically distinguished between religion and science, as in *The Future of an Illusion* where he'd also championed the powers of science to discover the world as it really was: 'scientific work is the only road which can lead us to a knowledge of reality outside ourselves'. Science had 'given us evidence by its numerous and important successes that it is no illusion'. 'No', Freud protested, 'our science is no illusion'.

That Freud should take up such a position wasn't surprising. But, while *The Future of an Illusion* had presented science as heroically pushing back the barriers of ignorance, *Civilization and its Discontents* confused the issue considerably by suggesting that civilization as such did the opposite. You'd have thought that civilization and the scientific projects carried out in its name would employ the same rational and demystifying powers of thought. But, Freud argued, this was not the case. On the contrary, civilization erected and sustained *illusions*. Moreover, these illusions included not only 'religious systems' but also – more problematically – 'speculations of philosophy' which included art and science. Reality was unbearable, and civilization helped man to bear it by means of 'powerful deflections, which cause us to make light of our misery'. Scientific activity, it turned out, was 'a deflection of this kind, too'. Confusingly, it looked as if science didn't reveal a reality 'outside ourselves' after all. An unexpected turn-around proposed that, quite the reverse, it too was a delusion – a mere idol of the mind. Science turned out not so much to examine truths as to be one of the many techniques for fending off suffering. 'The task here is that of shifting the instinctual aims in such a way that they cannot come up against frustration from the external world', Freud wrote. 'A satisfaction of this kind, such as an artist's joy in creating, in giving his phantasies body, or a scientist's in solving problems or discovering truths, has a special quality which we shall certainly one day be able to characterize in metapsychological terms'. Between them, the artist and scientist created patterns and systems of thought – and derived from them, it seemed, the far from illusory pleasure of enjoying illusions. 'If we assume quite generally', Freud suggested, 'that the motive force of all human activities is a striving towards the two confluent goals of utility and a yield of pleasure, we must suppose that this is also true of the manifestations of civilization which we have been discussing here, although this is easily visible only in scientific and aesthetic activities'.

Did this mean that scientific activity represented a withdrawal from reality into consoling paradigms? Was science dedicated to revealing reality or wasn't it? Could it be that science in fact inoculated the scientist against the pain of that reality? Was science devoted to utility or to pleasure? The question, needless to say, had implications for Freud's own science. And, although he tried to defer the issue to some un-specified 'one day', the niggling doubt about whether this could apply to his own work wouldn't go away. Was Freud's intelligence devoted to exposing illusions – as *The Future of an Illusion* had implied – or was his work merely the escape of the 'narcissistic man' who sought his main satisfactions in 'his internal mental processes' rather than in the real world? In 'The Question of a *Weltanschauung*', the last of the *New Introductory Lectures on Psychoanalysis* published in 1933, Freud was to make his most impassioned plea that psychoanalysis be considered a science. But, if art and science were just like religion in that they offered distortions and falsifications of reality, and if – again, like religion – they erected illusory structures of belief in order to console a discontented humanity, where did that leave Freud's pychoanalytic project? Was he, like the scientist, dedicated to solving problems and discovering truths or was he dedicated to pulling the proverbial wool over his own as well as everybody else's eyes? Were the discoveries of psychoanalysis true – 'it was discovered that . . .'? Or were they simply a deflection from reality like any other kind of 'scientific activity'? It was an important question. If the latter was the case, wasn't the proper course of action for Freud to give up his practice and finally to lay down his pen?

Civilization and its Discontents took Freud right to the door of theoretical man's insuperable dilemma. He came closer here than anywhere else to confronting the circularity of his argument and therefore to questioning his own status as a theorist who had something useful to say. Wasn't it rather a joke that theoretical man should derive his theories from – and deliver them back to – a theoretical culture whose very values he'd theorized as being, at the very best, a mixed blessing? This circularity – faced by Freud here in a way that it wasn't by Schiller, Huizinga, Caillois, or Winnicott – had disturbing and potentially silencing implications for his own work. Theoretical man was narcissistic man, looking into the mirror which reflected nothing so much as his own mind. And this, I'd suggest, is the real ambivalence to be found in *Civilization and its Discontents*. As Leo Bersani writes in *The Freudian Body*, the real subject of the essay is 'less the explicitly proposed antagonism between instinct and civilization than the moves by which that very argument is undone'; or not so much undone – since Freud didn't, after all, lay down his pen – as revealed to rehearse, in ways as poignant as they're comical, the possibility of its own undoing. Having opened the door on the potential pointlessness of it all, Freud stood hovering to and fro – the characteristic gesture of the true sceptic, one remembers – over the threshold.

Freud stepped back from the brink by pressing on in the essay to a more discussable kind of ambivalence – the struggle between the instincts of life and death. But he couldn't avoid noticing his own act of displacement. It came back to haunt him, and in the final section he was forced to admit that 'our discussions on the sense of guilt disrupt the framework of this essay . . . they take up too much space, so that the rest of its subject-matter, with which they are not always closely connected, is pushed to one side'. By way of defence, he continued: 'this may have spoilt the structure of my paper; but it corresponds faithfully to my intention to represent the sense of guilt as the most important problem in the development of civilization and to show that the price we pay for our advance in civilization is a loss of happiness through the heightening of the sense of guilt'. Indeed. What Freud as good as admits – guiltily – as he offers up the ruins of his spoiled, lopsided paper, is that he's pushed aside an ambivalence about his own position which is more profound even than the one he's settled for discussing. The real struggle isn't between the instincts of life and death. Strange as it sounds, that's a side issue. The real struggle is the ir-resolvable dilemma of theoretical man facing the illusoriness of all his best efforts.

IV

Freud stood with one foot on the threshold – poised to step out into a darkness which would deconstruct everything he'd done but drawing back at the last moment into the habitual comforts of thinking and theorizing. He'd never cross the threshold, but the prospect glimpsed through that open door was enough to hint to him that the pleasures of sense-making were illusory and to dent the serenity of theoretical man for good. In this respect, Freud's writing perfectly encapsulates the two-sidedness of play. For, on the one hand, play is creative – it makes order, it makes civilization, it makes theory. Of Freud's commitment to these things there's no doubt, and there's no conjuring away the mountain of words which, in all his papers and books, he bequeathed. But, on the other hand, these orders are illusory and vain – as perhaps no one knew better than Freud, who faced up to the limitations of the ordering mind in his theory and practice every day of his life. *Jokes* brought the two sides together in a way that wasn't quite like anything else Freud wrote. For there theory turned out to be made in very much the same way as jokes were made. Theory, psychoanalysis – it was all a joke. There was no getting round it. But Freud didn't lay down his pen, any more than David Hume – contemplating a similar possibility in the middle of his *Treatise of Human Nature* – had laid down his. A man who was overwhelmed by his scruples and doubts about the illusoriness of all that he was doing would indeed have admitted defeat and stopped at that point. But not Hume. For him, that would have been going too far – or not going far enough. It would have been taking things too seriously – or not seriously enough. He didn't stop but pressed on, in the 'careless manner' of the true sceptic – living up to his reputation as the most playful of philosophers by remaining as diffident of his philosophical doubts as he was of his philosophical convictions. And this is also, perhaps, the way in which we should interpret Freud. For he didn't stop either. He too would carry on theorizing. He theorized his own work as a permanent state of pleasurable spending . . . and just got on with it.

It was the same ultimately playful move beyond pleasure and back again which Freud made in *Beyond the Pleasure Principle* (1920) where – as Derrida speculates in his own playful reading of that text in *The Post Card* (1987) – Freud's own repeated steps forward and backward across the threshold found themselves repeated in the game of his little grandson, Ernst, whose cotton-reel toy went in and out of the curtained crib over and over again: gone! there! We'll come back to *Beyond the Pleasure Principle* later on. But, for the moment, the ambivalence of the joke book – its state of suspension, balance, or perfect poise between incompatible and conflicting positions – is best illustrated by looking at what others have made of it. It's almost as if Freud's two-mindedness is impossible to accept, is an affront to the intellect. For there's been a tendency in interpretations of Freud's book to try to resolve this ambivalence and to settle its precarious balance by making a decision either one way or the other. Play is either creative or it's illusory – it couldn't be both at the same time – and some readings try to resolve the doubts by tipping Freud's book decisively in one direction or the other.

On one side, for example, stand the psychologist, Ernst Kris, and the art historian, E. H. Gombrich (both, as it happens, namesakes of the solemn, game-playing grandson), who collaborated to produce – most notably in Kris's *Psychoanalytic Explorations in Art* (1953) – a theory of artistic creativity that was explicitly based on *Jokes and Their Relation to the Unconscious*. There were certain states like madness, drunkenness, and dreams, they said, where the ego was no longer in command but had temporarily abandoned its supremacy to those forces of illogicality and chaos that were the unconscious. Jokes, however, represented the 'opposite case' – for there, no longer overwhelming, the unconscious was brought under the ego's control and put at its disposal. Instead of being a helpless slide into the unconscious processes, jokes were willed or intended. They formed a kind of 'controlled' or 'voluntary' regression that was 'in the service of the ego'. Unconscious processes that, in themselves, were not only of no value but regrettable symptoms of intoxication, childishness, or mental illness, were in jokes put to good use. A confusion that would strike one 'as a defect' in a dream, for instance, became, in a pun, 'a valuable achievement'. When making a joke, a person dipped into the unconscious for a moment and the connections made there – punning, allusive, sarcastic, or smutty – were then drawn up again as a joke. In an essay on 'Freud's Aesthetics' first published in 1966 and closely based on his work with Kris,

Gombrich described the process with a striking metaphor:

> A thought which it would perhaps be rude or indecorous to utter plain is dipped as it were into the magic spring of the primary process, as one can dip a flower or twig into the calcine waters of Karlsbad where they emerge transformed into something rich and strange. In this new guise the idea is not only acceptable but even welcome.

This productive encounter between the ego's form-making capacities and the rich underworld of the unconscious recalls what Schiller said about the union of form and sense in the aesthetic, and it belongs with the same tradition which made play the beginning and exemplar of all human creativity. It was the same analogy that enabled Kris to use jokes as the basis for a discussion of 'the whole field of art and of symbol formation'. Standing halfway between the world of jokes and the world of art, moreover, caricature seemed to illustrate the case particularly well, and it was the account of caricature that constituted Gombrich's contribution to Kris's book. Caricature was the art of ridiculing human beings in graphic form, but it also had the higher aim of drawing out the essential character or true likeness of the person so ridiculed – of showing them up to be the fool, animal, or stereotype they really were. Caricature, that is, was explicitly an art not of surface but of depth. It had substance and value, penetrating 'behind the surface of appearance' into the 'innermost essence of reality'. No longer content with a merely slavish likeness, the artist was sufficiently confident of his own creating powers – his 'controlled use of the primary process' – that he could penetrate nature 'for the sake of a deeper truth', an ability that was to transform him from being a mere copyist or imitator of nature into being a creator, an inventor of new forms. This change represented one of the major developments in the art-historical tradition, and for Gombrich the art of caricature – unknown before the end of the sixteenth century – belonged to, if it didn't actually herald, the 'century of the Great Masters'.

Mastery, in fact, was the name of the game. For, in their account, Kris and Gombrich laid a special emphasis on the ego's agency in joke-making: 'unlike the dream, the pun is thought out, created'. That part of Freud's book which they took up and ran with, in other words, was what stressed the joke's *made* quality. In jokes, as in art, the ego wasn't overpowered by forces beyond its control but was a craftsman, artist, maker, creator – in charge of that happy conjunction of sense and form which made good the unconscious, redeemed it, and endowed it with meaning and 'depth'. The ego wasn't overwhelmed but in its element – sovereign and supreme, mastering not only the unconscious but pretty well everything in sight. Words, speech, language, experience, the body, pain, aggression, difficulty, fear, anxiety, the emotions, and inner danger were just some of the things said to be 'mastered' in these pages of Kris's book. This megalomania, furthermore, was positively thrilling, theorized as the true source of all comic and aesthetic pleasure. People who were unable to 'let themselves go' in laughter suffered from a weakness in the ego and could only acquire a sense of humour after 'the dominating power of the ego has been restored'. The ego's sovereignty was explicitly described as 'pleasurable' – pleasure arose from the 'sense of mastery' and the comic combined 'a sense of mastery with a feeling of pleasure'. The pleasures of shattering, rebellion, or release scarcely got a look in as pleasure was explained in every case to be the jubilant overcoming of such fearful extremities. Here, pleasure lay less in the breaking apart than in the gathering up and piecing together again of that exemplary ego: Humpty Dumpty.

Don't we see, in the form of this ego, a version of theoretical man – a wonderfully idealized self-portrait? Here the ego is a creator and artist – a Great Master, no less. He's purposeful, efficient, and workmanlike – a good citizen who takes something inherently worthless and converts it into something of use and value. He's a broker – a middle-man or entrepreneur – who's able to manage and balance the conflicting demands of the id and the superego, indeed, able 'to master the tension between the two' (an impressively omni-competent, rather superego-like ego, this). He's exemplary in his restraint and self-control. Kris cited the case of a woman patient – a teacher – whose inability to laugh at the clumsiness of her pupils was pathological – the result of disturbed childhood experience – and was to be distinguished from the 'praise-worthy pedagogic restraint' of the teacher who found it inappropriate to laugh at such things. Theoretical man evidently liked to consider himself the master of such admirable self-restraint. At one point, Kris described laughter as catching – as an 'attack' which one couldn't control unless, as the result of a 'victorious fight', this overwhelming desire to laugh was subjugated into a smile. The smile expressed 'moderate joy, a controllable quantity' and, best of all, it stood as 'evidence of the triumph of the ego'. Isn't the serenity of theoretical man summed up in just such a smile?

Kris could keep smiling because his obvious identification with and self-investment in this model of orderliness and rectitude went completely unnoticed. The circularity was complete. He'd theorized control, he was in control, and all was well in the world. No wonder he was smiling. He pulled Freud's book back from the brink into the safety of serene cogitation, neither hovering over the threshold nor peeking round the door, for he hadn't the faintest idea that the door was there. It's a quite different scenario, however, when we turn to another famous follower of Freud's – about as different from Kris as it is possible to be – the flamboyant French psychoanalyst, Jacques Lacan. Lacan presented himself as the joker in the pack whose mission – not unlike that of Nietzsche – was to wipe that smile clean off the face of theoretical man and to replace it with an inimitably mischievous smirk of his own. Lacan didn't only open the door out onto absurdity and alienation where all the lures of order and coherence went up in illusory smoke. He ventured forth – and it's his peculiarly diabolical laughter that can be heard issuing from the other side of the door.

For Lacan, the joke book, *The Interpretation of Dreams*, and *The Psychopathology of Everyday Life* were the most important of Freud's texts because they showed more clearly than any of the others those workings of the unconscious which – so weird and foreign to the waking mind – dismantled any pretensions the latter might have had to coherence or order. Of the three texts, however, it was the joke book which, in his paper on 'The function and field of speech and language in psychoanalysis' (1953), Lacan singled out as being the 'most unchallengeable' and 'most transparent'. For, more even than dreams and slips of the tongue, jokes revealed the inveterate ambiguity and instability of that element on which all man's claims to make sense so precariously rested – language. Puns lifted the veil on language in its natural state – slippery, fractious, mobile – annihilating our bids to make sense and exposing once and for all the 'the logic that is merely a lure'. If Kris had sought to bolster his own authority as a maker of theories by laying emphasis on the madeness of jokes, Lacan, by contrast, revelled in the fact that jokes were found. 'Nowhere is the intention of the individual more evidently surpassed by what the subject finds', he wrote. There had to be 'something foreign to me in what I found for me to take pleasure in it'. Jokes not only lay beyond intention but betrayed the feebleness of the intending mind, bringing home – in a way that nothing else quite could – the fact that, since he didn't know what he was going to find there, man was most definitely not master in his own psychic house.

For Lacan, famously, the human condition was not one of wholeness or self-mastery but of alienation and self-division. Any attempts to become a 'whole' personality – such as those offered by a sentimental, humanistic, largely American ego-psychology – were a mystifying con-trick for which Lacan reserved his own special venom. He had no truck with mastery – at least, not with the smug, self-satisfied kind – and in the introduction to his *Four Fundamental Concepts of Psychoanalysis* – based on his 1964 seminar and first published in 1973 – Lacan described his notorious expulsion from that respectable establishment institution, the International Psychoanalytical Association, in the following terms:

> if the truth of the subject, even when he is in the position of master, does not reside in himself, but, as analysis shows, in an object that is, of its nature, concealed, to bring this object out into the light of day is really and truly the essence of comedy.

The mastery that had been so precious to the likes of Kris was here debunked by Lacan in a characteristic gesture – by presenting himself as his own buffoon, whose excommunication, though neither a 'game', 'comedy', nor 'laughing matter', was, for all that, quintessentially comical. For the collapse of his own authority – signalled by his ex-pulsion from the IPA – could only vindicate the very principles of his psychoanalysis – that authority was a myth – granting him the not inconsiderable pleasure of having the last laugh. A pleasure which – again, in a wholly characteristic way – he enjoyed by proceeding to put the fundament back into the fundamental concepts of psychoanalysis that were his theme.

For all his playfulness – for all the manic punning which appeared on every page of his writings, to the despair of some of his readers (of which more later) – and for all the importance he attached to *Jokes and Their Relation to the Unconscious* – if any text could be canonical to such a schismatic, then that was it – Lacan in fact had surprisingly little to say about it. He didn't subject the book to lengthy analysis or make it the topic for one of his annual seminars. Indeed, his remark that *Jokes* was the most unchallengeable of Freud's works was prefaced by the comment that little interest had been shown in it and 'with good reason'. This throwaway remark was more than a playful contradiction.

Freud himself had shown little interest in the book after it had been published – barely returning to it again – perhaps because he'd confronted there, in an unavoidable way, the circularity that would have silenced his theoretical efforts for good. Wasn't Lacan merely following in Freud's footsteps: championing *Jokes* yet saying almost nothing about it – and with good reason – because the greatest accolade he could give it was to follow in the direction that it in fact led – beyond the pleasure principle, across the threshold, and out through the open door? If Lacan's relative silence on *Jokes* speaks volumes, it's because he was perhaps the only person in the world who had the sheer wicked panache to get away with it.

If this particular gesture of saying nothing remains – like most of what Lacan did – unrepeatable, it can still be appreciated and relished to the full. In *The Legend of Freud* (1982), the deconstructionist critic, Samuel Weber, put Freud's joke book at the heart – or hole – of the psychoanalytic enterprise, beginning his discussion with an account of secondary revision – that devious process by which the unconscious masquerades as logical thought: 'a kind of joke played by the unconscious against, or at the expense of, consciousness'. Secondary revision betrayed the instability of the border between the two, just as the distinction between what was found and made threatened to devolve upon itself. If Kris had emphasized that jokes were made and Lacan that they were found, Weber showed that it was their ambiguous position between the two that not only made jokes what they were but also looked uncannily like the account that was trying to theorize them. For Weber, Freud's decision to investigate jokes was bound to end up 'by making a laughingstock out of the theory'. For, just as a joke was made – and made to be heard by a third person whose spontaneous laughter (an unknown entity and wholly uncontrollable phenomenon) was alone what said it was a joke and a good one at that – so, by an irrepressible analogy, Freud's book (offered up to the scrutiny and examination of the reader) laid itself open to just such an uncontrollable, and possibly just such a hilarious, reponse. If you didn't respond to *Jokes* with Lacanian silence, you could respond with a Lacanian laugh.

Weber made the point that practically the only change Freud made – returning to this book, which otherwise seemed to have so little interest for him, in the second edition of 1912 – was to add a few lines to an existing footnote on nonsense jokes. Here Freud tried to describe a particular kind of joke for which he could find 'no appropriate name' but which we would class as shaggy dog stories: 'Life is a suspension bridge' – 'Why is that?' – 'How should *I* know?'. The point of such pointless jokes was to defraud the listener of his expectation. They played games with the desire for intelligibility, exactly, Weber noted, as secondary revision had done. The desire – here abused – to understand or 'get' the joke involved 'nothing less than the narcissistic striving of the ego to unify, bind, and synthesize, and thereby to construct that meaningful, self-contained *object* against which it can situate itself as an equally meaningful, self-contained subject, a self-consciousness'. For Weber, it was all too appropriate that just about the only revision Freud should have made to the joke book was to add a note on the kind of joke that pulled a fast one on jokes and, of course, on the theorist of jokes, with his own desire for meaning, as well. Having set out to gather together the scattered fragments of existing joke theories, Freud arrived, Weber put it, 'not so much at the organic whole he desired as at its shaggy fleece', leaving him to ask whether he, we, or Freud hadn't been fleeced in the process.

***

If there was one person who got the measure of Freud, it was, perhaps, Ida Bauer – better known as 'Dora' – the teenage hysteric whose father had brought her to Freud for treatment a few years earlier and whose case history Freud was to publish, as it happened, in 1905 – the same year as *Jokes* and the *Three Essays on the Theory of Sexuality*. The father – himself not a well man – had embarked on a liaison with a woman he'd met at one of the health-resorts he frequented – Frau K. as the case study styled her – and her husband, in what looked all too obviously like a pernicious exchange, had shown a sexual interest in Dora. Dora was 'overcome by the idea that she had been handed over to Herr K. as the price of his tolerating the relations between her father and his wife', wrote Freud, 'and her rage at her father's making such a use of her was visible behind her affection for him'. It was this rage, together with her response to Herr K.'s openly propositioning her in the course of a lakeside walk together, which had brought on, or exacerbated, the hysterical symptoms – coughing, loss of voice, headaches, weariness with life – for the relief of which she'd been brought to Freud.

Freud didn't get very far with Dora. She broke off the analysis after a few months, frustrating his desire to get to the bottom of her case. In analyzing her symptoms and dreams, Freud had tried to fit them round his theory of oedipal desire that would have required Dora to fantasize erotically about her father (or himself) – her horror at Herr K.'s sexual advances being read by Freud as a classically hysterical repudiation of such an idea. Freud notoriously tried to fit into Dora's gap-filled narrative the one missing element that would make sense of it all and identify her problem conclusively as oedipal – namely, the male organ which he pressed upon his patient, as being what she really wanted, no fewer than four times. This hypothesized penis appeared in the erect member which he supposed Herr K. to have pressed against her body, in the imagined scene of fellatio between her father and Frau K., in her inferred witnessing of a scene of parental intercourse, and in the defloration fantasy suggested (to Freud, at least) by the association made in one of her dreams to 'nymphs' (the *nymphae* or *labia minora* of the female genitals, he thought). Dora resisted his efforts, however, leaving Freud to put on record not his success but rather the story of an *analysis interruptus*. For what his urge to explain had missed – as footnotes added later acknowledged – was that beneath her oedipal desires lay something even deeper: her homosexual passion for Frau K. This, Freud admitted in retrospect, was probably 'the strongest unconscious current in her mental life'.

Dora left Freud, although she remained in touch with him and her later communications were noted in the postscript to the case history which Freud updated in subsequent editions. But Freud couldn't have anticipated how, many years later, Dora would end up. Having married – not very happily – and had a son, Dora was to be found, in the years between the wars, passing her time – indeed, excelling herself – in play. For Dora was to become a mistress of the newly invented game that was all the rage in Europe at that time: contract bridge. In the last chapter of *Homo Ludens* (1938), where he was discussing the play-element in contemporary civilization, Huizinga described how the more intellectual kinds of card game had recently reached their apogee in bridge, and how 'the paraphernalia of handbooks and systems and professional training has made bridge a deadly earnest business'. An 'enormous amount of mental energy' was expended on this 'universal craze', and it became the centre of Dora's life. 'In the private bridge circles of her world', write John Forrester and Lisa Appignanesi in *Freud's Women* (1992), 'she was a master, who would teach other middle-class women in their living-rooms'. Her partner in the game, moreover, was none other than Frau K. It was as if, 'across the years, they had finally dispensed with the superfluous men who had previously been their partners in their complex social games and contracts, yet they had retained their love of those games whose skill lies in the secret of mutual understanding of open yet coded communications within and across a foursome'.

Wasn't this a suitable ending for the mature young woman of independent judgement who, even in her troubled teenage years, had, as Freud put it, 'grown accustomed to laugh at the efforts of doctors, and in the end to renounce their help entirely'? Wasn't that, in fact, the only feasible response to doctors – and to analysts, professors, and philosophers alike, for that matter? David Hume had left the mortifying reflections of his study to go off and play backgammon with his friends. Couldn't Dora have been doing the same thing? And wouldn't Freud have found something irresistible in the sound of laughing girls, playing together, coming from the far side of that tantalizingly half-open door?

The Point of Puns

Wordplay was where it all began. The first joke Freud told in *Jokes and Their Relation to the Unconscious* was a play on words – the quip about Baron Rothschild behaving 'quite famillionairely' – and this was followed by other, similar witticisms – the 'anecdotage' of the old, the Christmas 'alcoholidays'. It was as if wordplay formed the loam or seedbed of all later, more sophisticated joke-making and so it was there, naturally enough, that the budding theorist would begin – grounding his thesis in the elementals of wit before branching out to consider more complex (and less translatable) word-jokes and eventually ex-panding out to jokes that weren't primarily verbal in nature but were either sarcastic or smutty. Emboldened, with a substantial body of well-developed jokes now behind him, Freud began to sketch in his theory about why jokes were so appealing, so pleasurable. Smutty and sarcastic jokes were a delight, he ventured, because they satisfied salacious or aggressive impulses which a person was otherwise forbidden to express. They saved on expenditure, giving the person a break from work, temporarily relieving him from the effort of being nice and polite all the time. But, on coming to consolidate this theory of pleasure in the the middle of the book, Freud went back to the specifically verbal jokes which he'd started with. Did the pleasures of economy apply to those as well?

On the face of it, economy seemed to be exactly what verbal jokes were about, for puns thriftily compressed words together giving you two for the price of one, whether an existing word or a portmanteau word like the – appropriately enriched – 'famillionairely'. But this wasn't the economy Freud was looking for. Although not negligible, this amounted in itself to little more than a joke's small change – the surplus of fore-pleasure that was to be found in the joke's external or technical form. That was an added bonus, but Freud wanted more than this, a greater economy. He wanted to find that verbal jokes, like the others he'd been analyzing, also relieved a person from a much larger outlay – from spending all those millions of psychical expenditure – thus affording him a greater degree of relief and so a greater degree of pleasure. To do this Freud went back to the world of children's play. 'During the period in which a child is learning how to handle the vocabulary of his mother-tongue, it gives him obvious pleasure to "experiment with it in play"', he wrote. 'And he puts words together without regard to the condition that they should make sense, in order to obtain from them the pleasurable effect of rhythm or rhyme'. But these early freedoms weren't to last long. They were brought to an end by the critical faculty and subjected to increasingly strict demands for comprehensibility. Illogicality, nonsense, and grammatical vagueness were at first frowned on and then punished until the child had learned his lesson and arrived at the no-nonsense adult world of strict sense-making and business-like communication. 'Little by little', wrote Freud with more than a hint of sorrow for those long-lost joys, the child was 'forbidden this enjoyment, till all that remains permitted to him are significant combinations of words'.

Wordplay was the prototype for all later and more developed forms of adult play. For long before he played with toys or games the child played with words – or, rather, long before he played with words, he played with sounds. Language was perhaps the first, the most pervasive medium in which the child was subject to constraint, the first thing he was given to control. By playing with sounds and words again, verbal jokes put the adult back in touch with his childish past – re-established old freedoms and shook off the burdens of an oppressive intellectual upbringing. Freud was thus able to conclude that they, too, were psychical reliefs and that his theory of expenditure was water-tight, holding good not only for 'all the techniques of jokes' but for 'all pleasure from these techniques' as well.

The satisfactions to be had from a whole, not to say totalizing, theory were unmistakably those of theoretical man. In order to be the master of his subject – the author of a self-respecting theory which, from the beginning, had declared its ambitions to create a new and 'organic whole' – it was essential for Freud to treat jokes as particular points, as distinct items or specimens to be bracketed off from the serious discussion that was going on all around them. If verbal jokes threw off the fetters of logic and reason, it was especially important to differentiate them from the 'serious use of words' and 'serious thought' which they broke through but within which the theorist was presumably situating himself – more necessary in a book about jokes, perhaps, than anywhere else. In the section on the comic, Freud described certain states that were antipathetic to the playful mood, including 'intellectual work that pursues serious aims'. 'There is no place whatever left for the comic in abstract reflection', he asserted, 'except when that mode of thought is suddenly interrupted'. Throughout *Jokes and Their Relation to the Unconscious*, jokes, jests, and comic moments were presented as just such momentary disruptions of what was, by implication, a contrastingly stable backdrop of seriousness. For good measure – and to make doubly sure that his readers were clear about the difference – Freud would highlight the punchlines of his jokes in bold or italic type, the typographical distinction serving as a visual reminder that, for all its joking subject-matter, the book in hand was eminently serious. This was no comic – no anthology of jokes to be consulted for the purpose of spicing up an after-dinner speech – but a serious contribution to the psychology of humour and wit and to the science of the unconscious mind.

By presenting the joke as a particular point and by highlighting the punchline – *Pointe* in German – Freud did his best to preserve the difference between jest and earnest and so to keep the dignity and integrity of theoretical man intact. The jokes had to be clearly visible, to be inserted into and clearly distinct from a discourse which, by definition, was un-joking. Something rather similar was going on, as the critic Sander Gilman has suggested, in Freud's treatment of the Jewish joke. A good many of the jokes in the joke book were Jewish, being drawn from Freud's highly valued personal collection because, he said, they'd made him laugh so much. Gilman makes the point that Freud treated such jokes in a very specific way – though 'they are labelled by him as "Jewish", they are written in good German'. Hilarious jokes – which often depended on Yiddishisms in word or accent – were embedded in the most earnest Teutonic prose as theoretical man tried to put a cordon round his ethnic roots, tried to demarcate the Jewish joker from the serious analyst of jokes. The same (and similarly questionable) attempt at demarcation was at work in *The Interpretation of Dreams*, where Freud again sought to distinguish his own theoretical language of analytic elucidation from the riddling, punning, and joking language of symptoms and dreams. 'Words, since they are the nodal points of numerous ideas, may be regarded as predestined to ambiguity', he wrote, and the neuroses, 'no less than dreams, make unashamed use of the advantages thus offered by words for purposes of condensation and disguise'. Neuroses and dreams – like jokes – exploited the inveterate playfulness of language for their own obscuring ends. But the theorist's words couldn't be predestined to ambiguity in the same way, or at least they had to work extra hard to resist this 'shameful' exploitation of the language. If 'our everyday, sober method of expression' began to be corrupted by puns or wordplay, he warned, 'our understanding is brought to a halt'. It was imperative that the language of theoretical man announce its clarity, health, and difference-in-kind from that of dreams or neurotic symptoms. The very fact that it marched serenely along and didn't grind to a halt was offered up as a sign of its seriousness and sense of purpose.

Keeping jokes to the point was a way of keeping them in their place – of pinning them down securely so as to prevent them from wandering off or from popping up in unwanted or unexpected places. Theoretical man needed to keep control of them. Jokes were thus clearly identified – flagged and marked off from his language of analysis like glittering jewels within an otherwise drab sea of theoretical prose. It wasn't only that, however. Freud's whole effort also went towards showing that jokes *had* a point – indeed, that they had to have a point in order to be jokes. It was true that it all began with play – 'play – let us keep to that name – appears in children while they are learning to make use of words and to put thoughts together', he reiterated. But, while wordplay certainly returned the wearied sense-maker to the lost freedoms of children's play, it wasn't just a return to the playground. There was more to it than that. Jokes were more than nonsense, mere babble. As Freud went on to elaborate, they formed a bridge between child's play and adult work. They went back to the linguistic liberties of those early days but on one important condition – they had to make sense: 'the meaningless combination of words or the absurd putting together of thoughts must nevertheless have a meaning', he insisted. 'The whole ingenuity of the joke-work is summoned up in order to find words and aggregations of thoughts in which this condition is fulfilled'. Jokes looked both ways, in other words. They evaded the work of adult rationality – the tedious business of having to make sense all the time. But, crucially, they also submitted to its demands – they were required to make sense. Jokes served two masters, allowing 'the old play with words' but in such a way that it could also 'withstand the scrutiny of criticism'. The joker could be a child again but only if – and when – he satisfied the demands of the adult that he'd since become.

Jokes were doubly pleasurable in that they allowed for the pleasures of rebelling against authority and for the pleasures of restoring that authority again to an equal degree. These twin purposes – continuing pleasurable play and protecting that play from criticism – were the 'two fixed points' which determined the nature of a joke. Jokes both played and worked. The best jokes did, in any case. For there were, after all, good jokes and bad. The very worst jokes – the totally meaningless combinations of words or shaggy dog stories for which Freud couldn't find a suitable name – were scarcely jokes at all. They were little better than babyish drivel. At an intermediate stage there were jests which played with sounds but not with sense – cheap puns, at best. But the very best jokes had to have an underlying point that could be 'got', a punchline that would be marked by a ripple, snort, or burst of laughter. A good joke absolutely had to make sense – the condition of intelligibility was binding on it. As Freud was to repeat later on, a joke could only make use of the distortions of condensation and displacement 'up to the point at which it can be set straight by the third person's understanding'. To go any further was beyond a joke.

The best jokes were the most pointed. They weren't stupid or childish but clever and ingenious. They testified not to the feebleness of the joker or to his shameful lapse into ambiguity but rather to his intellectual brilliance, panache, and technical skill. Because of their two-sidedness, jokes appealed to the joker and to the analyst of jokes alike. They made the joker roar with laughter as he rebelled against the unremitting demands of logical thought. But they also endorsed the sober theorist who sought always to restore the priority of rational thought and whose theoretical work was the self-justifying product of that worthy endeavour. Kept to the point, jokes could be redeemed. That was why they were 'good'. Apparent nonsense was shown to make sense – was brought over from riddling speech to everyday, sober speech and was straightened or translated back in the process. Verbal jokes – good ones, at any rate – revealed that what the child had suspected was true: connections between words that sounded the same did indeed exist. Lying behind this emphasis on the ingenuity and meaningfulness of jokes was the old idea of play as creative. Play didn't regress to childishness and nonsense. It only seemed to do so. In fact, play – and above all the 'developed play' of the very best adult jokes – was on the side of order and control. Play ordered, civilized, constructed, and built.

Wordplay suggested that the world was in fact even more orderly than it first appeared, that connections were there even when we didn't know it. Verbal jokes showed this to be the case and the theorist of jokes was happy to confirm it, establishing on the basis of it as orderly, stable, and coherent a theory as he was able.

Freud apparently set the greatest store by meaningful jokes. He had little time for pointless or nonsensical jokes, liking those with 'substance and value' best, not only because they made him laugh but presumably because they promised to shore up intelligibility as the bottom line and so to preserve the pleasures of theoretical man for a little longer. He didn't only enjoy jokes that had a point to them, moreover, but would often use jokes in order to make a point of his own. Indeed, if the testimony of Freud's friends and contemporaries is anything to go by, Freud *only* told jokes in order to illustrate some point or other. He was, it seems, most economical in his use of jokes, not telling them idly or for the purposes of mere amusement but only using them as a kind of lecturing aid. 'In my thirty years of friendship with Freud', wrote the psychoanalyst Theodor Reik, 'I heard him, of course, frequently tell a Jewish anecdote or quote a witticism, but it was never for its own end, never for mere amusement. In most cases the comical story was used as an illustration to a point he had made . . . It was as if he brought the joke forward as an example of how wisdom is expressed in wit, and – much more rarely, wit in wisdom'. For Freud's colleague and biographer, Ernest Jones, Freud was a 'chaste' and 'puritanical' person who'd tell smutty jokes 'only when they had a special point illustrating a general theme'. For the Hungarian analyst, Franz Alexander, it was the same – 'he liked to illustrate a point with anecdotes and jokes'.

Freud's joke-telling was always to the point. At least, it was to these colleagues of his – for we have to allow for the possibility that, in these respectful if not somewhat awe-struck accounts, it was Freud as genius and theoretical man who was being seen and honoured by other theoretical men. For them, seriousness had to be uppermost – and jokes redeemed as meaningful – in order to keep the psychoanalytical show on the road. In his own work on wit in *Surprise and the Psychoanalyst* (1936), Reik stuck closely to the orthodox line and worked overtime to separate jokes form the serious work the analyst was doing, hastening to assure his readers that a discussion of jokes would soon proceed to 'the most serious psychological problems'. The figure of the Austrian statesman Metternich appearing in a patient's dream, for example, turned out to be an Anglo-German pun on a failed rendezvous with a woman

– 'met her *nicht*'. There was no doubt about the pun being pretty terrible – but, Reik insisted, you couldn't ascribe the inanity of the joke to 'the process of interpretation' because, even if the analyst appreciated the wit, he would – in explaining it back to the patient – expend a great deal of labour and intellectual effort, thereby thoroughly redeeming himself in the process. On those occasions – which happened only 'rarely' and then only under 'special circumstances' – when the analyst hit upon a joke in his patient's unconscious, his momentarily exuberant mood would be quickly and discreetly repressed. 'The analyst will have no difficulty in overcoming the temptation to utter the joke', Reik thought.

As a theoretical man, Freud was bound to come up with a theory that would vindicate himself just as other writers who we've considered inevitably found themselves saying that play was creative because creative was what they were being, or at least trying to be. Jokes were 'good', accordingly, when they had a point. As such they were doubly pleasing. Meaningful and intelligent, they not only aroused the loudest laughter but they also satisfied the theorist as well, fitting in with his arguments and with his cherished wish to make sense of things and to make out of the scattered fragments of other theories a new 'organic whole'. Yet, as we've already seen, this was by no means the end of the story. For the very move Freud made to redeem jokes – to make them the products of ingenuity and 'work' which were then to be understood and appreciated by a third party – was inevitably going to rebound upon itself. Joking was for all the world like theorizing – for the condition of intelligibility was just as binding on that – and the better or more meaningful a joke was, then the more like the theory it began to look. The more Freud tried to keep jokes to the point, the more he tried to insist that they were ingenious, clever, witty, and worth theo-rizing about – 'good' in every respect – the more they threatened to slip and slide about, dilating out of all recognition until the joke book as a whole threatened to become one colossal punchline of a circular argument.

It's at this point that what we see isn't so much theoretical man as the 'other' Freud – the playful Freud who could sense, in spite of himself, the illusoriness of theoretical man's best efforts. This wasn't the official, orthodox Freud of biographical reminiscence but the Freud who emerged from the margins of his texts and from between the lines of his theoretical propositions. It was the Freud who, in the middle of his discussion on the pleasures of wordplay – and how a 'good' joke was one which, like 'Traduttore – Traditore!' ('translator – traitor!'), showed an apparently superficial connection to have a meaningful sense underneath – disconcertingly admitted, in one of those footnotes that has a way of tripping up the otherwise serene march of theoretical progress, that even 'bad' jokes – even jokes without much or any meaning whatsoever – could still in fact be good *as* jokes, could still, that is, produce pleasure and raise a laugh. As an example, he recalled the improvised joke that had been made at the dinner table of a friend when a roulade had been served up as dessert. Since this dish required some skill on the part of the cook, one of the guests had asked whether it had been made at home. 'Yes, indeed', replied the host, 'A home-roulade' – producing a storm of laughter and pleasure, which Freud could 'clearly recall', at what was in itself a superficial and totally meaningless connection between the kitchen and the world of politics.

Would this Freud have shown the worthy restraint of which Reik felt so sure? Would he really have mastered the urge to break down into helpless giggles at the most stupid, the most pointless of puns? Theoretical man would have set his jaw and done his best. But Freud was unable to leave the matter alone. He returned to it, worried it, fidgeted with it. Having apparently established to his satisfaction that jokes had to have a meaning in order to be jokes, he suddenly seemed uncertain again. The real pleasure of a joke was, he went on to say, derived from 'play with words or from the liberation of nonsense' and the meaning of the joke was 'merely intended to protect that pleasure from being doing away with by criticism'. The precious meaning of the joke was suddenly subordinated again – now a mere ruse with which to fob off the critical faculty – while the indulging of pure nonsense, of child's play, turned out to be the point of the whole exercise, after all.

In the to-and-fro between release and restraint – between the pleasures of rebelling against authority and the pleasures of putting it back again – it was all beginning to get rather confused. As Freud swung between those 'two fixed points' of his argument – that jokes relieved a person from making sense but also had to make sense at the same time – they seemed to be less fixed than ever. Freud was paying the price for trying to have it both ways. Often, he confessed, he was unable to decide what was 'good' – whether it was, as he'd been arguing, the inner meaning of a joke or whether it was the joke's purely external surface, the 'joking envelope', after all. We made mistakes, he admitted, and often over-estimated the worth of a joke. We could be misled, taken in. A joke could be deceptively 'good'. It could bribe the critical faculty with something which seemed 'more significant and more valuable' than it really was. A joke could promise an inner meaning when actually there was nothing inside it at all, for it was all pure surface – like the home-roulade – with nothing intrinsically to laugh about at all and nothing whatever to analyze. There was no plum of meaning to pull from the pie. And yet even when theoretical man was cheated in this way and denied the meaning he was looking for – even when the joke was pointless, just an empty envelope – it was still capable, as Freud knew from experience, of arousing laughter. The bad joke could still arouse pleasure – in which case, as things turned out, it was actually rather good. No longer kept to the point, the theoretical categories of good and bad began to slither hopelessly around. And the point of jokes – the one thing on which Freud had apparently been clear – dissolved into doubt again, as both jokes and the theory about them threatened to look increasingly pointless after all.

On the far side of theoretical man – proud author of a theory as creative and whole as it was to the point – stood the other Freud – author of a text whose categories were potentially as jokey and illusory as they were meaningless. Such instability would have seriously dismayed the theoretical men, who did all they could to look away and to limit themselves, like Theodor Reik, to a grim smile. But it was taken up with gusto by the demonically cackling Lacan who, by comparison, knew no restraint at all. And, if the maidenly Reik had never heard Freud tell a joke 'for its own end', Lacan did little else, flagrantly flaunting his own to the audience of his 1964 seminar on the fundamentals of his psychoanalysis. Lacan made no effort to keep wordplay to the point or scrupulously to separate puns from his own theoretical writing. Far from it, Lacan punned all the time. For him, as we'll come to a little later, a pun wasn't a *Pointe* – an isolated point, a little spot of trouble which punctured or punctuated the existing order of things. Puns didn't lie within a differentiated, supposedly non-punning field of 'seriousness' into which they could then be translated back – given a meaning, made good, and so redeemed. For Lacan, it was the other way round. Everything was a pun whether it was good, bad, or indifferent. Puns weren't items that could be pointed to or that had to have a point to be puns. Puns weren't the exception but the rule. Completely pointless, multilingual punning was the way the unconscious and language both worked – and Freud's ground-breaking work on the unconscious as it appeared in dreams, jokes, and slips of the tongue had, Lacan believed, first shown the way. From out of this teeming morass the exceptions weren't puns but, rather, the brief knots or provisional moments of meaning which sporadically raised their heads from time to time before sinking back into chaos.

Wordplay shows play in all its paradoxical aspects, and for this reason it's perhaps what exemplifies play best. On the one hand, wordplay is supremely creative. If language is, as it was for Huizinga, the 'first and supreme instrument which man shapes in order to communicate, to teach, to command', then wordplay shows his command over language. It makes connections which he didn't know were there, establishes hidden orders, makes the world seem more meaningful rather than less. Wordplay can become the basis for whole theories of human creativity, for out of it come not only jokes but poetry – for Schiller, the prime example of the play-drive. On the other hand, what could be more illusory? Man's command over language turns out to be a hilarious farce, as every bid to make sense, to establish meanings, to keep to the point breaks down in spite of everything into confusion and mess. No matter how hard you try to keep jest and earnest apart, they have a way of merging into one another for the distinction is purely notional. Connections pop up when you least expect it – and, since they're beyond your control, when you least want them – while connections which you've laboured to hold together – theoretical points, distinctions, categories – dissolve hopelessly into uncertainty and doubt.

Since you can't avoid using words to write about wordplay, the chances are that play's paradoxical nature – at once both creative and illusory – will show up there as well, whether you ignore it, sense but try to dodge it, or exploit to the full. I've concentrated on Freud because he took the middle position, torn between the temptations of theoretical man, tugging him back towards the undeniable comforts of knowing his own mind, on the one hand, and his doubts about the benefits or even the possibility of such a knowledge – which his own work only exacerbated – pulling him in the opposite direction, on the other. The resulting oscillation is made nowhere more visible than in the treatment of wordplay – and above all, of the pun – as a point. Did the pun lie within a field of straightforward, straightened speech – the terrain of theoretical man – as a bounded entity which could be pinned down and made to make sense? Was the pun a point that had to have a point – or *Pointe* – in order to be funny as well as interpretable? Or was it the other way round? Was it not puns which emerged from seriousness but rather isolated spots of meaning which emerged from an otherwise meaningless, totally punning field? What made a pun identifiable as such? What and where were its borders? Were they distinct or fuzzy? What made some puns 'good' and others 'bad'? What lay in between, and why?

Psychoanalysis is a particularly good place to reflect on puns because they're so ubiquitous in symptoms and dreams. They're everywhere, as Wilhelm Fliess complained, which was why Freud was moved to write about them – his book gradually turning into an account of jokes in general. Before returning to Freud, however, it's interesting to see how these questions are treated in another kind of interpretation – one that's just as concerned with wordplay as psychoanalysis – namely, literary criticism. For there, too, puns present themselves as points which, though sometimes stable, also have a habit of sliding disconcertingly around, posing the same quizzing questions about what's work and what's play, what's serious and what's trivial, what's worth doing and what isn't. Sometimes puns are clear and distinct – the objects of scholarly approval, admiration, and appreciation. But sometimes they're more ambiguous and vague, confusing the critic's categories and calling on him to exercise his powers of judgement and discrimination – 'is this a pun I see before me?' Sometimes they invade the critic's own writing, where they can be more dubious still. Are such puns put there by design – to be read as symptoms of the critic's own wit – or are they unfortunate accidents which prove more powerfully than anything else that he's not in control of his material? Are such puns made or found? If they're found, can the critic be said to have made them, and if so can he claim any credit for doing so? What if they're like the bad joke that's totally meaningless and yet, for all that, still quite good and rather funny? How on earth do you appreciate those? Is it possible to use words without playing with them? Are you dull and boring if you don't play with words? And, if you do, is that wordplay poetic and creative or is it just plain neurotic? Is the critic a worthy, earnest, theoretical man who has something useful to say, or is he just a joker who's conscious that every effort he makes amounts to little more than a pointless clowning?

II

It's as a point that's not quite a point, as it happens, that the pun is treated by that most serious of scholarly enterprises, the *Oxford English Dictionary*. According to the etymological note – added, as if by way of an afterthought, after the definition and historical examples – the word 'pun' is of 'unascertained origin'. It's possible, the dictionary continues, that the word 'might originally be an abbreviation of Italian *puntiglio*, small or fine point, formerly also a cavil or quibble . . . a pun being akin to a quibble; and that *pundigrion* might perhaps be a perversion, illiterate or humorous, of *puntiglio*. This appears not impossible, but nothing has been found in the early history of *pun*, or in the English uses of *punctilio* to confirm the conjecture'.

In a project whose avowed aim and mammoth task is to trace the heredity of every word in the English language, this shoulder-shrugging bafflement at the history of the word 'pun' is not without significance. In some ways, it served the etymologist's turn to present this word as untraceable – as having no point of origin – for it was another way of defining it, of keeping the pun in its proper place. The word's dubious history and unknown parentage could be seen to coincide with the pun's perfidious status as an aberrant element within the linguistic structure. As the critic Walter Redfern puts it, the word's obscure lexical background happily 'befits this trope which many consider illegitimate', supporting the view that puns are 'bastards, immigrants, barbarians, extra-terrestrials'. Puns play with meaning – they give the wrong names to the wrong things – and they disturb the proper flow of communication rather as the word 'pun' also disturbs the proper family lineage which etymology and genealogy mutually represent. 'Why bastard? Wherefore base?', asks the Edmund in *King Lear*, punning appropriately. Classed as a maverick – witty, daring, self-serving, and self-promoting – the pun's role as the anti-hero of literary history goes some way towards explaining why the Abbot of Calemberg – a legendary trickster at the German court – has in the past provided French etymologists with their conjectural derivation for the pun or *calembour*. Narcissistic, effeminate, showy – and lying too close to 'punk' (whore) to be productive of legitimate meaning – the pun represents a challenge to the stability of the linguistic order. For the eighteenth-century critic, Joseph Addison, puns had to be strictly differentiated from the more 'manly Strokes' of wit and satire. For Samuel Johnson, too, this word – for which he, likewise, could deduce no derivation in his own *Dictionary* (1755) –

139

was characterized by its deviancy. In the preface to his edition of Shakespeare (1765), Johnson famously described puns as the 'luminous vapours' which waylaid the unfortunate Shakespeare – the 'fatal Cleopatra' which inexplicably lured him away from the straight and narrow path of direct self-expression.

It's not inappropriate that the dictionary should present the pun as a bastard, for that was as sure a way as any of shoring up the legitimacy of the all the other supposedly non-punning words which are elsewhere being recorded and defined. But why *puntiglio*? The dictionary raises the possibility that 'pun' might derive from the Italian for a 'fine point' only to dismiss it again, or at least to refrain from granting the etymology the sanction of scholarly approval. Yet this strangely useless little note hasn't been edited from the dictionary. It's still there in the second edition, insouciantly suggesting that a pun isn't a *puntiglio* after all. If you're going to conjure a false etymology only to dismiss it again, then why choose *puntiglio* and not some other word – *punish*, for example, or *punaise*, a bed-bug? The reason, presumably, is to trail the pun's pointlessness. With *puntiglio* – a point that's not a point after all – the dictionary may not give the origin of the word 'pun' but it does perhaps give the origin of that old charge levelled against the pun – namely, its puposelessness. The dictionary appeals to etymology to fix the meaning of 'pun' only to record, somewhat helplessly, the failure of the attempt – 'nothing has been found . . . to confirm the conjecture'. The word's obscure lexical history is thus linked to its impertinence – its meandering frivolity. Just as the word 'pun' has no point of origin, so puns themselves have no point or purpose either. It's the dictionary which insinuates that the two are related.

Moreover – since *puntiglio* presumably suggested itself through its homophonic similarity to 'pun' – then to dismiss it as a false etymology is to admit that the connection was made, in the first place, through sound and not through sense, which is, of course, to do just what a pun does. Perhaps the purpose of the dictionary's little note was to show its readers the pun in action – to prove its point by exemplifying how a pun plays with sounds in order to suggest associations that are regardless of their sense – rather economically giving, as well as a definition, a demonstration of how the pun works. Like Jonathan Swift – whose *Modest Defence of Punning* (1716) delightedly mocked the learned etymologist by deriving pun from *fundum* (Lacan would have been pleased) – so the dictionary also implies that, in some self-evident way, the word 'pun' contravenes the otherwise sober business of etymologizing. It's somehow appropriate that the pun should display its subversive tendencies here in the middle of the dictionary, as if the etymologist were conceding that the role of the pun was indeed impishly to subvert the most patient endeavours of academic lexicography. As a folk etymology that would otherwise be accorded little room within a self-respecting dictionary, *puntiglio* is allowed to remain – a small trace of indecorum in which the science of etymology is temporarily allowed to betray its similarity to the dubious, suggestive, and altogether un-scientific play of puns.

The dictionary has every reason to present the pun as a pointless point. No longer the sharp end of a piercing wit, the pun is a bastard which, in confusing sense and sound, does what other words are presumed not to do, and is therefore cast off as a worthless liability. As it stands, the entry for 'pun' suggests a brief moment of disorder, a glimpse of frivolity during which the normal rules governing etymology and lexicography are temporarily suspended while speculation and fancy roam free. A small space is reserved within the vast project of the dictionary as a whole – an interval of demonstrated uselessness, a still small point of pointlessness. Presented in this way, 'pun' interrupts the serious work of recording and transcribing the language which is going on all around it and which is resumed with the very next entry – '*pun sb.*², a layer or bed of clay to prevent leakage'. The hole is patched up and that leaky element in the linguistic structure is fixed once and for all.

In any given language, according to the founder of structural lin-guistics, Ferdinand de Saussure, meaningful words are those units where a signifier and a signified emerge from the otherwise undifferentiated, jumbled planes of sounds and ideas, joining together to form a sign. But puns destabilize this neat formulation. For, while a particular sound announces itself as different from those surrounding it and so forms a signifier – *bat* is *bat* because it's neither *bit* nor *bet* nor *but* – it doesn't correspondingly differentiate a single signified but, on the contrary, two or sometimes more – in this case, a squeaky night-flying mammal and a thing for playing cricket with. It's not that puns expose the arbitrariness of signification – every sign does that – but that puns reveal the discrimination of meaning to be a haphazard, approximate, and error-prone affair. A pun subverts the one-to-one relation between signifier (*bat*) and signified (a bald, flying mouse or a stout piece of wood for hitting balls). It fractures the sign and disturbs those neat relations which, in Saussure's diagrams, tie signified and signifier together in tidily serried ranks. In a pun, one signifier is attached to two or more signifieds – the word can mean two or more things. It's because it ambiguates meaning that the pun disturbs the system of communication by which meaning is conveyed from speaker to listener, and upon which, in Saussure's view, any human society depends. That's why the pun has traditionally been treated as an anarchist, as a traitor who breaks rank with meaning. Since the mind 'naturally discards all associations likely to impede understanding', as Saussure suggested in the *Course in General Linguistics* (1916), he had nothing but contempt for 'feeble puns based upon the ridiculous confusions which may result from homonymy pure and simple'.

The dictionary's treatment of the word 'pun' might look like a happy accident – a pleasing quirk of etymological fate which vaguely corroborates the pun's widely held status as a literary picaro. But it's far from being unmotivated. For it articulates the same profound suspicion and distrust of any element that threatens to cause confusion and to impede understanding. Indeed, it's informed by a particular attitude toward literary language – a traditional poetics which finds its classic articulation in the *Poetics* of that supremely theoretical man, Aristotle:

> ... diction becomes distinguished and non-prosaic by the use of unfamiliar terms, that is, strange words, metaphors, lengthened forms, and everything that deviates from the ordinary modes of speech. But a whole statement in such terms will be either a riddle or a barbarism . . . A certain admixture, accordingly, of unfamiliar terms is necessary. These, the strange word, the metaphor, the ornamental equivalent, and the rest, will save the language from seeming mean and prosaic, while the ordinary words in it will secure the requisite clearness.

For Aristotle, literary language was characterized by its difference – its degree of deviation – from 'ordinary' words. Literary language was ordinary language defamiliarized, carnivalized, barbarized, made strange. As the smallest unit of linguistic deviation the pun was a microcosm of literariness since it contained ambiguity, polysemy, and frequently metaphor all within a single word. A pun is literariness writ small, and its supposed difference from so-called 'ordinary words' explains why it's traditionally been branded as illegitimate and treated as a barbarian – a foreign element or exotic intruder. The pun is marked as other and derives its status as such from being measured against an everyday, sober method of expression which is implicitly given as being the norm.

By associating the word 'pun' with a temporary relaxation of etymological and lexicographical rules, the OED, perhaps unsurprisingly, allies itself with the traditional view in which the pun's disorderliness is set against a norm of Aristotelian propriety and rectitude – the norm of lucid and explanatory prose with which the dictionary's scholarly etymologies and semantic classifications everywhere else identify themselves. Its account of the word isn't quite the piece of disinterested scholarship which it might at first have seemed. Rather, it's a tale with a bent – a corroboratory fiction which, in bastardizing the pun, implicitly supports a traditional poetics which is predicated on notions of order and legitimacy. The dictionary's note on *puntiglio* testifies not so much to the perplexity of the etymologist as to his interest in affirming this traditional poetics and in casting about for a story which obligingly represents 'pun' as both parentless and pointless. Within this particular literary history, the pun finds its home as a foundling child, and the small space that's made to accommodate it is carved out from within a larger paternalistic discourse which is contrastingly 'ordinary' – that is to say, stable, meaningful, and, by implication, punless.

Does literary criticism segregate the pun in the same way – keeping it to a point, assigning it to its lowly place as a poor bastard, as one of language's little accidents? Is the slipperiness, the elusiveness of the pun so easily contained? Some critics – like Addison or Johnson – liked to think so. They claimed to abominate the pun, insisting that it be quarantined from a properly regulated healthy and manly style. But others are less certain, more sensitive to the aura or fuzzy border around words which can make it more difficult to say with any accuracy whether they're puns or not. William Empson's *Seven Types of Ambiguity* (1930) is a case in point, being the classic study of the varying degrees to which the pun could be seen to differ from ordinary words – his seven types representing, like some family of folk-loric trolls, seven 'stages of advancing logical disorder'. Through a penumbra of associations, nuances, verbal echoes, and *doubles entendres* – all those 'subdued conceits and ambiguities' which Empson treats as variations on the pun – literary language announces in its depth and richness an ever-increasing distance from what, by comparison, is an increasingly impoverished plain style.

All the same, 'ordinary' words still remain a stable point of reference from which the remoteness of literary language can be measured and, although never specified as such, it's also the discourse to which Empson's own analyses and explanations are taken to belong. Moreover, to the extent that the critic aims to be interpretative and elucidatory rather than literary himself, the same turns out to be true even of the more playful critics who, like the deconstructionist Jonathan Culler, seek to put puns back into the centre of the frame – no longer as a 'marginal form of wit but an exemplary product of language or mind'. No matter how joyously the prodigal pun is welcomed back into the familial fold, it's still kept to a point – it can still be identified as a pun and differentiated from the language all around it – if only for the sake of the argument. Even if the difference between what puns and what doesn't is openly acknowledged to be a fiction, it's still a fiction which – for the purposes of having something useful to say – is in the meantime temporarily respected. Those critics who aim to show the ubiquity of puns by expeditiously inserting them into their own prose are doing the same thing, for if you're going to write about puns in literary criticism rather than write another *Finnegans Wake* you can't do anything else. Love them or hate them, the critic still has to keep puns to the point, still has to act as if some – or even most – words can be treated as relatively stable and taken to mean what they say.

However blurred or shadowy it acknowledges the border to be – and however extensive the no-man's-land in between – literary criticism still operates as if puns were on one side and the critic's language of explication (or most of it anyway) were on the other. Puns are identified, brought over the border, made to account for themselves, and shown to have something to say. Some critics may be more playful than others, more hospitable, more receptive to the pun. But they're still required to make sense – like the good joke, the condition of intelligibility remains binding on them. Every literary critic is a theoretical man to some degree or other. To analyze a pun – to track down its various meanings – is, one way or another, to recuperate the system of signification. However tentatively, apologetically, or provisionally, it's still to revert, even if only for practical purposes, to the routine business of making sense. It's to re-assign signified to signifier – to re-instate the pun as a sign, on the grounds that, after all, a sign is no less a sign for pointing in several directions at once. To understand a pun is necessarily to disambiguate it for you haven't got the joke otherwise. It's to put the linguistic house back in order, to straighten those oblique lines of reference, and to restore the everyday, sober method of expression. Puns may challenge meaning but to interpret them – if you want to make any sense at all – is *faute de mieux* to restore faith in the system of communication without which there'd be no understanding at all.

When discussing the puns in Shakespeare's *Sonnets* in his book *Beyond Deconstruction* (1985), for example, the American critic Howard Felperin writes about the potential the pun has to destabilize any system of meaning, describing it as the 'concealed fault-line' within language which, when it slips, has seismic consequences: 'the serene linguistic landscape is suddenly and totally transformed'. Yet, in his reading of the sonnets, Felperin shows little difficulty and indeed great delight in cracking the hidden codes and in itemizing the several meanings to which a given pun refers. His account of the puns in sonnet 129 seems in practice to be a matter of relatively straightforward translation: '"spirit" (ie. "sprit") . . . "heaven" (ie. "haven") . . . "well" ("will", and "Will" Shakespeare)' – his easy 'ie.''s contrasting with his claim that the puns cause him to 'oscillate dizzily' between their various meanings. In making sense of Shakespeare's puns, Felperin typically re-traces the 'trains of meaning they set in motion', a process which – in following the signifiers through to their various destinations – effectively re-stabilizes them, and which, it goes without saying, takes place within the serene landscape of the critic's lucid prose. Theoretical man doesn't give up his serenity lightly.

If puns threaten to destabilize meaning, couldn't interpreting them in this way be seen as a kind of damage limitation? Isn't reading a pun like this a way of bringing its dispersed or divergent signifieds back into place, of unpacking and sorting each of its alternative meanings? Doesn't interpreting a pun retrieve sense from nonsense, as if the disturbance in the linguistic order which the pun represents were most tolerable when its madness can be shown to be methodical? Whether the pun is cursed as a traitor to language or blessed as the welcome guest which brings two meanings for the price of one, its tendency to distort or to extend meaning is dealt with by the interpretative process which, however playfully, ultimately restores priority to the serious business of making sense, to showing what a pun finally means.

This would explain why the 'good' pun is traditionally the one which submits most readily to this treatment. A good pun poses no problems of recognition and is easily understood, obediently yielding up two stable and identifiable signifieds which can be seen to combine in a way that's fully relevant to the context. It suggests that the random associations which language throws up are not arbitrary but purposeful and motivated. The 'best' puns are those deemed to be the most pointed, Pope's lines from *The Dunciad* providing a classic and oft-quoted example:

> As many quit the streams that murm'ring fall
> To lull the sons of Marg'ret and Clare-hall,
> Where Bentley late tempestuous wont to sport
> In troubled waters, but now sleeps in Port.

'Port' points with equal directness to the peaceful haven and to the inebriating wine, as Pope's mock-serious footnote laboriously points out. Pope's pun is 'good' because its two meanings easily stabilize to form, in a single economical image, a satirical portrait of the drunken Cambridge don. A good pun is one in which the polysemy intrinsic to language is licensed – allowed to play for a strictly measured amount before being sorted out and tidied away.

Bad puns, by contrast, are less amenable to such interpretative straightening, dividing not into two neat signifieds which combine with satirical effect but rather into a plethora of half-suggested meanings which, if adding nothing obviously relevant to the context in hand, are branded as altogether extraneous. This is the home of those troublesome half-way houses – the subsumed pun, the stupid pun, the unmotivated, meaningless, gratuitous pun, puns that are dubious, accidental, or un-intended. Unlike its more tractable cousin, the bad pun doesn't suggest that wordplay can be contained but, on the contrary, offers an alarming glimpse of language gone out of control – of a perpetual play of signifiers yielding associations that threaten to impede understanding and to defy interpretation as they become increasingly disconnected and random. Traditionally, the criterion of a pun's acceptability is the degree to which its playfulness can be recuperated, brought back into the fold of meaning, and shown to have something useful or clever to say. If puns have historically been relegated to that supposed borderland between 'ordinary' and literary language, the good pun is the one which can most easily be naturalized, which has its papers most in order. The bad pun – in being less assimilable – is barely granted immigrant status.

The more strictly the pun is kept to the point – demarcated, diffe-rentiated, and defined – the more comfortable theoretical man feels about it. To be clear about what makes a pun a pun – and particularly what makes a good one good – is his way of mastering that sneaky element and of maintaining the all-important distinction between the puns that are under discussion and his own discursive prose. By dissociating himself from the pun – above all from the dreaded bad pun – the critic works to pre-empt or to remove any obstacle which might impede either his own or his reader's understanding. Limpidity, as always, is his aim. Allowing for puns but only within strict limits – keeping them on a tight rein – is as far as some critics are prepared to go. Umberto Eco, for example, thinks that Geoffrey Hartman goes too far in his reading of the following Wordsworth poem:

A slumber did my spirit seal;
I had no human fears:
She seemed a thing that could not feel
The touch of earthly years.

No motion has she now, no force;
She neither hears nor sees;
Rolled round in earth's diurnal course,
With rocks, and stones, and trees.

In Hartman's virtuoso analysis, words break up unexpectedly to reveal what he calls the poet's 'subliminal punning'. The phrase 'diurnal course', for example, suggests to Hartman the appropriately funereal words 'die', 'urn', and 'corpse'. The image of gravitational pull – 'Rolled round' – hints at a euphemistic displacement of 'grave', and he also suggests that the rhyme words 'fears', 'years', and 'hears' insinuate a subvocal word which, although itself repressed, is suggested by the anagram, 'trees' – namely, 'tears'.

Eco's objection is less that Hartman should read so much into the puns he's identified than that he should have identified them as puns in the first place. For Eco, Hartman is guilty of seeing puns where puns are not. Although Eco is prepared to accept 'diurnal course' as a good or at least acceptable pun, he's less willing to allow 'Rolled round' as a pun on 'grave' because the missing link – 'gravitation' – is supplied not by the text but by the critic. If puns are allowed to be simply the suggestions of suggestions – the implication seems to be – then where would it all end? Eco is similarly disinclined to accept 'tears' on the grounds that, although suggested by the rhyme words, it's not, strictly

147

speaking, an anagram of the word Wordsworth chose, 'trees'. If you're going to start being vague about what's an anagram of what, then anything could be said to be an anagram of anything else, and the same question arises again – where would it all end?

Eco's concern to restrict wordplay to the good pun – the pun which finds itself in the text and which, on being unpacked, yields meanings that are additional yet relevant to it – is the same as his desire elsewhere in his literary criticism to curb the limitless polysemy of language, and, as a corollary, the dangers of unlimited and, as he sees it, irresponsible interpretation. Implicitly, Eco would fix the limits fit to the potentially infinite suggestiveness of words by restricting it to puns, and specifically to good puns within whose limited scope the play of sense and sound can sensibly be contained. A good pun keeps to its appointed place, and it announces itself relatively unambiguously, according to certain criteria that are simple and manifestly reasonable – that it be in the poem, and that it lead somewhere meaningful. Isolated, itemized, categorized as such, the good pun demarcates itself clearly from the 'ordinary' words around it, shoring up the signifying efficiency of the latter as they proceed to identify and explain it. What makes a pun 'good' is its degree of recuperability – the extent to which, within certain fairly strictly determined limits, it can be managed, translated, and accounted for.

'Rolled round' and 'trees' are less obviously admissable, however, because the verbal echoes which they suggest aren't sufficiently tied to the text, and because puns which are so loosely defined can't be relied upon to lead anywhere. In Eco's view, bad puns are too ambiguous. They don't differentiate themselves from ordinary words straightforwardly enough, making any readings which they might suggest thoroughly debatable. Hartman's 'grave' and 'tears' are, Eco admits, relatively innocent examples; but, if defined any more loosely, the pun would ultimately threaten to lead the critic off into a labyrinth of totally unrelated associations. Bad puns can't be kept under control by interpretative reasoning but instead open up limitless possibilities and so jeopardize it, leading to some of the wilder excesses of what Eco calls 'over-interpretation'. As he would have it, bad puns aren't puns at all but accidental quirks of language which the reader is strongly advised to ignore. If a pun isn't good, readerly, and readily interpretable, then as far as he's concerned it's not a pun.

I've slightly caricatured Eco here – with his tight control over puns and his bid to retain meaning at all costs – as the anal theorist or good bourgeois whose passion for saving means that every pun has to be accounted for and redeemed in order to be good, indeed, in order to be passable as a pun. Hartman, by comparison, is much looser. More flexible and accommodating, he's willing to risk more, to venture more, to follow words in the direction which they lead, even if they sometimes go a little far. But this isn't to imply that Hartman's right and Eco's wrong, or that one reading is superior to the other. The point is that you can't legislate for suggestibility. If you picture a spectrum with theoretical man at one end and the joker at the other, then Hartman is further down than Eco, nearer to nonsense and play and further away from meaning and work. But what makes a pun a pun is nothing more definite or absolute than that – than a sliding scale. It's not a question of saying for certain what is a pun and what isn't – the difference is one of degree but not of kind.

It's almost as if what makes a pun a pun is less some objective criterion than the decision of a particular reader to make it so. It's true to say that 'tears' isn't an anagram of 'trees' because it contradicts the unambiguous rules about what makes an anagram an anagram – the rearrangement of the same letters to form a different word. 'Trees' and 'tears' don't have the same letters. But the same clarity doesn't apply to puns. 'Tears' may not be an anagram of 'trees' but there's nothing to say that it can't be a subsumed pun. It is if – on reading either Wordsworth or Hartman – you want it to be, but not if you don't. It depends where you are on the scale. The decision could almost be a matter of personal choice or private conscience – of nature or temperament, even of mood. It's possible to imagine a reader, for example, who was constituted slightly differently from either Eco or Hartman and who'd situate himself somewhere between them, more adventurous than the one, more conservative than the other, prepared to accept 'tears', say, but not 'grave'. But it's not a point of correctness either way. As every insurance house and gambling institution knows, some people are more risk-averse than others, or are more risk-averse at certain times in their life than at others. When it comes to deciding whether a pun's a pun or whether it's a good one or not, it seems to be less a matter of hard and fast rules than of how far a particular reader is prepared to go in giving scope to the suggestiveness of language – of the interpretative gamble he's willing to take.

As a test case for determining a particular reader's sensitivity to risk, one could use the following lines from Book IX of *Paradise Lost*:

O Eve, in evil hour thou didst give ear
To that false worm, of whomsoever taught
To counterfeit man's voice, true in our fall,
False in our promised rising; since our eyes
Opened we find indeed, and find we know
Both good and evil, good lost, and evil got,
Bad fruit of knowledge, if this be to know,
Which leaves us naked thus, of honour void,
Of innocence, of faith, of purity,
Our wonted ornaments now soiled and stained,
And in our faces evident the signs
Of foul concupiscence; whence evil store;
Even shame, the last of evils; of the first
Be sure then. How shall I behold the face
Henceforth of God or angel, erst with joy
And rapture so oft beheld? Those heavenly shapes
Will dazzle now this earthly, with their blaze
Insufferably bright. O might I here
In solitude live savage, in some glade
Obscured, where highest woods impenetrable
To star or sunlight, spread their umbrage broad
And brown as evening: cover me ye pines,
Ye cedars, with innumerable boughs
Hide me, where I may never see them more.
But let us now, as in bad plight, devise
What best may for the present serve to hide
The parts of each from other, that seem most
To shame obnoxious, and unseemliest seen,
Some tree whose broad smooth leaves together sewed,
And girded on our loins, may cover round
Those middle parts, that this new comer, shame,
There sit not, and reproach us as unclean.

In the famous pun with which Adam opens this speech, the homo-phonic syllables in 'Eve' and 'evil' are linked in a tendentious juxta-position whereby a freak coincidence in the English language becomes a causal and motivated connection. It's presented as lexically appropriate – not to say self-fulfilling – that Eve should have been the introducer of evil into the world. Moreover, this *bona fide* pun – which announces itself quite unambiguously, and which spells out the two signifieds which combine in a way manifestly relevant to the context of Adam's blaming speech – also prepares the way for a series of repeated 'eves' in the ensuing lines which confirm, with nagging reiteration, Eve's personal responsibility for the Fall: 'Both good and evil, good lost, and evil got', 'whence evil store; / Even shame, the last of evils'. Although less pronounced than the opening wordplay, these 'eves' are still obvious and readable enough to pass muster as acceptable puns. And a critic of Eco's persuasion would presumably also allow through other 'eves' which, crammed into this dense and punning passage, serve to drive Milton's point home with the sonority of a tolling bell: 'Which leaves us naked thus', 'brown as evening', 'broad smooth leaves'. Like the suggestive homophonic links between 'fall' and 'false', or between the fatal 'hour' and 'our eyes', 'our . . . ornaments', 'our faces', and 'our loins', so these various syllabic 'eves' combine to illustrate the secret wit of Milton's alliterative, punning style.

The question becomes more doubtful, however, when considering words which pun less obviously but which, in the context of this passage, begin to suggest *doubles entendres* or punning allusions and half-rhymes. Do we pass as puns, for example, the 'eves' hidden in 'whomsoever', 'evident', 'heavenly', 'never', or 'devise'? We've already been prepared for this question by an earlier passage in the same Book which similarly plays on Eve's name: 'O much deceived, much failing, hapless Eve, / Of thy presumed return! Event perverse! / Thou never from that hour in Paradise / Found'st either sweet repast, or sound repose'. The matter becomes more uncertain still as we move further away from the relative stability and obviousness of the inaugural pun which put the 'Eve' into 'evil' toward the increasingly twilight zone of the bad pun. Is there a latent 'eve' in the syllables – demonically reversed as if in a spell – of 'give ear'? Or what about 'live savage': do the vowels of the two words combine 'Eve' and 'Adam'? Does the 'ava' in 'savage' hint at Eve's name, or suggest that the serpent's address to her was an infernal parody of the 'Ave' with which a later mother would be saluted (after all, Eve's Hebrew name, *Havvâh*, meant 'life', and *ahavvah*, 'love')? Once we've gone beyond the common-sense limits with which an Eco would determine what makes a pun a pun, it's possible to see 'eves' everywhere: in 'counterfeit', 'eyes', 'cover', 'serve', 'each', and 'sewed'. Indeed, it's possible to see puns suggested that don't even appear in the text themselves. Does the play on 'Eve' and 'evil', for instance, insinuate an absent but complementary pun – that false etymology and bane of the lexicographer which links 'good' with 'God'?

A particular reader's willingness to accept some puns over others – and his reasons for doing so – could be used as a diagnostic test to establish his degree of aversion to linguistic risk. We could gauge, in quite a scientific way, just where on the spectrum or ludometer he'd fall. For one reader, these later suggestions might well seem totally preposterous, adding little or nothing to Milton's poem – not enough, anyway, to make them worthwhile. He might keep 'Eve, in evil hour' but discard the rest as too risky to have in his own portfolio. He'd be the safe investor, most comfortable with slow growth and with government gilts. But another reader might cash in and buy the stock, considering the poem vastly enriched by all those puns, and no doubt hoping that still more could be found – a further yield. This reader could also make the case that the fall of Man is quite appropriately marked by a descent into lexical chaos, and that the experience of words breaking down and splitting apart – as their signifying function deteriorates – is a wholly fitting symptom of the theological catastrophe that's just occurred. But it's not that one reader's better than the other. They're just prepared to take different degrees of risk. They may gain more or less, and may value what they gain more or less. Prices go up as well as down, down as well as up. But whatever position they take, whatever the kind of investor they are, the verbal exchange remains as volatile as it ever was. That never stands still.

There are good reasons for playing safe – for attempting to keep wordplay and its interpretation within reasonable limits and for restricting the pun to the good, clear, classic pun in which a writer exploits the felicitous conjunction of two identical homophones which preferably have two directly opposed meanings. Once limited to a certain point, the pun becomes masterable and pleasurable. A good pun's a security, a sound investment. The ingenuity and inventiveness of wordplay is exploited for the purposes of wit or satirical deflation. Nonsense is redeemed, the safe investor's vindicated, and theoretical man has his day. But to play safe isn't to control the market. That remains as unpredictable and volatile as ever. The player who's willing to expose himself to risk may stand a greater chance of losing – even of making a fool of himself – but he does perhaps have one advantage. He knows the nature of the market better, he's better attuned to its frantic instability. Whether he wins or whether he loses, he may in the end be better at playing the game. He may not want to think of what he does as a game or as a risk in which he stands to lose everything. But wherever he stands on the scale – whatever kind of reader he is – the literary critic is given the opportunity to test his nerve every day and to ask himself, with every text he reads (and writes), just how much and how far he's willing to venture.

As another test case, for example, one could take the following words addressed by the propositioning Angelo to the still novitiate Isabella in *Measure for Measure*:

> And from this testimony of your own sex
> (Since I suppose we are made to be no stronger
> Than faults may shake our frames), let me be bold.
> I do arrest your words. Be that you are,
> That is, a woman; if you be more, you're none.

Are 'made' and 'none' puns here? Why not? Isabella's both, after all, and it's highly relevant to the context that the lascivious deputy should be trying to seduce a virgin who's dedicated herself to the celibate life. Besides, why shouldn't a play that's so preoccupied with questions of exchange and value coin puns which show the linguistic currency to be particularly unstable? On the other hand, are they too slight or glancing – in comparison with other words in Angelo's neurotically punning vocabulary, otherwise much commented on – to make their way into the textual commentaries? Perhaps it depends, in the end, on the reader's disposition, on how playful or serious he happens to be feeling on a particular day? Or what about the moment when Horatio warns Hamlet not to approach the Ghost on the battlements lest he be lured

> to the dreadful summit of the cliff
> That beetles o'er his base into the sea?

Hamlet remains determined to obey its summons: 'It waves me still'. Dreadful, stupid, pointless though it may be, 'waves' is still a pun. Horatio – that eminently theoretical man – would have dismissed it out of hand, but hasn't Shakespeare's best punster started to play with words already?

Like it or not, puns are there. They're all over the place – good, bad, and very ugly. A reader can ignore them and turn aside. He can subordinate them, rank them, or discriminate between them. He can look for as many as he likes. But whichever he chooses, it has as much to do with the kind of reader he is or wants to be as with anything else – with how far he's prepared to go. Puns are like sounding boards or jumping off points from which the reader can pitch or gauge his own degree of sensitivity to risk at any one time. In *The Structure of Complex Words* (1951), for example, William Empson – whose sensitivity to nuance was as developed as anybody's – positions himself at a particular point along the scale when he deals with a possible pun that could be read into the final lines of *Hamlet*:

> Let four captains
> Bear Hamlet like a soldier to the stage,
> For he was likely, had he been put on,
> To have prov'd most royal; and for his passage,
> The soldiers' music and the rite of war
> Speak loudly for him.
> Take up the bodies. Such a sight as this
> Becomes the field, but here shows much amiss.
> Go bid the soldiers shoot.

Empson scoffs at the suggestion made by a German critic that there's a double meaning on 'stage' here – a deliberate joke or 'secret jeer' on Shakespeare's part intended to hint that Hamlet was no real soldier but – made effeminate by a German university education – was only fit to play at being a soldier on the stage. For Empson, 'few discoveries of a double meaning can seem more obvious nonsense'. Any hint that Shakespeare might have been joking here would clash with Empson's sense that these closing lines are 'enormously moving and whole-hearted'. And, although he admits that there's a case for seeing a double meaning here, given the intense and self-conscious theatricality of the play as a whole – and especially of this final scene where the dead Hamlet is now placed 'High on a stage . . . to the view' – Empson's whole move is to prevent any playful reading from running away with itself. He concedes that Shakespeare can't have helped noticing the double meaning, but in his view the playwright was 'letting his machine run away with him' and the best thing the reader or audience could do in the circumstances was to draw a discreet veil over this unfortunate tendency, turn a blind eye, and do their best 'to avoid noticing it'.

Empson's heading for the safer end of the theoretical scale here. Like Eco, he doesn't eliminate the pun but tries to keep it to the point. But, in a different mood, might he have been more generous to puns, more playful? How would he have reacted to those inadmissable puns – those suggestions of suggestions which don't themselves even appear in the text but for which – if stretching the point – a case could still be made? It might have struck him in an idle moment, for instance, that one word which is conspicuous by its absence in this highly theatrical final scene is 'rehearse'. According to the OED, Shakespeare was the first to use this word in the specific and now modern sense of 'to practise the performance of a play', using it twice with this meaning in *A Midsummer Night's Dream*. He was therefore presumably alert to the word's multivalency. Wouldn't his omission – or suppression – of it in the final scene of *Hamlet* rather befit a play in which so much hangs on the disruption of ceremonial, and where other characters are harrowingly buried 'hugger-mugger' and with 'maimèd rites' – without, that is, the pomp and dignity of a funeral procession or hearse? The action of the play is initiated, after all, by Old Hamlet's uncanny return from the grave – that place from which his 'canonized bones, hearsed in death, / Have burst their cerements'. The OED cites this line as the first example of 'hearsed' being used as an adjectival form, so Shakespeare was evidently experimenting with this word. Moreover, 'hearse' and 'rehearse' are, as it happens, etymologically related – via the Latin, *hirpex*, harrow. The agricultural instrument was similar in its form to the frame which carried candles and tapers over a coffin, and similar in its movements to and fro across the fields to the repeated rehearsals of a stage-play – an extremely harrowing tragedy, in this particular case. And – in a returning gesture which, in the circumstances, isn't at all inappropriate – it also transpires that Shakespeare was the first to use the verb 'harrow' in the metaphorical sense of wounding, vexing, paining, or greatly distressing – where? . . . in the first scene of *Hamlet*, where the terrified Horatio says of the Ghost that 'it harrows me with fear and wonder', the Ghost repeating the word, in an uncanny echo, to Hamlet a little later: 'I could a tale unfold whose lightest word / Would harrow up thy soul . . .'

This is a deliberately tall example and I'm not trying to put forward or defend a reading that would doubtless have harrowed up Empson's soul (and Eco's too, most likely). For Empson chose not to read any of this into Shakespeare's lines and, if he had, would almost certainly have called it the playwright 'letting his machine run away with him'. But is there nothing we can do with the crossed lines that result except avoid noticing them? Kept to the point as a discrete and bounded entity, the pun poses no problem to theoretical man. It's good. It exercises his ingenuity and expertise. It allows him to produce creative readings which make connections that actually amount to something and which add meaning to the literary text in question as well as to his own reading of it. It's additive and cumulative. It contributes substance, value, and weight – more meaning rather than less. But when the pun shifts from this position and begins to duck and to weave – to crop up in unexpected places, to elude the critic's grasp – then it's bad. Theoretical man begins unnervingly to lose his grip. Meaning looks more and more illusory – and not only in the literary text he's interpreting but, much more worryingly, in his own. He's been cheated and defrauded, handed an empty envelope. Even what he valued – his everyday, sober method of expression – turns out to be cheap and nasty. He may do all he can to overcome this. He may work harder than ever to separate jest from earnest, to keep puns in their place by studiously ignoring the bad ones and hoping quietly that they'll go away. But the repressed always returns. And the bad pun – that lightest of words – is like a ghost which can never be put to rest but which will keep on coming back from purgatory to haunt him.

III

Freud, as we've already seen, did all he could to retain the dignity of theoretical man and the substance of the good bourgeois theorist by treating the innumerable puns and plays on words which he analysed as points. In his habitual phrase, words formed the 'nodal points' of numerous ideas – particularly words 'the sound of which expresses different meanings'. Puns provided an opportunity for different meanings and associations to be crammed and blended together into a single unit, ready for the analyst to separate and sort. Freud's image of the nodal point – of the knot that required disentangling, untying, or unloosing (which is literally what 'analyzing' means) suggested that the pun was an element which needed to be straightened in order to be put right – 'set straight by the third person's understanding', as he put it in *Jokes*. And, in virtually every case, Freud's own method of interpreting was – albeit with varying degrees of difficulty – to unpack a pun's several meanings and to translate the dense, obscure, and mud-dled language of the unconscious back into the straight or straightened speech – *ortho-doxa* – of analytic interpretation.

The unconscious resorted to riddles, ciphers, and puns, but the secret of its disguised thoughts could be unlocked if you knew how to interpret these apparently baffling messages. Once translated and given a meaning, they could easily be elucidated and passed into the coherent currency of ordinary speech where they became 'immediately comprehensible', as Freud ventured in *The Interpretation of Dreams*, the text which most fully elaborated his revolutionary interpretative technique. However ubiquitous or commonplace in human psychic life, the pun was presented as a temporary and explicable departure from a differentiated language of sense – a language into which the pun was rendered back as soon as it was interpreted. As the interpreter brought what was dark and obscure into the light of rational day, moreover, there was a powerful suggestion that his recuperation of meaning brought with it a recuperation of health – and never more resoundingly than in those cases where the interpretation of a pun actually led to a clinical cure. The best example of this was the case of the 'Rat Man', a young man of university education who came to see Freud in the autumn of 1907 suffering from an obsessional neurosis which centered round rats, and whose case history Freud was to publish in 1909.

Freud's interpretative practice presumed two distinct orders of speech and the authority of his interpretations rested on preserving the difference between the two – between the 'nodal points' he analysed and the language of his own analysis, the everyday, sober method of expression. Freud worked to differentiate between the verbal tricks in which the unconscious indulged and his own comparatively lucid account of them. In the case of the Rat Man's baffling and unintelligible symptoms, for example, he wrote:

> Obsessional ideas, as is well known, have an appearance of being either without motive or without meaning, just as dreams have. The first problem is how to give them a sense and a status in the subject's mental life, so as to make them comprehensible and even obvious. The problem of translating them may seem insoluble; but we must never let ourselves be misled by that illusion. The wildest and most eccentric obsessional ideas can be cleared up if they are investigated deeply enough.

The secret to the Rat Man's various obsessions, it turned out, was puns. By understanding and deciphering these, Freud delivered them from ambiguity back into what was, by comparison, the valorized language of sense. Even the most gratuitous pun could be shown to be secretly motivated and meant after all. Puns which, on their own, made a 'purely external association' were 'obnoxious' to rational thought unless or until they could be redeemed in this way. The pun which Freud understood as linking the Rat Man's obsession with being fat (in German, *dick*) with his suppressed hatred for one Richard, an English cousin staying with his beloved, for example, justified an otherwise senseless and merely verbal link by finding for it a cogent explanation. It may have been a bad joke but it made perfect sense of the patient's behaviour. This didn't make it good, exactly, but it made the analyst rather expert in being able to spot the connection and consequently to clear up the symptom. In the course of such a 'straightening', a pun that seemed at first glance to make only a superficial or bastard association was redeemed by being shown to conceal a real or readable meaning underneath.

The patient's triggering obsession with rats was interpreted in a similar way. It turned out to have little to do with the parasite-carrying rodents. Rather, the word for 'rat' – *Ratten* – was a verbal bridge which brought together a whole series of unconscious associations, Freud's ferreting out of which proved the solution to the Rat Man's whole problem. The patient identified closely with his (by that stage, long-dead) father, a genial man who, in his soldiering days, had been much given to playing cards – to being something of a *Spielratte,* a gambler (literally, a 'play-rat'). One one occasion, he'd lost at play and, not having the wherewithal to pay the debt, he'd been obliged to borrow the money from a fellow officer. Later, having left the army and become a wealthy man, he'd tried to make contact with this generous friend in order to pay back the loan, but had never succeeded in doing so. The debt had remained unpaid and, years later, was still a source of pain and embarrassment to his son, Freud's patient.

The identification with his *Spielratte* father was what lay behind the Rat Man's obsession, as did other similar puns which Freud was gradually able to decipher and translate – *Raten*, instalments, and *heiraten*, to marry. His gambling father had forbidden the patient to marry his beloved but impoverished lady, and 'rat' had become the 'complex stimulus-word' which led Freud back to the patient's ancient infantile fury at his father's interference with his sexual desires. 'In his obsessional deliria', Freud commented, the Rat Man had 'coined himself a regular rat currency'. It wasn't an accident, perhaps, that it was the question of a gambling debt which first put Freud on to the right track. For the Rat Man's move to redeem an unpaid debt – which lay behind the crazy and virtually unintelligible behaviour which had brought him to seek Freud's help in the first place – was repeated by Freud himself as he too, the good bourgeois theorist, also moved to redeem language – to put sense back where it belonged. Translating the Rat Man's otherwise obscure and baffling associations, Freud was able to make sense of the whole situation. Meaning was restored and connections which in themselves were purely superficial or 'obnoxious' were made good – paid back. Theoretical man led the patient from darkness into light and the entrepreneur gained a definite return on his investment. Indeed, in this case Freud's interpretative gamble paid off spectacularly, for, as a direct result of his translations of the rat currency, 'the patient's rat delirium disappeared' and led – as he wrote in the introduction to the case history, not without a note of triumph, – 'to the complete restoration of the patient's personality'.

It was by keeping puns to the point that Freud solved the Rat Man's problem and got to the bottom of his case. He knew both what to focus his interpretative energies on – the particular pun that was highlighted by the patient's peculiar obsession – and how far he could afford to go – the point to which the pun could be set straight by his own under-standing. It was a gamble, to be sure. Freud had to set aside or suspend any idea of 'sensible' interpretation in order to bend his ear to the weird illogicalities of the unconscious and to see what meanings the particular pun in question would lead him to. In his openness to wordplay, Freud was closer to a Hartman than an Eco. But the pun was still contained. It didn't go on punning indefinitely. It eventually led somewhere – to some kind of solution, and in this case to a rather resounding one. However far and in however many different directions it led, the pun was still effectively kept to a point. It was still possible to tell the difference between the pun and 'ordinary' words. Freud didn't look for double meanings everywhere. That would have been pointless. He continued to exercise a degree of caution and common sense. He didn't behave as if everything punned. There were risks which, as a theoretical man, Freud wouldn't take, a point beyond which he wouldn't go. If he'd done so, it would have been difficult – if not impossible – to tell the difference between his own interpretation and the paranoid over-interpretations of the Rat Man himself, one of whose many symptoms was that he 'forced himself to understand the precise meaning of every syllable that was addressed to him'. To behave as if everything punned – as if every syllable were open to the play of meaning – would have been going too far. It would have been neurotic, frankly mad. So long as Freud kept puns to the point, the border between jest and earnest, between puns and ordinary words was re-instated. However permeable or leaky it may have been, the border was kept in place. Freud didn't go over it himself – he couldn't afford to, his reputation depended on it.

159

That connections which at first seemed superficial or pointless should turn out to be deep and meaningful underneath was a premise fundamental to Freud's whole interpretative technique. Indeed, it's possible to see this technique as a way of ensuring that meaning and seriousness – the good health of the language – were (or at least were capable of being) restored at any one time. The most stupid or arbitrary connections – the most empty, nonsensical jokes – could be found to make legitimate connections if only they were penetrated 'deeply enough'. If they seemed to be insoluble, this was just an illusion by which theoretical man wasn't to be misled. If he worked hard enough, meaningful connections would be found. The whole process was one of redemption, of making the bad come good. 'Whenever one psychical element is linked with another by an objectionable or superficial association', Freud wrote in *The Interpretation of Dreams*, 'there is also a legitimate and deeper link between them'. 'Superficial associations are only substitutes by displacement for suppressed deeper ones' – a belief which constituted one of the 'basic pillars of psycho-analytic technique'.

There was every reason why theoretical man should try to justify his intrepid quest for meaning. But he could still trip up or go round in circles, and his phallic mastery was still capable of taking a tumble – of being sucked down into a circular argument of his own making. We've already looked at how the 'other' Freud, the playful Freud, sensed the illusoriness of theoretical man's best efforts – at how the instabilities of his own theoretical texts betrayed his suspicion that there was a point lying beyond the end of the scale and beyond the pleasures of redemption. Freud didn't go there, but his texts peeped round the door. And in *The Interpretation of Dreams* this glimpse takes form in a particularly striking image. For it was there that Freud first admitted that a pun wasn't always a point but that its edges were capable of dissolving, melting, and turning in on themselves to leave only an endless tunnel, a bottomless hole. For, he wrote, there remained 'a passage in even the most thoroughly interpreted dream which has to be left obscure' – a pun which couldn't be pointed to or redeemed, a point where insolubility was no longer an illusion but a reality. 'At that point there is a tangle of dream-thoughts which cannot be unravelled and which moreover adds nothing to our knowledge of the content of the dream', Freud wrote. 'This is the dream's navel, the spot where it reaches down into the unknown'.

It was here – where the nodal point became a navel – that the pun finally got the better of theoretical man. No longer a stable point on which he could rest his case, the pun imploded into a reverse image of itself – an abysmal hole. No longer a knotty problem which, on engaging the interpreter's ingenuity, could be analyzed, straightened, brought out into the light and accounted for, the pun became a crepuscular tunnel which threatened to lure the analyst Alice-like down into a world which would defy all attempts at logical explanation. Here the pun added precisely nothing. The gamble didn't pay off and – having unmistakably lost the bet – theoretical man was forced to acknowledge defeat. What he saw here with sinking doubt was a glimpse of interpretation without end, of potentially interminable speculation – a series of word associations that could go on for ever and ever, leading nowhere and never getting to the point. Psychoanalysis was just another shaggy dog story.

The admission that there were elements within a dream that were incapable of being interpreted didn't quite tally with Freud's actual practice of following dream-analyses through to eye-opening conclusions. Though theoretical man's everyday, sober method of expression threatened to grind to a halt, it never quite did. The account of the dream's navel could be seen as a token gesture of inadequacy, designed to cover the analyst for any lapse or deficiency in his interpretation of dreams. If he worked even harder and penetrated still more deeply then perhaps he'd get to the bottom of this baffling obscurity and that dreadful insolubility would turn out to have been an illusion – a bad dream – after all. The navel gave the briefest glimpse of chaos, a mere hint of what might happen or what might be at stake if puns got out of control. Against the relentless drive toward elucidation, against the cherished belief that even the most absurd of connections had a reason and a motive, against the determination to prove of psychic events that there was 'nothing arbitrary about them' stood the smallest admission – a mere pin-prick – of the possible pointlessness of it all.

All the same, no matter how small he tried to make it, that mysterious and menacingly feminine navel finally stumped theoretical man and his claims to interpretative mastery. But for Lacan, who never believed in mastery in the first place, this was the opposite of a problem. Indeed, it only served to prove his point, for it was precisely puns which made the search for meaning a fruitless, not to say delusional task. Saussure had suggested that, once signifier and signified had emerged respectively from the jumbled planes of sounds and ideas, they bonded together to form a stable, meaning-bearing sign. But this didn't take account of those signifiers which bonded with two or more signifieds at once. For

Lacan, puns not only cast doubt on Saussure's formula but, more importantly, they pointed the way to the peculiar behaviour of the signifier itself. When a signifier emerged from the undifferentiated plane of sounds, it related, in the first instance, not to a signified but to other signifiers – to those other similar-sounding units within its immediate phonemic field – as *bat* would relate to *bit, bet, but, bête, bât, batte,* and so forth. A signifier didn't emerge naked, innocent, and spruce, but came trailing clouds of other signifiers – each of which related to others, and those to others still, and so on *ad infinitum*. Before a signifier had a chance to bond with a signified, it was off again like a butterfly chasing other signifiers. In place of Saussure's procession of relatively fixed, meaningful signs, Lacan saw a series of endlessly radiating chains of non-signifying sounds.

This was why puns were so important to Lacan – why he filled his own writings with them, why he had no problem with multi-lingual puns, and why, quite properly in his view, they disorientated and disconcerted the reader who was still unreconstructedly seeking meaning. Lacan betrayed a disarming lack of concern for the signified. He demoted it beneath the signifier and routinely represented its characteristic movement as one of slipping and sliding if not of disappearing altogether. The signifier in its bumbling flight might light momentarily upon a signified but any meaning that resulted would scarcely be more than provisional. Moreover, as one signifier related to others that were similar to but different from itself, those to still others, and so on down the Symbolic rabbit-hole, so language became not so much an image of the unconscious as the unconscious itself. It wasn't a question – as Freud had sometimes represented it – of the unconscious casting about for puns as a convenient way of expressing, through condensation and displacement, otherwise forbidden thoughts. For Lacan, the unconscious didn't have 'thoughts' to clothe in a riddling language which could then be deciphered and translated back into ordinary speech. For him, language and the unconscious were effectively one and the same.

In his analytic practice, Freud had treated the pun as a nodal point lying within a field of straight or straightened language and the pun which couldn't be interpreted as its opposite – as an endless, impenetrable hole. On balance, there are more knots than navels in Freud. But with Lacan the opposite's the case. Instead of standing at the periphery and looking dizzily down into the abyss, Lacan looked up cheerily from within it. For him, it wasn't puns which marked the nodal points within a field of ordinary speech but the other way round. It was sporadic sparks of meaning which lay dispersed within a field of otherwise detached and meaningless signifiers. Within the shimmering play of signifiers a proper Saussurean sign might occasionally show its head – for there were moments when signifier and signified joined together. It was just that these moments were the exception rather than the rule.

Moreover, of all the images which Lacan might have chosen to describe these momentary flashes of meaning, one can see why the one he finally opted for was the point – the 'quilting point' or *point de capiton* where the upholsterer buttoned down the sprawling fabric so as to pin it down more securely. For here – with the image of 'the point at which the signified and the signifier are knotted together' – we arrive at the mirror image of the 'nodal point'. No longer a point or *Pointe* whose function was to shore up everyday, sober speech, the pun disappeared into a universal field of signifiers – a field studded every now and then with a few scattered points of meaning. Without these there'd be nothing but insanity – but there wasn't a border between sense and nonsense. We weren't on one side of the line while ambiguity, incomprehensibility, and insolubility – fading out in varying degrees of tenebrosity – lay on the other. Rather, all was nonsense – a kind of primal psychosis – from which, if we were lucky, we were rescued only by a few small points of occasional meaning. 'I don't know how many there are', wrote Lacan in his 1955-56 seminar, 'but it isn't impossible that one should manage to determine the minimal number of fundamental points of insertion between the signifier and the signified necessary for a human being to be called normal, and which, when they are not established, or when they give way, make a psychotic'.

This is a question which might well be asked of Lacan himself. How many points of meaning would be required to rescue his texts from meaninglessness? Lacan ventured further and risked more in his wordplay than most, edging his way to the very end of the joking scale. But, though I've pictured him as looking up from the abyss or from the other side of a half-open door, he never quite fell off the end of the scale, or, if he did – gone! – he'd always, like a jack-in-the-box, come back again – there! For not even as manic a punster as Lacan would, when all's said and done, be mad. That wasn't his way, any more than it was David Hume's when he found himself faced with a choice between a false reason and none at all. To have given up on reason altogether would have been going too far, would have been taking things far too seriously. But trying to forget the pointlessness of it all wasn't an option either, at least not for the sceptical philosopher. Neither option was as gamesome as oscillating between the two. For Lacan it was the same. He didn't stop or lay down his pen. And though, for him, language would always begin and end with the play of detached signifiers, he didn't sink into silence or psychosis. For he still had a point to make – an important and eminently rational insight about the way the unconscious worked which, if accepted, would revolutionize psychoanalysis and jolt it out of the comfortably institutionalized practice which, from his point of view, it had become. If Freud had tried his hardest to keep the pun to a nodal point – fearful of its instability and its dreadful liability to turn into a gaping navel – Lacan didn't exactly disappear down the tunnel. In practice, he treated puns in a similar way. He just had a different attitude to them, a lower aversion to risk. He didn't fear puns or try to ignore them. His move wasn't to suppress, control, contain, or master them. But it wasn't his aim to be overwhelmed by them either, to be unreadable or unable to communicate. Instead, Lacan used puns for all they were worth – not only to spice up his texts, to entertain, and to subvert the solemnity of theoretical man but, above all, to illustrate his theme.

It was, after all, with a classic and technically 'good' pun that Lacan baptized the idea for which he remains, perhaps, best known – the *stade du miroir* or mirror-stage. The mirror-stage marked a decisive moment in the young child's life, being the moment – somewhere between six and eighteen months – when he first saw and recognized his reflection in the mirror, greeting it with signs of 'triumphant jubilation and playful discovery'. Unlike the chimpanzee – which, on discovering the image to be an illusion, quickly lost interest in it – the human infant would lean forward with narcissistic pleasure and hold the image in his fascinated gaze, producing 'a series of gestures in which he experiences in play the relation between the movements assumed in the image and the reflected environment'. But the mirror-stage wasn't only a point in time, a developmental phase. It was also a stage (the pun worked in English as well as in French) – a place for enacting a scene of discovery, a 'drama' whose story moved from 'insufficiency to anticipation'. For, on looking into the mirror, the child perceived a coherent, symmetrical shape which was – O joy! – himself, sublimely whole and together and quite different from the mortifying reality of a leaky, clumsy, dribbling body over which he still had a far from perfect control and which, as a little hommelette, he still experienced as existing in fragments or parts. The mirror-stage wasn't just a moment in time but a theatre – an arena or stadium (*stade*) in which 'two opposed fields of contest' met and where the struggle of identity and human subjectivity would be waged. The experienced reality of a fragmented, floundering body met an optical illusion – a body which presented a smooth and continuous surface to the eye, 'an ideal unity, a salutary *imago*', an Apollonian image of exteriority that was fixed, statuesque, and – to the eye of the beholder – beautifully formed.

The mirror-stage was a dramatic moment – Lacan's celebrated pun collapsing time and space together so that the point which inaugurated human subjectivity was also the place in which that subjectivity played itself out. For play was what it all boiled down to in the end. But this play wasn't particularly creative. It wasn't a first step on the way to progress, civilization, or maturity. Rather, it was illusory. It was *a* play – a drama or spectacle. From the beginning, the child's sense of identity rested on a theatrical conjuring trick that was quintessentially illusionistic because it was based on a fraud – on a fracture between real and ideal, between what was experienced and what was seen. Sight was the first sense of deception. The child's earliest impression of identity – his most rudimentary 'that's me' – was based from the start on a fiction, an externalized and objectified self-image, one which the chimpanzee, his intellectual superior at that stage, had immediately seen for the epistemological void that it was. For Lacan, this experience formed the basis for all later quests for and bids to wholeness. All the satisfactions of order or completeness – whether they took the form of a psychology, a religion, a theory, an ideology, a philosophy of life, or an over-arching world-view – had their origin in this wannabe. They were based on a foundation which from its inception was quite imaginary. The mirror-stage wasn't the beginning of great things so much as an ushering into the theatre, the start of a life of delusion and mystification.

It's a sign of how wedded he was to the idea of play as creative that Winnicott should have so misread Lacan's account of the mirror-stage in his *Playing and Reality*. For Winnicott, the child's finding an image of itself reflected back in the loving face and imitative gestures of its mother – its identity met, approved, and returned to it in that satisfactory act of maternal mirroring – was, like the transitional object, one of the most profound origins of the human creative spirit, the start of an individual's wonderful career as a maker, artist, and theoretician. But as Malcolm Bowie points out in his book on Lacan, what Winnicott, like many others, edited out from Lacan's account was the sense the child was being taken in, that 'something derisory is going on in front of the mirror'. In idealizing that moment, Winnicott betrayed himself as a theoretical man and, from Lacan's point of view, was merely repeating the groundless jubilation of the infant who was mistaken enough to think that he'd hit on something – that there was something substantial, profound, and meaningful in what he saw. Whether it was himself or his theory that he saw made no difference, for theoretical man was a narcissist who was so devoted to proving himself right that he'd always come up with a self-reflecting and so self-fulfilling argument. That was why he felt so fulfilled, so serene. Theoretical man didn't want to know he was in the theatre. The fact that he was deluding himself was the last thing he wanted to know, and he did all that he could to deny it – to go on deluding himself. For Lacan, the human subject had a perverse desire to remain deluded, to seek out and chase after a notional perfection and wholeness that had never existed except in the mind's eye. Human subjectivity perpetuated the peculiar pleasure of the theatre audience which chose to be captivated by what it knew very well was a fiction but which it still liked to believe in all the same.

The mirror-stage wasn't a one-off. Like a stage-play, it would be endlessly repeated for – since it marked 'the threshold of the visible world' – it inaugurated a way of seeing that was so ingrained from the earliest stage as to become *the* way of seeing, *the* human way of being in the world – deluded. All the world's a stage since the theatre – from θέατρον, to see – was literally a looking place, a place for seeing, which is something we'll come back to when we consider Shakespeare in the following chapter. Lacan drove the theatrical point home, not leaving it at the pun on 'stage' but taking his wordplay further, so that the child's act of looking in the mirror or speculum became a form of spectating, the enthralled witnessing of a spectacle. The 'specular image' and 'specular I' of the mirror-moment became the child's 'spectacular captation' of that image and his 'spectacular absorption' of other objects of sight, as, in Bowie's words, the mirror was suddenly 'punned into a spectacle, a specialized moment of seeing into seeing at large'. The stage pun was doing a lot of work. With all its associations, that single, economical image compressed together a time, a place, a thing for seeing, and an act of seeing. And all the while it was also demonstrating Lacan's underlying point that looking for a stable meaning in language was as deluded a task as looking for a stable identity in the mirror.

Lacan didn't need to spell that out laboriously because it was all contained within his witty and allusive pun. The proof of the pudding was, as always, in the eating.

Lacan's pun was 'good' in the sense that it was economical, rich, and laden with meaning. It worked hard for him and gave an exceptionally high yield. It was also 'bad' in the sense that it undermined meaning, revealed words to be slippery and unstable, and showed language to have got the better of the writer rather than the other way round. But since this, in turn, only proved Lacan's point – that mastery, like identity, was an illusion – he was, as he saw it, guaranteed to have the last laugh every time. He'd made his case. He had his pudding and had eaten it too. As a sceptical philosopher, it wasn't a question of choosing between jest and earnest or trying vainly to differentiate between the two. Oscillating to and fro was infinitely preferable – at once the most serious and the most playful move. Lacan didn't give up, didn't stop. He played the most serious game of all – and he played hard, played to win. If Freud had swung rather unsteadily between those two not-so-fixed points of sense and nonsense which made a joke a joke or a pun a pun, Lacan carried the gymnastics off with greater panache. A dare-devil who perhaps had less to lose, he managed to maintain a more perfect balance between the two.

Lacan was like the joker or the cheat who never needed to pay his debts because he knew he was destined to win. His speculations would always pay off. Perhaps that was why he was so unpopular and controversial a figure, and why he did everything he could to live up to his reputation as the *enfant terrible* of a psychoanalytical establishment which could only cope with this unruly pupil by expelling him altogether. Perhaps that's also why Lacan – for him, so uncharacteristically – passed in silence over another pun that was just waiting to be made. For speculating wasn't only something which the mirror-drawn infant or the theatre-audience did as they gazed wonderingly down on the spectacle of themselves. Nor was it only something which the theorist or philosopher did, as he reflected, pondered, and speculated in his own mind. Speculating was also something the gambler did, and which Lacan, in his own gambles with language, did better than any. Could it have been out of a kind of entrepreneurial embarrassment at the size of his jack-pot – out of a reluctance to be seen to cash in too greedily on his pun's over-abundant windfall of meaning – that Lacan played down that other meaning of speculate: to invest in a risky business venture in the expectation of considerable gain? Was Lacan's coy resistance to drawing out this particular meaning that of a gambler who didn't want to give away too easily the secret of his success?

Oscillation was the secret – to and fro, back and forth, in and out, up and down – just as it was for Hume, and for Nietzsche and Heraclitus who didn't go back to the sandpit but who settled on the image of the sand-playing child whose castle was for ever going up and coming down. Lacan saw himself as that child – a terrible child. Above all, he saw what he was doing as encapsulated in that particular game which has by now accrued something of the status of a parable – the game played by the little boy in Freud's *Beyond the Pleasure Principle* who threw his cotton-reel toy back and forth, into the folds of his crib and out again: gone! there! In 'The function and field of speech and language in psychoanalysis' (1953), one of his longest, most important, and most influential papers, Lacan presented his whole argument as being summed up by that now legendary game. For, in the articulation of those two syllables 'o' (*fort*, gone!) and 'a' (*da*, there!) – a 'pair of sounds modulated on presence and absence' – all was contained with the most beautiful and economical simplicity. There you had it – the way language worked by means of the pure relation of sounds or signifiers to one another. Every language could be reduced to these most basic of building blocks, 'a very small number of these phonemic oppositions'. Lacan's whole theory of language, of the unconscious, and of puns was all there – issuing from the mouths of babes – just as his own talk claimed, in its opening breaths, to be no more than 'an infantile cry', being first delivered, as it was, to the Psychological Institute in Rome, on the Vatican hill which derived its name from *vagire*, 'the first stammerings of speech'.

Lacan described the cotton-reel game as a 'game of occultation'. Since it epitomized the working of language – a signifier being identified by difference, by what it wasn't, 'o!' by 'a!' and *vice versa* – it was only appropriate to christen the game with a pun. A game of presence and absence, of having and not having, it was also a game of seeing and not seeing, of peekaboo – of now you see it, now you don't. It was a matter of seeing with the eyes, of ocular proof that something was present – there! But it was also a matter of not seeing, of absence, invisibility, and occlusion – gone again! 'Occultation' both saw and didn't see, was a kind of seeing that was also blind. It also presented another chance for playing with 'speculation', though it wasn't one that Lacan took up. For that we must turn to the only person, perhaps, who could be said to play harder with words than Lacan – the French philosopher, Jacques Derrida. For, in a fit of the disinterested and gracious generosity in which he has such a philosophical investment, Derrida gave the game away. His entire reading of *Beyond the Pleasure Principle* in *The Post Card* centres round the puns on speculation. And it's a sign of his own degree of playfulness and openness to risk that he should have placed Lacan among those who'd taken Freud too seriously and 'constructed an entire discourse about the seriousness of *Beyond*' – Lacan being, of all these, 'the most interesting and spectacular case'.

Derrida, by contrast, announced himself as following in the footsteps of Freud himself, who'd offered up *Beyond the Pleasure Principle* as one of the most speculative of his texts. 'What follows is speculation', Freud had written at the beginning of the fourth and middle chapter, 'often far-fetched speculation, which the reader will consider or dismiss according to his individual predilection. It is further an attempt to follow out an idea consistently, out of curiosity to see where it will lead'. Derrida followed Freud's strange, circuitous, and ambulatory path where it took him, extending 'the "properly Freudian" usage of "speculation"' – a way of thinking, a mode of research – to mean also 'specular reflection (the pleasure principle can recognize itself, or no longer at all recognize itself, in the reality principle)', the 'production of surplus value, of calculations and bets on the Exchange, that is, the emission of more or less fictive shares', and finally, 'that which overflows the (given) presence of the present, the given of the gift'. As Freud had anticipated, whether you consider or dismiss speculation – his own or anyone else's – in the end it comes down to individual predilection, nothing more nor less. It's as personal and inescapable as your astrological nature – your goatish disposition laid to the charge of a star – or your name. There's nothing you can do about it. You're born a gambler, or you're christened one. At least, Derrida was. For beyond pleasure – beyond the end of the scale – the punning machine will always run away with itself producing endlessly crossed lines which will, whether they like it or not, 'come to deride all those, men and women, who are worried by the question of knowing *what carries the day* in the end, and what *commands* in this world'. If such a question exists, Derrida adds, citing Nietzsche, it should be abandoned to the philosophical dilettantes, to the poets, and to women.

Shakespeare's Play

It was in the second chapter of *Beyond the Pleasure Principle* that Freud told what has since become the legendary and oft-repeated story of the *fort! da!* game. In the midst of his scientific and metapsychological speculations, he lifts the curtain on a scene that's remarkable for its homeliness. He describes observing a small child of one and a half – his grandson, Ernst, no less – play and untiringly repeat what Freud eventually recognizes and entitles as a game. The child's game consisted of throwing his toys to the furthest corners of the room so that hunting them out and giving them back to him was often 'quite a business'. The little boy perfected the game, moreover, when, possessed of a wooden cotton reel attached to a piece of string, he deftly threw it within the folds of his curtained crib, uttering his habitual 'o-o-o-o!' (*'fort'*, gone!), only to pull it out again and hail its reappearance with a joyful 'a!' (*'da'*, there!). 'This', says Freud, 'was the complete game – disappearance and return'.

This small domestic scene is presented candidly – artlessly, even – its very ordinariness offering a glimpse of normal, on-going family life, the intimate domesticity of which serves to shore up the writer's appeal to universal human experience. It's to the same fund of shared cultural knowledge that Freud appeals when, having identified it as a game, he draws from the little boy's action what seemed to him to be its most 'obvious' inference. In making the cotton reel alternately disappear and reappear, the game staged and re-enacted a key event in the child's life – the disappearance and return of a by all accounts much-loved mother. Passive and powerless in the adult world – with all its mysterious comings and goings – the child had converted his impotence into would-be executive action. In the face of contingency and un-predictability, he sought to master his condition in play, transforming the brute 'it was' into an empowered 'I willed it so'. The pain and fear of his mother's absence were objectified and controlled. The child's gesture incorporated both revenge – 'All right, then, go away! I don't need you. I'm sending you away myself', as Freud paraphrased it – but also, more consolingly, a heady control over the mother's reappearance, something which could now be governed by the merest twitch on the thread.

The experience of an otherwise unfathomable, arbitrary, and un-predictable world was thus ordered and brought under control. Play converted passivity into activity, unpleasure into something that con-soled, that pleased. In Freud's interpretation, the whole procedure could be put down to the child's 'instinct for mastery', an instinct which was constituted, moreover, by his earnest repetition of the game. For, in unceasingly repeating his action, the child didn't merely re-experience the wished-for moment of return. The pleasure of the game didn't lie in multiplication alone. He mastered his condition most effectively by conceiving of it as a narrative which had already reached its conclusion and which could therefore be repeated. His 'great cultural achievement' lay in converting his experience into something rounded-off and com-plete – a finished play – proof of which exemplary transformation lay in the fact that the same story, already completed and known, could be reiterated any number of times and with any number of local variations on its basic theme.

Repetition was one of the defining characteristics of play – perhaps *the* thing which elevated play to the higher realms of art and culture. As Huizinga wrote in *Homo Ludens*:

Play begins, and then at a certain moment it is 'over'. It plays itself to an end. While it is in progress all is movement, change, al-ternation, succession, association, separation. But immediately connected with its limitation as to time there is a further curious feature of play: it at once assumes fixed form as a cultural phe-nomenon. Once played, it endures as a new-found creation of the mind, a treasure to be retained by the memory. It is transmitted, it becomes tradition. It can be repeated at any time, whether it be 'child's play' or a game of chess, or at fixed intervals like a mystery. In this faculty of repetition lies one of the most essential qualities of play. It holds good not only of play as a whole but also of its inner structure. In nearly all the higher forms of play the elements of repetition and alternation (as in the *refrain*) are like the warp and woof of a fabric.

With its action taken out of time and made repeatable, the game which Freud described was the nearest thing to being a work of art. It did indeed reflect the child's mastery of a great cultural achievement. As Hannah Arendt suggests in *The Human Condition*, the repetitions of art differ crucially from the brute repetition of the biological cycle – the swinging rhythm of the life-processes, the inert and ever-recurring treadmill to which the *animal laborans* is condemned, endlessly repeating the monotonous routines of consumption and reproduction – the preservation of the species being its sole aim. Against the deterministic and self-programmed perpetuity of nature, *homo faber* constructs a 'world of durability' – of useful tools, primarily, but also of artifacts, monuments, stories, fictions. Like Freud's grandson, *homo faber* fashions, forges, and fabricates. And by such means he segments his experience, removing it from the relentless open-endedness of the biological cycle, punctuating it so that it can be repeated as a completed event, retrospectively mastered, narrated, and controlled. Although adults, unlike children, require novelty for their enjoyment – for them a joke or a stage-play encountered a second time would, Freud suggested, produce 'almost no effect' – all the same, local variations between one joke and the next, or between one play or production and another, make no difference to the mere fact of their repeatability – to the structural organization of these events which ensures their status as play. Man's constructed, durable world is the second world of art, and its repeatability is what distinguishes it from the blind and grinding momentum of nature. The *animal laborans* is imprisoned within continuous repetition, but the artful repetitions of *homo faber* are, by contrast, continual – like beads on a string, identical if need be, but each one end-stopped, rounded, and complete in itself.

Within the mind-made field of art, play is quintessentially creative. It takes the disorderliness of life and, like Freud's grandson, transmutes it – makes of it a repeatable story, a work of art. Within play, the disorderliness of a contingent world is folded into the game, so that unpleasant experiences of uncertainty, loss, surprise, absence, even death are taken charge of, managed, and organized. Play orders experience. It re-creates it, which is why play is recreative. It divides experience into completed, tellable narratives, making it repeatable and masterable. Play consoles by transforming an otherwise impervious and impersonal world into one that's authored, made sense of, and humanly controlled. The second world of art 'is the playground, laboratory, theatre, or battlefield of the mind, a model or construct the mind creates, a time or place it clears in order to withdraw fom the actual environment', writes the American critic, Harry Berger. 'It presents itself to us as a game which, like all games, is to be taken with dead seriousness while it is going on'.

Of all the various art forms which human beings have created, what the cotton-reel game resembled more closely than anything else was the drama. Although simple in its structure, the game contained in miniature – in the barest outline – drama's most basic plot. Child's play was the first stage-play. The disappearance and return of the reel performed the same mimetic action of a play in which events that are irreversible and consequence-ridden in the real world are transmuted into the second world of art and made repeatable within the con-sequence-free world of play. Drama takes the contingencies of human experience and orders them, bringing them under the control of a narrative logic and a scripted outcome. It takes the vicissitudes of life and transforms them, allowing for them to be ludically simulated, usually under the strictest conditions. What the child's game exemplified with a peculiarly eye-opening clarity was a play's transfiguring of unpleasure into pleasure. 'Suffering of every kind is . . . the subject-matter of drama', Freud wrote in 'Psychopathic Characters on the Stage' – an essay he never published but which he wrote in the aftermath of *Jokes* late in 1905 or early in 1906 – 'and from this suffering it promises to give the audience pleasure'. Because drama enacted that suffering – actualized it in visible form – it explored emotional possibilities 'more deeply' than any other art form, including either lyric or epic poetry.

Drama could be said to represent human play at its most sophisticated because, instead of simplifying or stylizing the experience of uncertainty – as games or lotteries do – it treats that experience in the round. Drama can figure in its plots the whole range of individual experience and personal vicissitude. Above all, drama creates a world that's designed to be repeated. Drama cancels the irreversibility of real human actions. It has a built-in repeatability – its stories are made to be played and played again. And, while the same could be said of any game, drama repeats the myriad different ways of experiencing uncertainty in all their complexity and variety. Drama imitates life's unknowability – playing on the audience's susceptibilities by means of shock tactics or dramatic irony. But it does so, all along, with knowledge – for the ending, or the existence of an ending, is already known ahead of time. Within the safe haven of play, death isn't death and the most terrible misfortunes can be undone, for in the end it's only a play. Disorder is ordered, and authorial motivation and design is found for the disorganization and arbitrariness of real life, down to its most absurd and least comprehensible outcomes.

For the anthropologist, Victor Turner, theatre as we know it originates in 'social drama' – in society's characterization of certain events *as* events because they're emergent, isolable, and discriminable from the environing field of the uneventful, from 'the peaceful tenor of regular, norm-governed social life'. 'Social drama' refers to those colourful or noteworthy incidents which society perceives to stand out from an otherwise drab and indeterminate backdrop because they constitute a breach in the latter – on whatever scale, from a domestic argument to a full-scale revolution. Breach gives way to crisis, a situation which then requires redress and which summons all that society's adjustive and self-regulatory machinery – ritual, law, and dispensation. By such means, a society organizes its private and collective experiences into discrete units with a beginning, middle, and end – an organization which, as Aristotle perceived in the *Poetics*, it was theatre's function to imitate. For what drama copies is society's predisposition to divide its experience into storied segments – crisis and resolution – whence those enduring forms by which theatre has anciently staged society's systems of redress: revenge tragedy, and the many versions of the court-room drama.

In its manipulation of suspense and surprise, relief and disbelief, or uncertainty and recognition, drama mimics the unforeseeability of real life. But it presents an unforeseeability which – paradoxically – has already been seen in advance, has already been 'taken in by the eye', as Aristotle put it. It's this seeing of the unforeseen, perhaps – an especially creative kind of seeing – that could be what's most truly invoked by the 'seeing place' or θέατρον from which the theatre takes its name. For Schiller, too, man's delight in semblance – in the imitation of life, which was Aristotle's working definition of the drama – arose directly from the sense of sight. For, while the sense of touch was something to which we were passively subjected, the sense of sight was something we actively engendered or made. 'What we actually see with the eye is something different from the sensation we receive', he wrote in the *Aesthetic Education*, 'for the mind leaps out across light to objects'. The savage or troglodyte who didn't rise to this level of seeing remained bound to the animal world of purely creatural sensation. But once he began to 'enjoy through the eye' he became a human being – 'he is already aesthetically free and the play-drive has started to develop'. Child's play marked the start of this aesthetic vision where passive seeing became active looking, and later adult appreciations of the drama inevitably referred back to that inaugural and wondrous sightfulness. 'Being present as an interested spectator at a spectacle or play does for adults what play does for children', wrote Freud in 'Psychopathic Characters', hyphenating the normal German word for a dramatic performance (*Schauspiel*) to emphasize the word's two component parts – *Schau*, spectacle, and *Spiel*, play or game.

Moreover, if, out of all the art forms, what the child's game in *Beyond the Pleasure Principle* most closely resembled was the drama, then of all the dramatic forms what it most closely resembled was tragedy. The game repeated and mastered a story whose ending was already known. Freud's description of the 'complete' game echoed Aristotle's description of a tragedy as representing an action that was 'complete in itself'. The pleasure special to tragedy lies in the fact that it doesn't simply repeat any experience but specifically repeats unpleasure – loss, catastrophe, sacrifice – in order to master it, and, with each repetition, to reverse the consequences of human action and to redeem an otherwise uncaring and aleatory world. Above all, tragedy repeats death – that categorically unrepeatable occurrence – palliating its blank finality with the promise of being able to play it again. Tragedy gives a particularly striking example of how art makes pleasure out of unpleasure by means of repetition. The reiteration of any event presupposes that its ending is already known – devoid of fate, chance, or unforeseeability. A story that's repeatable is a story already finished, waiting to be re-told. It needn't necessarily be a story of loss. But tragedy gratifies its audience with what Aristotle calls its own 'proper' pleasure because it doesn't triumph over just any disorder but over the very worst kind – death.

In feigning death, tragedy cancels, mitigates, and so compensates for death's crushing finality, providing a consolation which goes far beyond the elementary pleasure of survival. It's true that, as Elias Canetti writes in *Crowds and Power*, the 'moment of survival is the moment of power. Horror at the sight of death turns into satisfaction that it is someone else who is dead. The dead man lies on the ground while the survivor stands'. This moment fills the survivor with a special strength, and there's nothing 'which more demands repetition'. But this consolation belongs to what Freud called the game's 'first act' only – 'gone!' As a rule, he noted, little Ernst played this single act most often, for ever throwing his toys away – playing 'gone' with them. But tragedy's deeper consolation lies in its staging of the 'second act' – 'there!' – and Freud was in 'no doubt that the greater pleasure' lay in that. For here death is feigned. It's not for real. Tragedy promises that its represented deaths can be repeated – that the dead characters will revive without fail and that they can do so any number of times: gone! there! gone! there! gone! there!

Tragedy is *fort! da!* for grown-ups. Tragedy laughs in the face of death because a represented and repeatable death is a non-death. Tragedy cheats death – even the most catastrophic – when at the end of the performance the actors get up and walk away. This moment is invariably performed, however engrossing the scene, and however emphatic the actors' denials:

> Haply you think, but bootless are your thoughts,
> That this is fabulously counterfeit,
> And that we do as all tragedians do:
> To die today, for fashioning our scene,
> The death of Ajax, or some Roman peer,
> And in a minute starting up again,
> Revive to please tomorrow's audience.
> No, princes, know I am Hieronomo,
> The hopeless father of a hapless son.

Hieronomo assures the stage audience of Thomas Kyd's play, *The Spanish Tragedy* (1582-92), that the deaths which they've just witnessed in his masque aren't merely acted but are in earnest – for real – the fulfilment of his long-vowed revenge. But his gesture of naturalization doesn't alter the fact that, of course, the deaths are acted, and that reviving 'to please tomorrow's audience' is exactly what the players will go on to do. For all the ironic frame established by the play-within-a-play, the game's second act will take place without fail and with utter predictability. That's why – or one of the reasons why – tragedy pleases.

That his grandson's game was indeed a prototypical tragedy was the conclusion Freud came to himself, closing his account of it with the observation that in artistic productions carried out by adults and intended for an audience – 'for instance, in tragedy' – the spectators were no more spared from the most painful experiences that were nevertheless felt by them to be 'highly enjoyable'. Nobody watched a tragedy in order to suffer themselves but rather to experience the particular pleasure of identifying with the suffering of someone else, and, in so doing – according to Aristotle's classic definition, which remained the mainstay of the western aesthetic tradition – to purge themselves of unpleasant feelings and so to feel better. The powerful alchemy by which something painful was turned into something pleasurable called, Freud said, for some explanatory 'system of aesthetics'. He didn't pursue this question in *Beyond the Pleasure Principle*, but he'd touched on it elsewhere, as in the 'Psychopathic Characters' essay where he'd specified that the first precondition of all art – but especially of tragic drama – was that it shouldn't cause suffering to the members of the audience but rather 'compensate' them aesthetically for any sympathetic suffering which was aroused through their identification with the hero or heroine.

What we recognize in this compensatory aesthetic is what Leo Bersani has called the 'culture of redemption'. Play redeemed human experience. It took the worst aspects of human experience – loss, un-certainty, surprise, and, in the case of tragedy, death – and transported them to a second world where they could be played out and, in the process, taken out of time, de-realized, and put under human control. 'A crucial assumption in the culture of redemption', Bersani writes, 'is that a certain type of repetition of experience in art repairs inherently damaged or valueless experience'. Human suffering may have been acute or overwhelming, but art was understood to take that as the raw material of experience and to transmute it in a way that imparted value to it, gave it meaning, and ultimately redeemed it. In tragedy, even death – that greatest wound to man's narcissism – could be re-played, repeated, and so redeemed in this way. The culture of redemption was, Bersani adds, above all else the creation of theoretical man – that creature who, as Nietzsche put it in *The Birth of Tragedy*, held fast to the belief that thought could 'plumb the farthest abysses of being and even *correct* it'. The culture of redemption implied that the bad could always be made good, that, however painful, human experience could always be redeemed in art, and that – since the aesthetic realm is the one area under human control – it would always be within man's power to do so. It implied that the imperfect could be perfected – the meaningless made intelligible, the unknown known, the unpleasurable pleasing – and that theoretical man would be able to effect the transition and to work his wondrous magic every time.

That the broken could be mended, the sick healed, and the partial made whole was presented by theoretical man with unblinking con-fidence as the most natural and ethical thing in the world – as his whole *raison d'être* and unchallengeable self-justification. It's a winning philo-sophy and one which continues to hold sway in the moralized rhetoric of health and wholeness that daily beats at our door. But, as Nietzsche never tired of objecting, that doesn't in any way prevent it from being a myth – a 'grand metaphysical illusion' – and not only for the obvious reason that the consolations of tragedy are illusory: that death is death and no amount of tragedy is ever going to obviate that. For Nietzsche, the culture of redemption was also an illusion – a pernicious fiction – because it couldn't deal satisfactorily with any exceptions to its rule. If a work of art for some reason failed to give aesthetic pleasure or to benefit the audience with some uplifting moral or other, theoretical man could only respond by saying that it wasn't art or, if he couldn't get away with that, then by saying that it was 'bad'. Writing of the drama that it must, by definition, compensate the audience with some kind of aesthetic satisfaction, Freud added, with a faint note of disapproval, that 'modern writers have particularly often failed to obey this rule'. There are echoes of the bourgeois theorist here who was determined to get his money's worth and who demanded of the art he'd paid good money for an unambiguous yield of pleasure without which he'd have felt cheated or had.

But theoretical man's 'rule' was highly reductive and obliged him to classify a great deal of art as non-art or as bad. Such was the rigorously logical conclusion Freud was forced to come to regarding *Hamlet* – a play which, since it represented the development of a neurosis in the hero (the inability to repress oedipal jealousies and desires) could arouse nothing but 'aversion' in anyone who wasn't a neurotic themselves. Freud's position in the 'Psychopathic Characters' essay – the solid position of theoretical man – was that art should strengthen and improve. In order to be art, it had to help a person master his own neuroses and maintain his repressed, cultured, civilized self. From such a perspective, any play which did the opposite, such as *Hamlet*, could only be characterized as bad. If it didn't have something to show for itself – something meaningful, improving, or pleasurable to exchange – then art was either not art or 'bad' in exactly the same way that a pun which didn't mean anything was either not a pun or 'bad'. If something failed to obey theoretical man's rule, then it was beyond redemption. But that ruled out quite a lot of art, much of it – like *Hamlet* – by no means bad.

The culture of redemption brought art down to what Bersani calls a 'superior patching function', its compensations designed to do little more than to round off or fill in experience that wasn't quite complete – to strengthen a little here, reinforce a little there. It didn't only reduce art, however. The culture of redemption woefully reduced experience, too. It implied that, however unsatisfactory, human experience could always be embellished, straightened, or improved upon by art – an idea which, if taken to its logical conclusion, was capable of producing an invidious irresponsibility if not a callously *laissez faire* attitude to suffering. As Bersani puts it, 'the catastrophes of history matter much less if they are somehow compensated for in art'. Moreover, just as theoretical man had no name or place for an art that failed to compensate, so he had no way of describing experiences that couldn't be compensated for – experiences that were so bad they couldn't be redeemed. Yet, as even the most cursory survey of human history could demonstrate, there manifestly were experiences of unpleasure so extreme that they couldn't be made good and which clearly couldn't be declassified as not existing. There were experiences of brokenness so acute as to be beyond repair, occasions when the gap between unpleasure and pleasure widened out into a chasm that proved unbridgeable. Perhaps death came into that category, putting in doubt the ability of tragedy finally to compensate for the bleakness of that absolute. For play didn't always redeem. There were some things that were beyond it – some experiences that play couldn't master. And even the most optimistic of theoretical men was forced to acknowledge that there were exceptions to his rule, when he had no choice but to admit defeat.

Winnicott, for example, described just such an experience of irrecuperable loss. If a mother left her baby for x minutes, the infant would feel distress since – as Freud had said of his grandson – it couldn't possibly feel its mother's departure as something 'agreeable or even indifferent'. If the mother returned in x + y minutes, the distress was 'soon mended' and the baby suffered no lasting damage – its state wouldn't have been altered for the worse. But there was a place beyond pleasure – a point of no return, a zero degree of suffering that couldn't be mended or healed. In x + y + z minutes the mother's absence would have constituted a decisive break – a trauma. A gap would have opened up in the infant's sense of life's continuity, inducing in it a state which the normally sunny Winnicott did nothing to euphemize. In that state, as he saw it, the baby was mad. It endured a condition of 'unthinkable anxiety' which amounted to the disintegration of its nascent ego structure. This was a gap not mendable by play – a 'gone!' that couldn't be redeemed by a 'there!' 'We must assume', Winnicott wrote, 'that the vast majority of babies never experience the x + y + z quantity of deprivation. This means that the majority of children do not carry around with them for life the knowledge from experience of having been mad'.

But for the unfortunate few, that deprivation was irredeemable – a wipe-out, an experience that could never be got over or creatively built upon afterwards. 'After "recovery" from x + y + z deprivation a baby has to start again permanently deprived of the root which could provide continuity with the personal beginning'. Henceforward, the child's play wouldn't be cumulative – a gradual, creative mastery of his environment, a testing-out of his limitations, a coming to terms with a reality beyond his control. His play would be lifeless, joyless, and inert.

After an experience such as this, the transitional object which normally defined the 'potential space' between the child and its mother would lose its value and begin to become meaningless. No longer a creative tool, it would be used as a form of denial. As an example, Winnicott cites the case of a clearly disturbed seven-year-old who'd been traumatized by his mother's withdrawal from him on several occasions – at the birth of his younger sister, on her absence to have an operation, and on her lengthy hospitalization for a severe depression. The boy had an obsessive preoccupation with string, and in his play – which immediately struck Winnicott as pathological – he'd use string to tie pieces of furniture together or, more alarmingly, to tie round his sister's neck or to hang himself upside down from a tree. For Winnicott it was clear that in his play the boy was 'dealing with a fear of separation, attempting to deny separation by his use of string'. Some improvements were made when the mother then talked to the boy about his anxieties, but the damage had been done, and he grew into a troubled adolescent, unable to separate from his mother, to leave the family home, or to set up a life of his own. In another, admittedly less severe case, Winnicott saw a boy of two and a half who'd developed a stammer and, frightened by it, had stopped talking altogether. He too indulged in string-play, making a gesture in which he seemed to plug one end of a piece of string into his mother's thigh, as if it were a 'symbol of union' with her. Freud's grandson had substituted a cotton-reel for his mother – had made his first metaphor. But in Winnicott's two cases, the children had failed to take that first, creative step, too fearful of loss to risk re-creating the experience in play. For them it wasn't a substitute but their actual mother that they needed to have on the other end of that patently still umbilical cord.

Not every experience was masterable by play, not every 'gone!' redeemable by a 'there!' When it was, then, in Winnicott's well-known phrase, the child's environment had been 'good enough'. Healthy play was a sign of that sufficiency, the indication that a critical line hadn't been crossed. But not every environment was good enough. Sometimes 'gone!' meant 'gone!' and no amount of play would overcome or compensate for that loss. In those cases, play was no longer reparative but a desperate attempt to deny reality and to hold on to an illusion. Play wasn't necessarily healthy, creative, and spontaneous. It could also be compulsive, neurotic, and ill. Perhaps theoretical man would respond at that point by saying that such play wasn't what he meant by play – it wasn't 'true' play, the creative, ordering, meaningful play which he was engaged in himself. But whatever you called it, play wasn't always a form or mastery, a learning experience in which a child came to terms with his lack of omnipotence by means of role-play or imaginative make-believe. Indeed, far from being something the child mastered, play could master the child. Instead of coming from within – a making over of distress, as Freud's grandson converted unpleasure into control – it could come from without. An over-controlled child, for example, would submit compliantly to another person's rules rather than making up his own. This was the case with the patient of Winnicott's who, as the youngest of her family, had entered into a world 'already organized' before her and had therefore never learned to play her own games – an inability which expressed itself in her adult life in the compulsive playing of boring games like patience. Instead of building her own world through play, she'd submitted to someone else's, developing not her true potential but only the empty shell of a false self.

Unhealthy play proved more powerfully than anything else that the culture of redemption was flawed. Not all experiences were masterable. Not all play was masterly. And this remained the case whether you called it play, not-play, tragedy, art, not-art, 'bad' art, or whatever. It was, of course, in order to pursue that elusive beyond – the z factor – that Freud had embarked on writing *Beyond the Pleasure Principle* in the first place. The account of little Ernst's game turned out to be some-thing of an irrelevance – beside the point – for, having judged that the child had converted the experience of unpleasure into pleasure by means of his 'instinct for mastery', Freud was still left with the need to go further into the penumbrous 'beyond' of his title. What was on the other side of mastery? What lay beyond pleasure? If nothing else, there might lie the answers to those unquiet questions which so troubled theoretical man – not only his relation to art and culture but, more urgently from Freud's point of view, the undeniable fact that human beings not only experienced unpleasure but also found themselves repeating that experience over and over again – and not always in a way that could be redeemed. Why should they do this? What drove them to it? How could you account for the 'mysterious masochistic trends of the ego'? For the drive towards mastery and control, powerful and pleasurable as it was, still didn't quite square with what Freud saw in his consulting room (and not only there) every day – the equally powerful if strangely inexplicable urge which drove human beings towards unpleasure, unhappiness, and self-destruction.

Little Ernst had repeated unpleasure – the distressing experience of his mother's departure – and had mastered it in play. But Freud was interested in repetitions that weren't masterly, in experiences that couldn't be so redeemed. The best example he found to illustrate his case wasn't child's play but what he called the neurotic 'compulsion to repeat'. Neurotics repeated a past experience instead of remembering it and consigning it to history. Failing to relegate it to its proper place, they re-lived and acted out in the present an attachment, relation, or trauma which belonged to the past. They didn't know that they were doing it – that was the point. Hopelessly caught up in a loop, replicating the same thing again and again, they compulsively repeated an identical situation – one not necessarily forgotten but whose connection with the repetitions of the present had been severed and which was therefore to all intents and purposes repressed. Freud cites as an example the case of a woman who'd successively nursed three husbands to their deaths. Neurotics weren't in command of their repetitions – as little Ernst had been – but were in their grip. They weren't active, creative, and playful but passive, helpless, and possessed by what felt to them to be some alien or 'daemonic' power. What neurotics repeated was invariably some repressed infantile sexual experience, but what Freud found so 'remarkable' was that they repeated something which had *never* been an occasion of pleasure. Instead, they re-experienced on a daily basis the scorn, humiliation, and failure to which all infantile sexual researches and desires had been doomed. 'No lesson has been learnt' from these failures – no moral drawn from the tragedy. Instead of deriving a stern but improving lesson about reality (as, by implication, the good bourgeois theorist or theoretical man of culture would have done) it was as if neurotics remained stuck in a bad play, and the result was mental illness.

If child's play was creative – the first step on the march of progress towards culture and civilization, a testing-ground where the proto-adult learned to master his environment, subdue anxiety, and make good use of otherwise 'unserviceable' desires: if play was primarily active, converting – like little Ernst – 'the passivity of the experience into the activity of the game', then the compulsion to repeat showed its other side. Here repetition was the opposite. Neither creative nor masterful, it was neurotic and pathological. It didn't usefully convert unpleasure but uselessly repeated it. Above all, it wasn't active but passive. The neurotic wasn't a master of repetition but a slave to it. He'd mastered neither his unpleasant experiences of failure nor his compulsion to repeat them but felt the victim of some external, demonic force which drove him to re-enact certain patterns of behaviour seemingly against his will. It was this passive aspect of the repetition compulsion which Freud took up and which – in following it through to its logical conclusion out of a desire for thoroughness – brought him to what for some still remains one of the most contentious of his propositions – the idea of the death drive.

As Freud saw it, the compulsion to repeat unpleasurable experience in a way that delivered no compensatory pleasure could only be explained by some principle that was somehow 'more primitive, more elementary, more instinctual' than the drive towards pleasure or self-preservation. What the neurotic demonstrated with a peculiar visibility was a profound passivity – a constitutional inability to fight, to work, to overcome, to take arms against a sea of troubles. It was as if – as well as a noisy, busy drive that led towards activity and liveliness – there was also in human beings an equally powerful yet more conservative, regressive tendency – a pull away from activity towards stillness, a move to reduce tension, to fend off stimuli, to keep agitation and excitation to a minumum. It was as if there were a tendency towards stability which, at its furthest end, would become what Freud called 'an urge inherent in organic life to restore an earlier state of things'. At the beginning of the evolutionary scale, the most elementary organism had been prodded into life and had had to exert energy, effort, expenditure, however minimal, to stay that way. But all things being equal – if conditions had stayed the same – it would have done no more than constantly repeat the same course of life, preserving its energy and keeping it to the barest minimum. It was this near-primaeval state to which, Freud guessed, the neurotic compulsion to repeat bore witness, as a throw-back to an unimaginably distant creatural past. The elementary organism lived, but all the while it nurtured an urge – a veritable principle of inertia – to revert to the stasis of the inanimate, inorganic state. What kept it alive – rather than fading out at once into blissful oblivion – was only the fact that it wished to avoid returning to that state by any means other than those immanent in itself. 'What we are left with', Freud hazarded, 'is the fact that the organism wishes to die only in its own fashion'. On the far side of the pleasure principle lay the most profound silence of all – the absolute silence of lifelessness, the awesome silence of stone.

From the point of view of the death drive – an instinct which preceded life and to which, it couldn't be denied, all living things were destined to return – the instinct for development and change couldn't look anything but puny and insignificant. Theoretical man was forced to stop in his tracks as before a Gorgon that would turn him to stone. No longer some splendid inner quality which had brought men to 'their present high level of intellectual achievement and ethical sublimation', the striving towards perfection in human beings could only seem trivial and slight – an evolutionary latecomer, an up-start, a mere blink in the eye of nature with its universal tendency to revert to the stasis of death. For the author of *Beyond the Pleasure Principle*, the instinct towards perfection was nothing more than a 'benevolent illusion' with which men sought, however vainly, to deny or at least to palliate the blank of that otherwise heart-stopping truth. All theoretical man's best efforts – his trials, strivings, and conquests, which had to include *Beyond the Pleasure Principle* itself – were, in the light of this ponderous eternity, reduced to humiliatingly irrelevant specks. Absent in the plant and animal worlds, the drive towards development 'upon which is based all that is most precious in human civilization' was the result of a freakish repression of the instincts which peculiarly affected human beings. The life instincts – embodied in the sex drive – were, for whatever unfathomable reason, submitted to repression by the human creature. But they never ceased to strive for complete satisfaction, whence the driving force that impelled man ever forwards in his quest for advancement and success. This drive came from the eternal shortfall between the degree of satisfaction which the life instincts demanded and the degree of satisfaction which man attained. Man was permanently short-changed, and civilization – a paltry attempt to make up the difference – was the result.

This dim or at least ambivalent attitude to what could have been thought of as man's highest achievement anticipated the line Freud was to take ten years later in *Civilization and its Discontents*. After a decade in which his idea of the death drive had been variously criticized, deplored, and rejected 'even in analytic circles', Freud found it 'more serviceable from a theoretical standpoint' than ever. Coming to consider order itself – something incontestably useful and beautiful, civilization's whole redemption and rationale – Freud again saw it as less than the glorious sum-total of all human endeavour and more as 'a kind of compulsion to repeat'. Civilization was humanity's neurosis – one which the plant and animal kingdoms had, in nature's wisdom, been spared. Civilization was a sickness – an illusion, a pretentious lie – distracting humanity from the true aim of life which was death. As one of a number of 'powerful deflections' designed to distract man from this reality, art, like science, could offer a consolation no more substantial than, in the final analysis, could Freud – for there was no consolation to be had. 'Thus I have not the courage to rise up before my fellow-men as a prophet', Freud concluded, 'and I bow to their reproach that I can offer them no consolation: for at bottom that is what they are all demanding – the wildest revolutionaries no less passionately than the most virtuous believers'.

Standing dwarfed before the immensity of the death drive, theoretical man faced the annihilation of everything he stood for. His cherished order was but a freak of nature, an abnormality which perversely pulled against nature's overpowering and ultimately inconquerable tendency towards death. Daunted, theoretical man peered up at the blankness and galactic silence which defied all thought – indeed, which was unthinkable, not unlike the 'unthinkable anxiety' to which the baby who suffered the zero degree of deprivation was exposed. Freud's argument impelled him to this frontier, to the end of the scale, right to the very brink. But he didn't proceed. He couldn't and didn't go further. He stopped short at the limits of the possible with a mixture of relief, dissatisfaction, and dread. He didn't lay down his pen or revert to stony silence. Instead, he played. For, although he could offer no consolation at the end of *Civilization and its Discontents* – nothing to redeem or compensate for the grim message which he'd brought back from the other side – what he did offer was a telling and curiously theatrical gesture. Like an actor at the end of a tragedy, he bowed . . . still hoping, perhaps – after everything and against all the odds – to defy death to the last.

What we get in *Beyond the Pleasure Principle* – as in *Civilization and its Discontents, Jokes and Their Relation to the Unconscious*, and indeed in everything Freud wrote – is not a lapse into silence but play, the sceptic's back and forth or to-and-fro. Freud didn't opt for silence, madness, and death – for what Nietzsche called the 'ghastly absurdity of existence' – any more than David Hume, the playful, careless, dile-tanttish philosopher who also chose to alternate between reason and despair. In this playful oscillation, the sceptic perhaps lives up most truly to the etymological meaning of play. For the word which derives from the Old English *plegan* originally meant to move with lively, irregular, and capricious motion, to spring, to fly, to dart to and fro, to gambol, frisk, flutter, flit, sparkle – as in the play of light upon water. From the glinting to-and-fro between 'the instinct of life and the instinct of destruction' came human civilization, Freud proposed in *Civilization and its Discontents*. And out of the same oscillation – as a representative of that civilization, as a part of that greater whole – came *Beyond the Pleasure Principle*. The life instincts – creative, progressive, compre-hensible – lay alongside the instincts of death – mysterious, masochistic, counter-intuitive – producing an opposition or tension between the two which, for Freud, spelt the human condition. 'It is as though the life of the organism moved with a vacillating rhythm', he wrote. 'One group of instincts rushes forward so as to reach the final aim of life as swiftly as possible; but when a particular stage in the advance has been reached, the other group jerks back to a certain point to make a fresh start and so prolong the journey'.

It's in the way that Freud's own argument repeats this vacillating movement itself – running helter skelter towards the silence beyond the pleasure principle, 'gone!', and jerking back again at the last minute into the comfortable satisfactions of theoretical thought, 'there!' – that Derrida sees the true play of *Beyond the Pleasure Principle*. What repeats itself not only in the account of little Ernst's game but in the text as a whole, he suggests in *The Post Card*, 'is the speculator's in-defatigable motion in order to reject, to set aside, to make disappear, to distance (*fort*), to defer everything that appears to put the PP into question'. Freud was determined to go 'beyond', to move on and to press ahead. But his attempts to advance step by step were inevitably thwarted by his own instinct for perfection – an instinct which he couldn't shake off even if its grandiosity was mocked in the process and if the final product was less than perfect. Every gesture of progress redoubled and devolved upon itself – a false start followed by false starts. Moving back and forth, dithering this way and that, going round in circles, theoretical man could get nowhere. His text 'mimes walking, does not cease walking without advancing, regularly sketching out one step more without gaining an inch of ground'.

Out of the meandering, circuitous path of a theory which seeks an end – but only in its own fashion – comes a strange text in which the theorist can't quite believe and yet whose implausibility is, for all that, not totally unconvincing. 'It may be asked whether and how far I am myself convinced of the truth of the hypotheses that have been set out in these pages', wrote Freud. 'My answer would be that I am not convinced myself and that I do not seek to persuade other people to believe in them'. Conviction, he added – a note of defensiveness creeping in – needn't come into it. Theoretical man should be free to follow through a line of thought, however implausible, to play devil's advocate if necessary. Besides, it was impossible to pursue an idea of this kind without 'repeatedly combining factual material with what is purely speculative'. At bottom, it was all a game. It couldn't be anything else. Theoretical man came up with theories that didn't persuade him and which he didn't expect would persuade anyone else. But, in the play of the theorist's mind, that didn't matter. The theorist and the child collapse into one another since both are, as Derrida puts it, 'playing so seriously'. At the end, Freud is left extending to this strange creature of his brain a 'cool benevolence' – the mixed feelings of a man who finds he's fathered a prodigy. Perhaps this text – like any product of theoretical man – was a 'benevolent illusion' after all. But then wasn't that true of all art?

As Freud takes his bow at the end of *Civilization and its Discontents* – a gesture of humility that also seeks applause – doesn't he, like some latter-day Prospero, leave us with a body of writing which offers us the same strange pleasures as play? Play has to be creative – for without that there'd be no writing, no speculating, no game. But play is also illusory – a fiction, a pretence which only fills in the brief interval before life's longed-for return to silence. In the pull towards tension and release we find again that 'peculiar pleasure' which, so many years earlier, had piqued Freud's curiosity and prompted him to investigate jokes. For jokes – the 'developed play' of adults – also pulled in opposing directions – towards the tension of meaning, of purpose, of the *Pointe*, and of getting the joke, on the one hand, and towards release into nonsense, child's play, babble, and meaninglessness, on the other. This pleasure – defined by its oddness, its resistance to theoretical classification – differed from the much more straightforward pleasure for which the sexual act offered the most obvious model: a build-up of tension which was then relieved by discharge, satisfaction temporarily extinguishing desire. Laughter looked a bit like that discharge. But the

pleasure which jokes had to offer was more complicated, more com-
promising than that. It didn't seek extinction or even satisfaction. If
anything, jokes seemed to prolong and perpetuate the interplay between
tension and release – moving back and forth between the two, delaying
if not infinitely postponing the satisfactions of satiety – of silence, death,
or *petit mort*. The pleasure of this adult play was more like the
pleasurable unpleasurable tension in which, in the *Three Essays*, the
polymorphously perverse infant indulged, curiously seeking not to
resolve that tension – the supposed satisfactions of goal-orientated adult
genitality still being a long way off – but rather to perpetuate it and, in
Leo Bersani's image, to shatter itself into sexuality over and over again.

On the last page of *Beyond the Pleasure Principle* – still indefatigable
after all those false starts – Freud throws out what could be 'the starting-
point for fresh investigations', namely the sensation he feels in himself
(the result, no doubt, of his running for so long on the spot) of a 'peculiar
tension' – peculiar because it 'can be either pleasurable or unpleasurable'. Theoretical man pulls himself together one last time – there!
– for here, at the end of his book, he'd reached that certain point where,
as he'd earlier remarked, the life instincts jerk back 'to make a fresh
start and so prolong the journey'. But it's a journey not of progress but
of play – not of the adult but of the child – not of a tension which
satiates itself in discharge but of a tension which strangely wishes to
prolong itself 'to no good end'. A 'peculiar pleasure' that's both pleasant
and unpleasant at the same time – both tense and relaxed, both meaningful and meaningless, both reasonable and mad, both creative and
illusory. That's what play has to offer. A peculiar pleasure indeed. And
one which, for Roland Barthes, is best exemplified not by jokes, games,
philosophy, or theoretical speculations but by what all those things
perhaps come down to in the end – tragedy:

> Of all readings, that of tragedy is the most perverse: I take pleasure
> in hearing myself tell a story *whose end I know*: I know and I don't
> know, I act toward myself as though I did not know: I know perfectly
> well Oedipus will be unmasked, that Danton will be guillotined,
> *but all the same* . . . Compared to a dramatic story, which is one
> whose outcome is unknown, there is here an effacement of pleasure
> and a progression of bliss.

In Yeats' poem, 'Lapis Lazuli' – a prolonged meditation on the repeatability of art – the exquisite craftedness of the artifact carved in the blue stone is, like the poem itself, set apart from disorder – from cataclysm, cycle, and change, from the decline of whole civilizations 'put to the sword'. Art doesn't intervene in life, or busy itself to avert war, or contrive to make the world a better place – misguided views that are attributed to a few 'hysterical women'. Rather, the peculiar pleasure of art lies in repetition – in the repeated entry into the mind-made field – just as the poet's own contemplated, imagined scene of the Chinamen carved in lapis lazuli is itself presented as timeless, as removed from the urgency of real life. Art immures itself, impervious to the passing of time or to the collapse of empires, and destined in its self-repetition to remain for ever art:

> All perform their tragic play,
> There struts Hamlet, there is Lear,
> That's Ophelia, that Cordelia;
> Yet they, should the last scene be there,
> The great stage curtain about to drop,
> If worthy their prominent part in the play,
> Do not break up their lines to weep.
> They know that Hamlet and Lear are gay;
> Gaiety transfiguring all that dread.
> All men have aimed at, found and lost;
> Black out; Heaven blazing into the head:
> Tragedy wrought to its uttermost.
> Though Hamlet rambles and Lear rages,
> And all the drop-scenes drop at once
> Upon a hundred thousand stages,
> It cannot grow by an inch or an ounce.

Tragedy doesn't break its lines and weep because to do so wouldn't be tragedy. It would be the obliterating response to the pathos and catastrophe of the real, discrete, time-bound event – to the unthinkable anxiety of a universe that's indifferent and impervious to human pain. Tragic play, on the other hand – whether it's Shakespeare's play or the 'mournful melodies' played by the Chinamen – is 'gay'. It's consoling not in its confrontation with the world, in its resolving of tension, or in its answering of questions – for, like Freud in *Beyond the Pleasure Principle*, tragedy cannot advance by an inch. It's consoling rather by its knowing escape into an eternal repetition of itself.

The rest of this chapter goes on to consider four plays by Shake-speare – *Julius Caesar, Hamlet, Antony and Cleopatra*, and *The Winter's Tale* – four texts chosen because they each draw particular attention to the mechanics of repetition while remaining profoundly aware of their own status as repeatable play. These plays stage the deaths of a king, a father, a queen, and a wife – each one an insufferable, cataclysmic, and shattering event, causing 'Black out; Heaven blazing into the head'. What happens when these events are turned into play? What happens to the characters and what happens to the audience? Is either consoled, and, if so, with what kind of consolation? Is it pleasurable as such? What kind of pleasure does tragedy evoke? These four plays each explore the relation between the consolation which the audience derives from watching the represented scene and the represented consolation of the characters who find themselves faced with the finality of death and yet who are also compelled to re-play or to speculate on re-playing it. As horrific and otherwise irreversible happenings are staged and re-staged both within these plays and in recurrent performances of them, Shakespeare and his characters not only create but also meditate deeply upon the alchemy by which drama makes order from disorder and tragedy, gaiety from dread.

II

Julius Caesar centres round a tragedy. At the heart of the play the con-spirators stab Caesar to death and then perform an extraordinary and in some ways quite unnecessary action. Stooping over the dead body, they wash their hands and swords in his blood, meaning, subsequently, to display them to the terrified populace in the market-place (an event which in the end never happens, at least not on stage). This action is unnecessary in the strict sense that it doesn't render Caesar any more dead. It's not a question of delivering the *coup de grâce* but an afterthought, an addendum to what has already definitively occurred – Caesar's murder. Moreover, in Plutarch's *Life of Caesar*, Shakespeare's otherwise closely followed source, this action is unnecessary because the conspirators are by this stage already blood-soaked. In the unseemly scramble of the killing, as the historian describes it, they not only get spattered by Caesar's blood but also by their own, having accidentally wounded each other in the fray. Shakespeare's conspirators, by contrast, are coolly controlled in what they do – they cover themselves in blood on purpose – and it's clear that, in their deliberation, they're doing the same thing that the playwright is doing. Both are engaged in transforming a wild and messy scene into a tragedy, in turning it into a work of art.

Pointless in the strictly practical sense, what is clearly signalled as the conspirators' ritualized action fulfils (or is intended to fulfil) a function of a most serious kind. For the sword-smearing serves to transfigure the dread action of the murder – to make it 'gay'. From amid the confusion of the assassination itself emerges a stage-managed moment of pure theatre, one which dignifies and privileges the scene, and which is designed to perform that all-important reclassification upon which the political justification for the conspirators' action depends. Ceremonialized in this way, murder becomes not a murder but a work of art, to be duly attended by 'all true rites and lawful ceremonies'. The ritual act transforms what would otherwise have been mere butchery into a sacrifice, moralizing the raw material of the happening, converting history into story, and story into a re-tellable event. Ritual transmutes the 'savage spectacle' into something quite different – into a 'piece of work', or, more specifically, into a 'piteous spectacle', that is to say, a tragedy. And, since the conspirators are here manifestly engaged in the same project as Shakespeare himself, it's only appropriate that they should, at this moment, explicitly think of their action as play:

Brutus: . . . Stoop, Romans, stoop,
And let us bathe our hands in Caesar's blood
Up to the elbows, and besmear our swords;
Then walk we forth, even to the market-place,
And waving our red weapons o'er our heads,
Let's all cry, 'Peace, freedom, and liberty!'

Cassius: Stoop then, and wash. How many ages hence
Shall this our lofty scene be acted over
In states unborn and accents yet unknown!

Brutus: How many times shall Caesar bleed in sport,
That now on Pompey's basis lies along
No worthier than the dust!

It's a remarkable moment. In these few lines, Shakespeare collapses the distinction between the 'many times' and 'now', between the actors performing his tragedy of *Julius Caesar* and these self-styled actors who describe their murder of Caesar as itself a performance, a tragedy. The self-consciousness of the conspirators' words, moreover, invites the following question – are we witnessing the original, inaugurating scene or one of its subsequent repetitions, repetitions which are held like seeds in the pod of the initial moment, anniversaries which retrospectively justify that first moment as an inaugural one? The answer, naturally, is the latter, for the 'now' which we are watching is at the same time one of the 'many times' the same scene has been, is being, and will continue to be acted over. At the same time, Shakespeare accentuates the immediacy and proximity of the scene by emptying the stage of all but the conspirators and their victim at this point, so that our view is uncluttered, unmediated by the represented points of view of other characters. We're made sole witness to the conspirators' ritual act. As the theatre-audience of the present, confronted with this spectacular scene, we're invited to see it both as the original moment and as a repetition of the same.

What arises is a blending of past and present whereby 'then' anticipates the repetition which is 'now', and what we see 'now' is what happened 'then' – creating a curious overlap between the two equally theatrical moments. We trust that the actor playing Caesar will revive to please tomorrow's audience. But there's a sense in which the conspirators half believe this too. For, in killing Caesar, and immediately speculating on the repeatability of their action, the assassins seem to inaugurate an unending *fort! da!* game themselves, the very evidence of which is being played out before our eyes. It's as if they haven't really killed Caesar at all but have only pretended to do so – which, at one level, of course, is exactly the case. Their act of transfiguration coincides exactly with Shakespeare's in that he too is making gaiety of dread, pity of savagery, sacrifice of butchery. The conspirators' tragedy serves to turn the event of the murder into a non-event, repeatable because removed from time, and provably repeatable, furthermore, because the tragedy which they act out and which they postulate as being eternally repeated in 'accents yet unknown' is being done so here and now in Shakespeare's repeatedly performed play.

By turning death into play, the conspirators seek not only to justify what they have done but also to derive some consolation from the supposition that theirs is no ordinary murder but a work of art. They would be artists not killers. The 'gaiety' of their ritual attempts to release it from the brute causality and consequentiality to which any event in the real world is subject. It's not a death which they perform, but – for the very reason that they perform it – a non-death, a spectacle arousing pity and terror, a tragedy. Moreover, Shakespeare's artful enfolding of their work of art within his own colludes in the same consolation. The conspirators' tragedy blends so perfectly with Shakespeare's at this point as to suggest that their Caesar ('then') will revive as surely as our Caesar will ('now'), transforming their heart-stopping and epoch-making action into the repeatable gaiety of the second world of art.

In paralleling so closely the conspirators' killing of Caesar with the actors' feigned murder of a fellow actor, however, Shakespeare implicates his characters in what amounts to an act of denial. For, what threatens to disappear beneath the simulacra of the original moment and its subsequent repetitions in play is the actuality of the murder – any sense we might have of the first and only time that it happened. If the conspirators are behaving just like actors, then how far are we expected to believe in their conviction that what they are doing is for real? If, in their assassination of Caesar, the conspirators do as actors do – that is to say, play – then how can it be said that Caesar really died? He clearly doesn't die in any of the 'many' repetitions of the scene, because the actor is always expected to revive. So when is assassination assassination and when is it play? Caesar, it appears, can be murdered over and over again, 'in sport'. Indeed, his killers say so and evidence of this miracle is to be found in the fact that we are watching it happen. But the conspirators' sense that they can repeat their action and kill Caesar again is, of course, an illusion, albeit an illusion in which we participate. What disappears within the encircling tautology of play – the repetition of a repeatable act – is the blunt and unrepeatable reality that Caesar really did die, once and for all, never to return, and never reviving to please the audience of tomorrow.

Shakespeare's meditation on the repeatability of play in *Julius Caesar* not only consoles insofar as all tragedy does but also speculates on the nature of that consolation. For, by a series of ironies and reversals, he prepares the audience alternately to imbibe and to question the pleasure which tragedy produces. The conspirators' highly theatrical and incantatory act of ritual, for example, comes somewhat oddly from men who, in the first half of the play, are remarkable for their resolute anti-theatricality – a political stance by which they differentiate themselves from the gamesome, play-going Antony, and from the theatrically adept Caesar, who exploits spectacle so well and who makes the Romans write his speeches in their books. Against the blatant manipulation of appearances, the conspirators self-consciously adopt a what-you-see-is-what-you-get ethic, their supporters' first action in the play being, significantly enough, to 'Disrobe the images, / If you do find them deck'd with ceremonies'. Moreover, given their high degree of staginess later in the play, it's all the more ironic that, in the opening line of *Julius Caesar*, members of the conspirators' party are so suspicious of theatricality that they deny the very theatre in which they stand. To begin a play with the words: 'Hence! home, you idle creatures, get you home!' is tantamount to dismissing the audience before the play has even begun.

The conspirators begin by setting themselves against show, and by paying allegiance to what lies behind it – to the raw reality which can only deceivingly be clothed by word or image. Theirs is a doctrinaire suspicion of images, an affiliation with the 'low' as opposed to the 'high'. In the first half of the play, their world is shown to be secluded – a small, intimate cabal which contrasts strikingly with Caesar's highly public presence. Indeed, they refuse, at this point, even to countenance their own actorliness. Cassius disdains to be a 'common laughter', a mere object of audience appreciation, while Casca deplores Caesar's crowd-pleasing antics, as if the 'tag-rag people' whom he reports as cheering Caesar were a thousand miles from the audience to which he delivers these lines.

The conspirators' principled rejection of show undergoes an ironic u-turn when they later find themselves impresarios of the play's most impressive piece of theatre – a reversal which gives rise, in the circumstances, to an irony greater still. For, like the playing child, the conspirators ritualize the killing in order to master the event. In attempting to signify that the death is play rather than murder, they seek to mitigate the finality of what they have done and to master fate by proposing a repeatable narrative, one already completed and known in advance. But, in seeking to master reality by such means, they not only adopt the once-despised theatricality of their victim. They also perform exactly what they wanted to destroy – mastery. The tyrant-killers turn tyrants, in other words, their attempt to master the murder – by means of consummately calculated actions – being the artistic equivalent of what they fear to be Caesar's growing political mastery over themselves.

The conspirators' bid for mastery ironically devolves upon itself, for they do what they would destroy and destroy what they do – an unending and unendable cycle to which their own sense of innumerable future repetitions looks ahead. Furthermore, the conspirators fail to master reality not only for the simple reason that death is death and reality is not masterable, but also because, as Shakespeare suggests, they are bound to do so. In their earlier, play-hating phase, the conspirators had reacted to the drama of the crowning episode – with all its visual spectacle and symbolic gesture – as 'mere foolery', scornfully reducing it to something of no consequence, mere child's play, no more than a deplorable playing-to-the-gallery on Caesar's part. And yet, by the time they themselves come to dramatize an event – the assassination – so as to denude it of consequence, they not only engage in the same showmanship as their enemy. Their action is itself a consequence of that showmanship. The theatricality which they had formerly dismissed as mere play – safely relegated to the harmless, escapist second world of art – turns out to be massively consequential. Their own action proves it because their fear that Caesar 'would be crown'd' results directly in their assassination of him. Any attempt which they subsequently make to transform the latter into consequence-free, repeatable play is bound to fail, and to sabotage any further foray – including the one we're watching – into the second world of art. The assassination, in other words, is no more mere 'sport' than the coronation is mere 'foolery'. It would be foolery to think otherwise.

As actions turn out not to be repeatable but all too real and consequence-ridden, so the preserve of art gives way to historical necessity. Gaiety returns to dread, play to cataclysm. To emphasize this point, Shakespeare doesn't leave the conspirators in the final act of their own carefully constructed plot. He doesn't end with their moment of high drama. Instead, the play goes on. Shakespeare incorporates the conspirators' tragedy within his own, the growing fragmentariness and bittiness of which – with its broken scenes, crossed messages, misunderstandings, incompetencies, and bunglings – increasingly contrasts with the brilliant precision of the conspirators' own work of art and deposits them in the chaos and unpredictability of a world which their own artistic efforts can only fail to control. Whereas at the mid-point of the play the conspirators' heavily ritualized tragedy had coincided with Shakespeare's play, in the second half the two plots diverge, Brutus' stage-managed play becoming ever more remote from the messy and seemingly unplotted world which Shakespeare has provided for him. For all its desired repeatability, the conspirators' play is shown to have consequences just as surely as Caesar's crown-play did – consequences which bear an uncanny resemblance to each other: plotting and death. And the consolation for which they looked – in the closed-off, repeatable action of play – is revealed to be illusory indeed.

Repetition's deceptive mastery over reality seems, in the last, disillusioned scenes of *Julius Caesar* to have been thoroughly deconstructed. The conspirators' attempt to make a tragedy – to transform the killing into a work of art – fails miserably when they find themselves having to face the consequences of their action. High drama gives way to petty squabbles, tragedy threatens to descend into farce. Yet one further twist, one crowning irony remains in this play's rocking, alternating, to-and-fro speculation on repetition. For, ultimately, even Shakespeare's plot – naturalistically chaotic and unplanned as it seems – is itself, of course, repeatable play. Shakespeare's own representation of designed chance, of scripted unpredictability, and of foreseen unknowability returns us to the very thing which it has taught us is an illusion – to the idea, that is, that play repeats, that repetition masters, and that mastery consoles.

Having denied the conspirators the solace of their own play by plunging them immediately afterwards into the contingencies consequent upon it, Shakespeare nonetheless doesn't and can't go beyond play himself. He doesn't kill Caesar, after all. Play is all there is – but play which never goes beyond itself, which never passes through the pleasuring but also falsifying illusion to which it always returns us. Play's mastery is an illusion, but there's no way out of it – at least, not in play. For to say that play perpetuates illusion is to repeat the tautology that play is play. Play can't release us from repetition because it enslaves us to it. And this, perhaps, is why poets have such a difficult time in *Julius Caesar* – either lynched for their 'bad verses' like Cinna, or dismissed for their 'jigging' rhymes like the well-meaning but incompetent poet who's brusquely sent packing by Cassius. For, in the end which is no end neither they nor their inventor can finally deliver us from play's pleasing but pernicious double bind.

III

Hamlet mourns the passing of a world which used to know how to play – a stately, ponderous world where, as glimpsed briefly in Horatio's account of the combat between the old king and Fortinbras senior, even matters of conquest and death were as formalized as in a game. The complicated legal article – a 'seal'd compact / Well ratified by law and heraldry' by which each king agreed to forfeit land should he lose the fight, and their mutually recognized token of the 'gage' – succinctly evokes the whole complex code of chivalric etiquette. For Huizinga, the single combat of archaic culture exemplified the nature of human play almost better than anything else, encapsulating that whole 'inextricable complex of ideas covering anything from the game of chance to the lawsuit'. Nostalgically recalled at the beginning of *Hamlet*, this was a world in which even adversaries played by the same rules, their conflict almost choreographed in its slow deliberation. The brutalities of killing and conquest were subsumed beneath a code of valour and courtesy which regulated – even beautified – actions, transforming them into works of art. There was no question of either party unilaterally changing or subverting the rules for personal gain because the intrinsic rightness of the system was so utterly taken for granted that it went without saying – a rule-bound, predictable, and emotionally secure world, according to whose mutually monitored ethic everyone – including enemies – knew where they stood.

It's to the same stately, ceremonial world that Shakespeare's play reverts at its close, the dignified ritual of the soldier's funeral – that formal 'rite of war' which, as a last act, Horatio and the young Fortinbras arrange for Hamlet – harking back to those earlier days of chivalric solemnity, striving to convert the surrounding mess and gore into spectacle, and to transfigure the dreadful chaos of the preceding, wild scene. Music and procession dignify death, serving to make what is otherwise 'amiss' decorous, and to return us to the world that existed prior to the play's beginning. Placed 'high on a stage' to be the better seen – never before so pointedly the observed of all observers – Hamlet here achieves his most authentically theatrical moment, as our act of seeing combines with an act of mourning – for the loss of the prince, but also for a pure theatricality which is itself so imminently about to cease with the play's close.

By placing such moments of high drama and visual spectacle at the terminal points, the very edges of *Hamlet*, Shakespeare situates his play in an ambiguous middle-ground – an uncanny place where the nature of theatricality and playing is famously put in doubt. Sorrowful heir to a world that once knew how to stage its happenings and dramatize its actions, the Elsinore into which the first scene ushers us is, by contrast, lost and disorientated – 'out of frame' and 'out of joint'. The gamesmanship of former times has been irrevocably disrupted by 'foul play' – by young Fortinbras' unceremonious disregard for the honoured terms of his father's forfeit, and by Claudius' hasty dispensing with the equally honoured rules of consanguinity. It is appropriate, therefore, that what is projected as a prior, stable world – one which understood the relation between human actions and their formalization – should give way to an antic world whose emotional confusion is represented in terms of a confusion above all of ceremony. For this is a place where funerals are accompanied with mirth – *mirth*? – and weddings with dirge – *dirge*? – a place emblematized by Claudius' image of the laughing / crying face, whose 'auspicious' and 'dropping' eyes squint grotesquely in opposite directions. In so distracted and distorted a world where joy and sorrow look like one another, ceremony's dignifying of human emotion is horribly lost, and the dead are buried hastily, 'hugger-mugger', and with 'maimèd rites'.

The result is a nightmarish lawlessness. What has been forfeited by the greedy actions of Claudius and the young Fortinbras is rule – the fundamental understanding that the world is ordered and that it is only according to such an order that life and death, heredity and enmity can make sense. In that old, ordered world – irretrievably lost by the time the play begins – life and its attendant rituals had been perfectly understood as relating to one another. This event was accompanied by that form, this reality by that appearance. When everyone knew their parts and understood the same thing by 'seems' and by the 'actions that a man might play', then life's events were interpretable and their consequences relatively predictable. Everything – life, love, war, death – could operate with the precision of clockwork, the formal beauty of a courtly dance. But, when the rules of the game are broken and when appearance and reality are disjoined, we enter into the crazed and punning world of *Hamlet* where signifier is divorced from signified, where the rules of social and ethical grammar have been so thoroughly subverted that it's no longer possible to be understood, and where the contractual exchange which once made language meaningful gives place to a world in which dialogue is, from the opening scene, habitually thwarted by people giving the wrong answers or speaking out of turn.

The horror which confronts Hamlet is not only that of his father's death and mother's over-hasty re-marriage but the fact that both these occurrences arise from a refusal – principally by Claudius – to play by the rules. The reason that Claudius' iconoclasm is so revolutionary is that it exposes the former world to have been nothing more than culture's fragile architecture of consensus. The stability of the old world – which had depended on a collective agreement to play fair – gives way, in one scandalous and opportunistic stroke, to an ontological cataclysm which entails a loss of faith in all structure, all rule, all obedience. Claudius' rule-breaking bursts the illusion that life is inherently rule-bound, revealing that the latter's 'natural' systems and hierarchies were so arbitrary as to be easily, if shatteringly, dispensed with. When experience ceases to be paced and timed according to a collectively inspired script, then the consoling fiction that the world is ordered like a work of art is revealed for what it is – a deceiving figment, an idol of the theatre.

It's in order to simulate the artlessness of a world which has abandoned its aesthetic moorings and lost the will to play that Shakespeare presents what T. S. Eliot notoriously described as an 'artistic failure' – a rambling play full of confusions, impertinencies, and postponements which complicate the otherwise simple causality of its source-stories. In such a context, Hamlet's own attempts to play are, as one might expect, doomed from the start. Like his prototype, Brutus, Hamlet too would play. He too would construct a 'piece of work' designed to tragedize a death, his 'Mousetrap' being as creative a work of art as Brutus' would-be ritual and, like it, promisingly repeatable. Hamlet poisons 'in jest' rather as Brutus stabs Caesar 'in sport'. His inset play transfigures the dread of the actual murder into the gaiety of the enacted scene where death is only feigned and where the revival of the player king to please tomorrow's audience wishfully denies the finality of the murder of Hamlet's father.

Since a radical disturbance in the relation of reality to play, however, is what has caused Hamlet's problem in the first place, then his attempt to master that reality through play is comically, catastrophically self-defeating, and takes its place among the series of self-cancelling acts which make up the plot of Shakespeare's play as a whole. To begin with, to attempt to master reality – especially death – through play is to submit to an illusion the desperate sustaining of which is not so very far from pathology. Even if Hamlet's sole purpose in staging his father's death were to theatricalize it – to accord it the dignity of being seen which the stealthiness of the murder denied both him and ourselves – he still cannot undo what has been done. An infinity of repetitions wouldn't restore old Hamlet, any more than the child's consoling game could ultimately relieve the anxiety of his situation. He remains, like Hamlet, inconsolable.

In the second place, what makes Hamlet's play doubly self-defeating is that he knows this. The events which inaugurate the action of Shakespeare's play have already taught him that what once passed as a natural order was but a game, a social and political construction which depended on all the participants playing by the rules. It's because he finds himself beyond the confines of a world which was once sustained by a collective belief in its own practices that the latter now appears to Hamlet as man-made – as an illusion – which is why he is so thoroughly disillusioned by the time the play starts. His soliloquies speculate on the frightening power of the mind to believe in illusions, and, worse still, to belive in illusions of its own making. When these illusions are revealed to be the fabrications that they are, how can a culture set about constructing a new reality? What is to prevent that from being as illusory as what went before?

It's with bad faith, therefore, that Hamlet tells the players that drama mirrors a given reality, for he knows full well – indeed, he's shown as having experienced – that reality is only a distorted picture, a dubious projection of the mind. Man is just as much a 'piece of work' as a stage-play is. Since the capacity of the mind to embrace its falsifying images as true is Hamlet's whole problem, then his attempt to master a reality which he's already experienced as illusory by using what is itself illusory – a play – only compounds the problem, and leaves him floundering in a world in which less and less can be believed or taken on trust.

Evidence of Hamlet's bad faith is to be found in the queasy logic of his soliloquy in Act II, scene ii. Moved by the player's tears over the story of Hecuba, Hamlet develops the idea that he might verify what he fears could be a story of his own morbid imagining by means of another story, 'The Murder of Gonzago':

O, what a rogue and peasant slave am I!
Is it not monstrous that this player here,
But in a fiction, in a dream of passion,
Could force his soul so to his own conceit
That from her working all the visage wann'd,
Tears in his eyes, distraction in his aspect,
A broken voice, an'his whole function suiting
With forms to his conceit? And all for nothing,
For Hecuba!
What's Hecuba to him, or he to Hecuba,
That he should weep for her? What would he do
Had he the motive and the cue for passion
That I have? He would drown the stage with tears.

If the player can be so visibly moved by what is scarcely of personal concern to him, then how much more should Hamlet – and, as the soliloquy continues, should Claudius – be moved by what concerns them both most intimately: real murder and guilt-ridden incest? As a direct result of witnessing the player's emotional engagement with the Hecuba story, Hamlet resolves to put Claudius to the test, and to use his uncle's emotional response to the play as a way of settling the matter of his guilt once and for all: 'the play's the thing / Wherein I'll catch the conscience of the king'.

Yet there's a flaw in Hamlet's argument which stymies the whole enterprise from the start. For, the player's tears are conjured up, of course, by a fiction – by a story that's of no immediate relevance to himself or to his companions. What is Hecuba to him, after all? His tears don't corroborate anything. They certainly don't prove that the story is true, still less that he killed Priam. All they prove is the admittedly large matter that fiction is capable of rousing powerful feelings, just as our own emotional response to *Hamlet* itself – which is as remote from our own lives as Hecuba is to the player's – obviously says nothing about the strict truth-content of what we're watching. The player's factitious tears are the result of his temporary suspension of disbelief – his willing entry into the field of make-believe and his imaginative empathy with the character of Hecuba. But if real feelings – wet tears – can be conjured by illusion, then Hamlet's scheme to conjure those feelings by means of play clinches nothing, or at least only the tautology that play has the power to conjure feelings. This logical flaw is concealed beneath Hamlet's vague 'I have heard' which – in assuming that Claudius' guilty reaction to the representation of a murder will un-equivocally indict him – fails to take account of the inspiring moment which he's just witnessed: the ability of fiction to move as powerfully as fact.

It doesn't follow, therefore, that if Claudius reacts emotionally to a given scene, that scene can be taken as a correct record of his brother's murder. All Hamlet can forensically read into his uncle's response or lack of it is his degree of sensitivity to plays. Claudius might start, gasp, and weep or he might remain utterly indifferent – two responses, in fact, which Shakespeare allows for, the dumbshow proceeding without interruption, while the spoken play is broken off by the king's hasty exit. But neither response in any way alters the fictional status of the story which has been presented for his viewing. The only firm conclusion which can be drawn from Claudius' reaction is the pointless tautology with which Hamlet does in fact conclude:

> For if the King like not the comedy,
> Why then belike he likes it not, perdy.

The play about Gonzago remains what it always was – as much a fiction as *Hamlet* itself, and equally capable of being rehearsed, adapted, and repeated, or of having lines added or subtracted. Play by definition illudes – play is play. As a formal miming of life, play is only an approximate simulation – never more than 'near' or 'something like' what it represents. And, since responding emotionally to a mimetic representation is what we are being invited to do, along with Claudius, then Hamlet gets no nearer to mastering reality – what really happened, and what he is going to do about it – than provide entertainment for his uncle and, by extension, for us. Like the child, Hamlet occupies himself fully with a game which is destined interminably to repeat itself.

Tautology is the stuff of *Hamlet*, a play in which the hero's suicide suicides itself leaving him living, and in which even his will to kill gets killed leaving him innocent. 'Who calls me villain . . . gives me the lie i'th'throat . . . Who does me this?' Hamlet asks rhetorically, before answering, pat: 'Bloody, bawdy villain! / Remorseless, treacherous, lecherous, kindless villain!'. He means Claudius, of course, but, in the ever-encircling play of tautologies, Hamlet's self-answering question also implicates himself, killer and killer's killer merging with much the same ambiguous economy as they do in Lucianus, the player-revenger who collapses the roles of Claudius and his nephew into one. The nightmarish tautology which Hamlet has occupied from the beginning of the play can only come to rest, appropriately enough, with another tautology – when Claudius' treachery betrays itself. Only then – with the failure of his devious plot with the poisoned sword, the ultimate 'foul play' – does playing, in the sense of sword-fighting, come to mean the same thing as killing. Only then does Hamlet die.

Hamlet's 'Murder of Gonzago' is a set-piece which dramatizes a story known in advance, a tragedy whose final act has been scripted ahead of time. Like all tragic endings this is a pseudo-ending because the players are all expected to revive again afterwards. But the illusory nature of Hamlet's play isn't limited to the fact that the player king will never die in the strict sense that the king his father did. Hamlet's illusory play flirts with a grander irony. For, if a tragedy's ending is known, then what's Hamlet doing using a tragedy to find out the ending of the story in which he finds himself? Paradoxically, he employs something which is already known – end-stopped and epilogued – in order to discover something which he doesn't yet know: the Ghost's veracity and what to do about it. Hamlet's play can only find resolution by coming to the end which 'The Murder of Gonzago' – as a representation – could not – namely with a death that's not 'in jest' but, at last, for real.

The last laugh, however, is Shakespeare's. He no more kills Hamlet than Lucianus kills the player king, for even Hamlet's death – longed-for release from the bad dream of repetition as it might seem – is only a jest after all. Hamlet will revive to please tomorrow's audience as surely as night follows day. It's the last, clever, echoing joke of this 'miching mallecho' to leave us where we always were and where we have been for the duration of the play – with our willingness to indulge in illusions intact, even though, if we've entered into the spirit of the game, we've had it thoroughly disillusioned along the way. And, by an inverse relation that's positively fiendish, the more we've enjoyed the play, the more prey we've been to its illusions, and the more effectively caught – jestingly, despairingly, pathologically – in the circular pleasure which is play: caught fairly in a mousetrap, indeed.

IV

Antony and Cleopatra kill themselves rather than take part in Caesar's play – the triumphal procession, or 'imperious show' which he's deter-mined to stage on his victorious return to Rome. With the defeated pair held aloft and paraded before the censuring eye of Rome, this masque-making Caesar clearly envisages the pageant as a piece of theatre, and calculates his effects with the eye of an impresario whose show-piece, Cleopatra, will render the spectacle 'eternal' – rather as Ben Jonson hoped that his court masques would leave a lasting impression on the memory, long after the visual splendour of the particular occasion had 'perish'd like a blaze, and gone out, in the beholders eyes'. It becomes evident as the play progresses that the optimum staging of this brilliant show assumes so great an importance in Caesar's mind that it subordinates his political decisions – how to treat the vanquished Cleopatra – to his theatrical ones – how to ensure showing her alive – so that he emerges more as a fussy stage-director than as the conquering hero and emperor of Rome.

It's in order to escape playing in Caesar's triumphal pantomime that Antony and Cleopatra take their own lives. 'Wouldst thou be window'd in great Rome', Antony asks Eros, 'and see / Thy master thus with pleach'd arms, bending down / His corrigible neck, his face subdu'd / To penetrative shame?' – an unthinkable fate, and one that Eros 'would not see'. Death is preferable. Cleopatra too would sooner die than be so seen, whether paraded to the 'shouting varlotry' or parodied by the Roman players with their comic rendering of her 'Alexandrian revels'. Like the faithful Eros, Iras also balks at her sovereign's predicted fate, refusing to countenance so blasphemous and shaming a visibility: 'I'll never see't! for I am sure mine nails / Are stronger than mine eyes'.

There's strategy as well as shame behind Antony and Cleopatra's action, however. For their deaths don't merely get them out of an embarrassing situation. They also pre-empt Caesar's theatrical plans by staging what amounts to an alternative show. As against Caesar's *tableau vivant,* Cleopatra mounts a rival production of her own – the burial of Antony and the performance of her own self-staged death. Caesar's play will, she fears, be the first in a series, her own humiliating appearance in his triumphal procession inaugurating a wake of burlesque repetitions to be 'extemporally' staged by the comedians of Rome. It's in direct competition with Caesar that Cleopatra presents a tragedy – a 'high event' worthy of pity. But she also goes one step further in forestalling him, for this culminating death of hers is not feigned but, she protests, for real. By killing herself, Cleopatra would in effect cancel her rival's opening night. When she tells her women, therefore, that once relieved of their duty they might 'play till doomsday', they interpret her 'play' accordingly – 'Your crown's awry, / I'll mend it, and then play', Charmian remarks, before taking up the asp herself – for in Cleopatra's tragedy to play and to die have come to mean the same.

Both Cleopatra and Caesar know that play masters, and both bid to be the master of ceremonies, to produce a drama to their own best advantage. In this battle for mastery, not only are the players playing the same game. The very pieces of this game are plays – Caesar's comedy of triumph versus Cleopatra's tragedy of defeat. Cleopatra bids for finality, pitting her own version of a unique tragic action – her death – against what she fears will be Caesar's parodic repetition of it. And, at one level, it's a contest which Cleopatra wins. For, in doing the one thing which Caesar wanted to prevent, she thwarts her enemy's theatrical ambitions and denies him his dazzling show-piece, keeping it for herself.

Her play successfully trumps his, and Caesar – who normally wins at play – finds himself dramatically outmanoeuvred at the end, up-staged by the queen's superior cunning. His play never happens, at least not in the form that he wanted, so that Cleopatra's mastery over him is complete.

If Shakespeare takes sides in this play of plays, he must be seen to throw his weight behind Cleopatra. It's 'The Tragedy of Antony and Cleopatra' which he presents, after all, a play sufficiently identified with the latter's as to end with her ending and to hand the stage over during its closing minutes to her own superb direction. Cleopatra theatricalizes her own death rather as Brutus had theatricalized Julius Caesar's – so as to master its outcome in advance. But, whereas Brutus' moment of drama came in the middle of *Julius Caesar*, leaving him to face the uncontrollable consequences of his action in the second half, there's no equivalent follow-up in *Antony and Cleopatra*. In aligning the death of Cleopatra with the conclusion of his own play, Shakespeare provides no succeeding scenes in which to undermine the mastery of her *coup de théâtre* but gives us an ending to end all endings. In so doing, he pays homage to Cleopatra's showmanship and leaves us with an image of Caesar as thoroughly discomfited as the queen herself could have wished.

Shakespeare emphasizes the impact of Cleopatra's final scene by saving up for the last moment a stunning visual spectacle for which he's prepared us up to now with only verbal descriptions. Seeing Cleopatra arrayed 'like a queen' for the first time, we witness something akin to the coronation scene which Agrippa had earlier described to a scandalized Caesar, our own bedazzled eyes seeing now what the 'public eye' had seen then. More specifically, Shakespeare allows us at this moment to share in the most privileged and consequential of visions. For in death Cleopatra is 'again for Cydnus', once more the visual icon and object of the universal 'gaze' that she was on the day when first beheld by Antony. Shakespeare has prepared us for this moment by means of Enobarbus' famous speech: 'The barge she sat in, like a burnish'd throne, / Burnt on the water . . .'. Enobarbus' apparently unconscious drift from the past into the present tense here – 'A seeming mermaid steers . . . A strange invisible perfume hits the sense' – anticipates the overall movement of Shakespeare's play as it visualizes and makes present in its final minutes the moment of vision which the soldier here recalls. For, by beholding the dying Cleopatra in all her regal splendour, we come closer to seeing for ourselves what Antony once saw, and we replicate in our own act of looking the captivated gaze without which the tragedy of Antony and Cleopatra would never have begun, and to which Shakespeare alludes in the opening lines of the play:

> *Philo*: Nay, but this dotage of our general's
> O'erflows the measure. Those his goodly eyes,
> That o'er the files and musters of the war
> Have glow'd like plated Mars, now bend, now turn
> The office and devotion of their view
> Upon a tawny front.

Antony's truant vision is here made an object of our gaze, as we too are enjoined to behold and see. In a play that's so conscious of the multiple acts of looking which constitute it as a piece of theatre, it is appropriate that Shakespeare should begin by making us look at two characters taking a critical look at Antony's own enamoured looking. By the final scene, however, these ironic, distancing frames have all collapsed in on one another so that we see with our own eyes a version of what has captivated Antony – an image such as Leon Battista Alberti might have approved. Cleopatra's 'infinite variety' induces a sense of wonder which, like the best of paintings, captured the eyes of its beholders. 'The *istoria* which merits both praise and admiration will be so agreeably and pleasantly attractive', Alberti wrote in his treatise *On Painting* (1435-6), 'that it will capture the eye of whatever learned or unlearned person is looking at it and will move his soul. That which first gives pleasure . . . comes from the copiousness and variety of things'. Antony is just such a captivated beholder. 'Would I had never seen her!', Antony exclaims early in the play, all too aware of the irresistible power of Cleopatra's image. But, as Enobarbus retorts, 'you had then left unseen a wonderful piece of work'. Having kept this spectacle from us until the closing moment of the play, Shakespeare finally presents it for our own wondering sight, inducing in our eyes that same optical truancy with which the play began. He thus demonstrates that Cleopatra's play is self-contained, its end bound up with its beginning like the serpent with its tail in its mouth – a tragedy 'complete in itself', as Aristotle had defined it, and designed to be 'taken in by the eye' almost more literally than the philosopher could have meant by that phrase.

Cleopatra successfully beguiles Caesar, leaving him an 'ass / Unpolicied' and without a pageant to play. By concluding his own play with Cleopatra's grand finale, moreover, Shakespeare seems to participate in the queen's foxing of the Roman leader. She wins the contest outright, it would appear. Or does she? Antony and Cleopatra kill themselves to avoid appearing or being represented on Caesar's humiliating platform – a determination in which they succeed. But they don't avoid being so represented on Shakespeare's stage. His *Antony and Cleopatra* doesn't take the form of a triumphal procession through Rome, it's true. But it does represent its eponymous characters in those very humiliated and prostrate postures which they apparently did everything they could to prevent being staged. Antony takes his life rather than appear in Caesar's train with head bowed, a living emblem of the latter's conquest. Yet Shakespeare has no compunction in showing us an Antony just so cowed and shamed. Indeed, he lays before our eyes the spectacle of Antony's botched suicide – a sight quite as demeaning as the flight from Actium which had so sickened the eyes of Enobarbus. Cleopatra too, if not the centrepiece of Caesar's tableau, appears defeated in Shakespeare's play. She does, after all, lose the war, and presents to Caesar's messengers an image of 'sweet dependency', the vision of a queen who would kneel and kiss his 'conqu'ring hand' and learn from him the 'doctrine of obedience'.

In showing us the shaming scenes of Antony and Cleopatra's military defeat and its disastrous aftermath, Shakespeare makes us see the very thing which they dreaded and sought to avoid – being exposed to public view, being shown vanquished and at a loss. Moreover, Cleopatra had intended by her death to trounce Caesar once and for all – to annul not only his own play but any subsequent repetitions of it. She means her death to be a catastrophic, unrepeatable event which will resist and pre-empt the 'gaiety' that would be consequent upon its reiteration in play. In literalizing her tragedy – in dying for real – Cleopatra aims to call Caesar's bluff. This isn't a tragedy which can be re-played but the real, dreadful thing – 'Black out; Heaven blazing into the head'. It's her idea to make herself unrepresentable, for she intends her removal from the world, like Antony's, to be on the scale of universal cataclysm where 'All's but naught' – unsayable, undiscussable, and thus secure for ever from the dodges, adaptations, and compromises which representation entails. The real token of Cleopatra's victory would be to have no play at all.

Shakespeare goes half way toward meeting Cleopatra's idea by according her the dignity of an ending which has been designed according to her own most careful specification. But he only goes halfway. For every performance of his play gaily transfigures the dread of that final scene, flying in the face of the queen's declared ambition not to be re-played, and countering her bid for finality and un-repeatability as effectively as if the tyrant Caesar had got his way after all. Play is death for Cleopatra. But with every reiteration of his drama, Shakespeare turns her death back into play again, repeating the un-repeatable and giving the lie to her grandiose self-mastery. Cleopatra does all she can to avoid being in the play she is in, an absurdity to which Shakespeare draws cruel attention:

> *Cleopatra*: Now, Iras, what think'st thou?
> Thou, an Egyptian puppet, shall be shown
> In Rome as well as I. Mechanic slaves
> With greasy aprons, rules, and hammers shall
> Uplift us to the view. In their thick breaths,
> Rank of gross diet, shall we be enclouded,
> And forc'd to drink their vapour.
>
> *Iras*: The gods forbid!
>
> *Cleopatra*: Nay, 'tis most certain, Iras. Saucy lictors
> Will catch at us like strumpets, and scald rhymers
> Ballad's out a'tune. The quick comedians
> Extemporally will stage us, and present
> Our Alexandrian revels: Antony
> Shall be brought drunken forth, and I shall see
> Some squeaking Cleopatra boy my greatness
> I'th'posture of a whore.

Just as the assassination in *Julius Caesar* looks ahead to the same repetition of which the play is itself an example, so here Shakespeare collapses past with present and alerts us to the fact that the theatrical event in which we are engaged is precisely one of the repetitions which Cleopatra foresees. In so doing, Shakespeare impresses upon us that he has succeeded where Caesar has failed. He gets to do what Caesar can never do – to master Cleopatra in play, to bring her squeaking forth and in the posture of a whore. At the very moment when she most voci-ferously asserts her independence from another's stage-direction, and when she resolves to stage her own play as a true version of herself, Cleopatra is more than ever the representation of another – an impersonator who has assumed her role for that fleeting performance. Never so poignantly and never so self-defeatingly does Cleopatra appear the very thing that she wanted to avoid.

Like it or not, the act of looking in which we're engaged implicates us in Cleopatra's defeat. For the rank and sweaty audience which she describes as being entertained by her show is a mirror image of the Jacobean audience to whom she first uttered these lines. While Cleopatra would master her fate and, with her final spectacle, inspire in us the doting gaze which brought Antony to his knees, the fact that we also see her in the posture of defeat suggests the extent to which we may fail to be coerced by her brilliant manipulation of appearances. We're made witness to that which Iras would not see – the representation of Cleopatra's story on the stage. And, insofar as Shakespeare doesn't require us to do as Iras threatens – to scratch out our own eyes – he gives us no choice in this scene but to look on Cleopatra's failure. The act of looking which constitutes us as a theatre audience positions us in our stance toward her and identifies us willy nilly with the hostile and deriding eyes of Rome.

In this, Shakespeare is as manipulative of theatrical illusion as Cleopatra herself – more so. For his decision to show Cleopatra defeated, and above all to show her making a speech as mockingly self-defeating as this one, can only have one effect – to undermine her authority and to reveal her last, heroic bid for finality as having already failed. Having appeared to support Cleopatra in her struggle for mastery over Caesar, Shakespeare doubles back upon himself. While there's no denying that he gives Cleopatra the benefit of the last word, his undertaking to repeat that last word renders the gift a contradiction in terms. He appropriates for himself the imperial satisfaction of showing Cleopatra on stage which Caesar would have enjoyed had the queen stayed alive. Taking pleasure in his own masterful play, Shakespeare assumes the mantle of the impresario himself – a dramaturgical move which anticipates *The Tempest*.

Instead of the simple if devious contest with which we began – Caesar's comedy pitted against Cleopatra's tragedy – the issue is complicated by the intrusion of a third figure, Shakespeare, whose own play presents itself as an amalgam and digest of the other two. *Antony and Cleopatra* is not so straightforwardly the polarized play which it's so often characterized as – divided between Egypt and Rome and all the political, ethical, and aesthetic standards by which those two places are symbolized. Rather, it's a triangulated play, with Shakespeare's

London forming the third point of its pyramid, a third – and rogue – point of perspective on the scene. While the various tableaux of Caesar and Cleopatra – each an 'eternal moment of disclosed presence' – could be seen, like classic perspective paintings, to inspire in their beholders a reverential, awe-struck, and submissive gaze, Shakespeare's play, by contrast, might be seen to inspire what the art historian, Norman Bryson, differentiates as the glance. Flickering, mobile, and ungovernable, the glance jumps from point to point and builds up a sense of a picture's unitary whole only from its multiple and often fragmentary acts of looking.

The struggle for mastery turns out to be divided not between two but between three would-be playwrights, and between their three versions of the same events. Of the three players, Caesar scores lowest, for he loses to both the other two. He not only fails to get Cleopatra for his triumph (he has to bury her instead). He also finds that, for all his reluctance to be made a spectacle of himself – such as being 'stag'd to th'show' in a hand-to-hand combat with Antony – he meets just such a fate in Shakespeare's hands, put on a stage for all the world to see. Cleopatra comes second in the ranking, successfully outwitting Caesar, yet outwitted herself with every reappearance of her Egyptian puppets on Shakespeare's stage. Which leaves Shakespeare, the player king, in possession of the field – the grand master of illusion, with Caesar and Cleopatra immortalizing his own pageant as the centrepieces of his show.

V

In each of the plays discussed so far, Shakespeare brings characters on to the stage who speculate on the denial of death that's implicit in any representation of it and on the fact that tragedy's consolatory power rests upon a falsification of life's grim realities. In doing so, Shakespeare exposes to our view the deceptions that are created by his own play-world, inviting us to enter into the second world of art while revealing the pleasures and consolations of that world to be based upon a pleasing lie. *The Winter's Tale* is just as closely concerned with the representation of death. The story of Hermione's disappearance and return forms a tragedy within the play as complete in its finished action as the *fort! da!* game. Hermione's tragedy plays for two Acts – for as long, that is, as we and the other characters believe her to be dead. But it ends, as every tragedy ends, with the revival of the actor to please tomorrow's audience, and with the accompanying realization (or reminder) that her death was only feigned. By containing the threshold between the play-world and the everyday within his own play, Shakespeare dramatizes the reversal which occurs at the end of every tragedy when the representation of death is revealed to have been an illusion all along.

The Winter's Tale differs from the other plays discussed so far, however, in one important respect. Instead of including a character who – like Brutus, Hamlet, or Cleopatra – speculates on the imponderabilities of representing death, Shakespeare here leaves the speculating to his audience. He does this by organizing the play in such a way as to take us by surprise, making us participate emotionally in the marvellous statue-scene at the play's close. Manipulating our discovery of Hermione's survival, Shakespeare works to arouse in us all the gratification of that discovery and invites us to hail her reappearance as joyfully as little Ernst was to hail the reappearance of his wooden reel – there! Shakespeare makes us feel within his play the consolation that's more usually reserved for the end – for the moment, that is, when a tragedy is signalled as being over and when the actors get up to take their bows. By including this terminal point within his play, Shakespeare allows us to speculate for ourselves on the nature of that pleasure and on the power of tragedy to produce it.

Shakespeare achieves this end very simply – by not telling us what's going on. Exceptionally, Shakespeare keeps us in the dark, neglecting to inform us that the account we're given of Hermione's death is a fiction. *The Winter's Tale* is full of other tales in which the audience is not deceived but kept fully informed and granted, by means of dramatic irony, the advantage of being in the know. We know all along, for example, that Perdita is truly 'the King's daughter', and neither the daughter of Polixenes, nor of a waiting-gentlewoman, nor of the shepherd, nor of Smalus, the king of Libya, as she is erroneously believed to be by different characters at different times in the play. We know, too, that Leontes' fantasy about his wife's infidelity is likewise a tale, spun entirely by his jealous and clue-catching imagination. Yet we're granted no such command of the truth where the account of Hermione's death is concerned, and only in the final moments of the play do we discover that we, like the other characters, have been fooled. When news is brought that Hermione is dead, we have no reason to suppose anything different. She faints on hearing of her son Mamilius' death, and, when her own death is announced by the distraught Paulina a few lines later – 'the Queen, the Queen, / The sweet'st, dear'st creature's dead, and vengeance for't / Not dropp'd down yet' – we have no reason to suspect Paulina of telling anything other than the truth. Leontes reacts to the double blow with a profound remorse, finally taking responsibility for his actions – and the terrible consequences to which they have given rise – by embarking upon a 'saint-like' and self-punishing sorrow. He has the legend of his wife and son's deaths inscribed upon their tombs – 'upon them shall / The causes of their death appear (unto / Our shame perpetual)' – and he vows to visit the grave every day, his tears shed there to be his 'recreation'.

One could regard Leontes' action as extreme, pitiable, or justly deserved. But not until the last scene of the play can we look back and see that it was deluded. It's only with hindsight that we know he's been mourning a wife who's not dead – a realization which necessarily alters our sense of the penance which he's been undertaking for sixteen years, since it now transpires that Leontes has been believing in a fiction all that time. Indeed, he has been living out the 'sad tale' of the man who dwelt by a churchyard which Mamillius had begun earlier in the play but hadn't been allowed to finish. We now see that Leontes' grief has taken the form of living inside a tragedy, of relentlessly repeating its plot, of daily re-creating it with his tears. His response to catastrophe, like that of Richard II, is to sit upon the ground and tell sad tales, 'in winter's tedious nights' to tell 'tales / Of woeful ages long ago betid'. Moreover, Leontes has been repeating the same story, reiterating the sequel-less account of how he came to be without an heir – something which induces in him a profound melancholy, a kind of self-induced neurosis which is clearly signalled as being sterile in its obsessive repetitions since it perpetuates and guarantees his heirlessness. We not only see Leontes grieving for the loss of his family. Our discovery that Hermione never died in the first place allows us to see him as a character who – like some doomed figure from Dante's *Inferno* – is condemned for his sins endlessly to repeat to himself the same tale.

It's fitting that Leontes should suffer this particular punishment, since it was his misplaced credulity in a fiction which set the whole tragedy in motion from the outset. The story of Hermione's adultery is clearly a figment of his imagination – a catastrophic confusion of fiction and fact in which he interprets the actions of his wife and best friend as if they were taking place in some hackneyed cuckold-play. 'Go play, boy, play', he tells Mamillius, 'Thy mother plays, and I / Play too, but so disgrac'd a part, whose issue / Will hiss me to my grave'. At her arraignment, Hermione helplessly declares that her unhappiness is more than 'history can pattern, though devis'd / And play'd to take spectators'. Her misery exceeds the kind of thing that might be narrated in a story, yet Leontes' mad fabrication gives her no choice but to represent it as a story, as a play to be performed before an audience. Cast as the dishonest wife in her husband's jealous drama, Hermione is forced to plead for her life, yet finds herself reduced to the role of a fictional character, a phantom who exists only 'in the level of [his] dreams'.

In his nightmarish confusion of fiction and reality, Leontes takes for true what other characters in the play clearly regard as an incredible tale – as a 'jest' or as 'sport', as a folly more worthy of laughter than anything else. Yet, as a maker of fictions, Leontes is also a type of poet, since the title of 'poet' was derived from his ability 'to make' (from ποιεῖν) – to make things up and to make-believe. Although Leontes clearly doesn't make things 'better than Nature', as Sir Philip Sidney described the poet doing in his *Apology for Poetry* (1595), nor deliver a golden world, this lunatic lover-king does give substance to airy nothing, and does make things 'quite anew, forms such as never were in Nature, as the Heroes, Demigods, Cyclops, Chimeras, Furies, and such like' – his image of an unchaste Hermione belonging not inappropriately amid the catalogue of monsters which Sidney here lists. In his text, Sidney glosses over the implications of the poet's ability to fabricate from nothing, his defence of poetry resting more heavily on the power of the poet to idealize and improve on Nature and to delight and teach his readers. The true poet will 'bestow a Cyrus upon the world to make many Cyruses', but won't be 'wholly imaginative, as we are wont to say by them that build castles in the air'. In the figure of Leontes, however, Shakespeare sketches the career of just such a 'wholly imaginative' man, one who builds upon foundations light as air and who tyrannically affirms that which is false to be true. As a kind of anti-poet, Leontes embodies the charge anciently levelled at poetry – namely, that it lies. Whereas Sidney's text aims to redeem poetry from this old charge and (in the words of one of its first editors) to chase away the 'stormie Winter' under which poetry had for so long languished neglected and accused, Leontes' fiction recalls it, and fittingly brings about the 'winter / In storm perpetual' of his guilt-ridden sixteen-year remorse.

Since Leontes is guilty of making a story up and believing in it, it's only fitting that Paulina should punish him by making up another story and making him believe in that – the tragedy of the dead queen. Paulina casts him as a penitent – quite as 'disgrac'd a part' as the role of cuckold which he had earlier assigned to himself – and she counters his cuckold-play with a curious revenge-play of her own: a drama, in the very repetition of which her leading player is made to take revenge upon himself. It's unclear whether Paulina is simply tormenting the king – like some kind of perverse therapist who prevents her patient from working through his trauma, inducing, instead, a pathological repetition of it – or whether she instigates his psychological suffering as a means of healing him through a long-learned patience. Either way, we discover only in the final scene that Paulina too is a tale-teller, another anti-poet who's affirmed that which is false to be true, and who has successfully conjured everyone (including ourselves) to believe it.

When Leontes first sees the statue, he still believes Hermione to be dead. What he sees is an effigy of his long-dead wife which, like the tomb, he regards as another – if more intense – venue for his continuing grief over her loss. Only in the magical moments which then follow is he led, wonderingly, into the knowledge that the statue is not a statue and that Hermione never died at all. Only then can he begin to see Paulina's fiction for what it is. For, in bringing the statue to life, Paulina reveals for the first time that the story which Leontes has been believing and repeating during the preceding sixteen years was, all the time, 'only' a story, 'only' a play. The revival of Hermione shows that she no more died for real than an actor dies in a tragedy. Paulina's story of the dead queen is no more true a representation of reality than mimetic drama is a true representation of life, or the seemingly life-like statue is a true representation of Hermione. Indeed, this supposed effigy is not, as it transpires, a representation at all. What first appeared to be a representation of Hermione in stone turns out to be the representation of a stone by Hermione. In one stroke, the whole existence of the sculpture and its supposed maker – Giulio Romano – vanishes into thin air, for there *is* no statue. As the non-sculptor of a non-statue, Giulio – the famous illusionist, within whose own *trompe l'oeil* paintings art was (at least for the chronicler of Renaissance painters, Giorgio Vasari) indistinguishable from life – is himself revealed to be an illusion, a mere fabrication to be consigned to oblivion together with all the other false trails and tall stories in the play. In place of an artifact, a fashioned object capable of being 'taken in by the eye' and surveyed – like the lapis lazuli carving in Yeats' poem – in all its permanence and re-peatability, Leontes is here given his queen in person – moving, breathing, ageing. Instead of a work of art, he experiences the immediacy

214

of the lived moment – the unique and unrepeatable reunion with a long-lost and long-lamented wife.

It's a wonderful moment. And, since our discovery of the truth is made to coincide with that of Leontes and the other characters on stage, the scene seems designed to evoke in us the same stunned reaction that we see in them. For Hermione's reappearance is no mere wish-fulfilment. It's the real thing. The marvel of the scene derives from its rejection of fictions in favour of reality. Hermione's appearance is a lived moment and not a work of art, a happening and not a statue. By constructing his play in such a way as to make us participate in the same moment of discovery, Shakespeare invites us too to experience the joyful reappearance of Hermione as if it were for real and to feel all the relief and consolation which accompanies so unexpected and so gratifying a denial of death.

The wonder which this scene so visibly arouses in the characters could be argued to surprise and arrest us too, to turn us into stone – Milton's conceitful tribute to the overwhelming power of Shakespeare's art:

Thou in our wonder and astonishment
Hast built thyself a live-long monument.
For whilst to the shame of slow-endeavouring art,
Thy easy numbers flow, and that each heart
Hath from the leaves of thy unvalued book,
Those Delphic lines with deep impression took,
Then thou our fancy of itself bereaving,
Dost make us marble with too much conceiving.

But, since the statue comes to life in *The Winter's Tale*, to remain for too long in so immobilized a state of wonder – however fittingly – would be to miss the point. 'It is owing to their wonder', writes Aristotle in the *Metaphysics*, 'that men both now begin and at first began to philosophize'. Wonder is that blank state of incomprehension and bafflement which precedes inquiry, since 'a man who is puzzled and wonders thinks himself ignorant'. It's wonder which provokes us to work out for ourselves the things which we've failed, on a first encounter, to understand. And Shakespeare's arousal of our wonder in the last scene of *The Winter's Tale* is an invitation to do the same.

If we take up that invitation, our speculation leads us to see what Shakespeare has playfully obscured from view. For the revival of

Hermione which we've been made to experience as real is, of course, no such thing. If the statue isn't a statue, then it isn't, strictly speaking, Hermione either. 'Hermione' is only a part played by an actor – and not even, on Shakespeare's stage, by a female one. Hermione is no more a living character than she was a dead one. To learn that Paulina's fiction was, all along, only a play and that Hermione is 'really' alive is still to submit however irresistibly to another fiction, this time, Shakespeare's. For our experience of this reality is conjured by a fiction, and our coming to know the truth is brought about by narrative and theatrical devices on Shakespeare's part which are quite as manipulative as anything which he reveals Paulina to have been using. In unmasking Paulina as a tale-teller, Shakespeare works to cover his own traces and tricks us into believing that Hermione is indeed 'living', a story which (as he bluffingly makes Paulina say) 'were it but told you, should be hooted at / Like an old tale'.

The last scene of *The Winter's Tale* seems to privilege life over art, to put the unrepeatability of the lived moment above the static repeatability of the work of art. Leontes could have visited a statue any number of times, but he can only be re-united with his wife once. There can only be one first time. Yet Shakespeare makes future repetitions of this wonder-inspiring moment possible by putting it into a play, a text that's been written to be repeated. The fact that we're given an opportunity to re-experience that scene with every successive performance of it gives the lie to the very inspiration of that wonder. For the work of art – the statue – which turns out not to be a work of art – Hermione – still is a work of art – *The Winter's Tale*. While Leontes is released from repeating the tragedy of Hermione's death when he discovers that she has really been alive all along, there can be no comparable release for us insofar as we're continuing to watch a represented and repeatable scene. By willingly entering into the second world of art, we find ourselves embroiled in the same repetition of which Shakespeare gives us a glimpse in Leontes' sterile, sixteen-year penance. The king's belief in and repetition of the winter's tale of his wife's death is a grim parody of what the audience has been and will be doing every time it suspends its disbelief in and returns to or re-reads Shakespeare's play.

Shakespeare signals in his title that the play we've been watching is as tall a tale as any of the others in the play – the same fabulous and belief-beggaring 'drollery' which Ben Jonson was to accuse it of being in the Induction to *Bartholomew Fair* (1614). As three different characters within the play remind us, a winter's tale is proverbially an old wives' tale – a sensational, incredible, yet compelling fiction, of the kind which, as Sidney writes, 'holdeth children from play, and old men from the chimney corner'. Throughout this play, believing in tales is associated with a credulity which varies only in its degree of culpability. The simple shepherdesses might be forgiven for believing in Autolycus' monstrous ballads ('Is it true, think you?'), or the shepherd for believing in fairy-tales ('it was told me I should be rich by the fairies'). But other examples of believing are shown to be more serious in their consequences. For all his hesitations – 'I have heard (but not believ'd) the spirits o'th'dead / May walk again' – Antigonus lends sufficient credence to the vision he has of Hermione's ghost as to believe that Perdita is 'indeed the issue / Of King Polixenes', and consequently exposes the infant to what he sees as an almost certain death. Leontes loses his entire family as a result of believing something untrue. And, so long as they remain in circulation, the various, erroneous stories of Perdita's origin prevent her from taking up her proper place in the social, sexual, and dynastic framework. For only when she is universally known to be the daughter of Leontes can Perdita legitimately become Florizel's wife. Several characters find themselves entangled in the dangerous web of deceptions which surrounds Florizel and Perdita in Act IV. Not only do the lovers dupe the shepherd with a tale, obscuring Florizel's princely identity with 'a swain's wearing' in the best tradition of pastoral romance, as a result of which the shepherd is very nearly executed as a traitor. They, in turn, are duped by the disguised Polixenes and Camillo – 'not appearing what we are' – as a result of which they have to flee the country. Camillo subsequently advises the lovers on how to deceive Polixenes, by devising a 'scene' in which they must disguise and play parts, all the while planning to deceive them. 'What a fool Honesty is', remarks Autolycus aptly. For in this play believing in tales manifestly makes for deception, mystification, and betrayal.

Everything that goes wrong in *The Winter's Tale* is a result of believing in tales and is put right only by the play's repeated shifts from falsehood to truth as, one by one, inauthentic stories are exchanged for true ones. But Shakespeare's story about the dangers of believing in stories necessarily calls into question our readiness to enter into his second world of fiction and to suspend our disbelief in *The Winter's Tale* itself. How, logically, are we to suspend our disbelief in a play that's so systematically undermined belief and so consistently shown it to entail loss? By drawing attention to the fictional status of his own tale in this way, Shakespeare raises like ghosts all those questions about make-believe and the consequences of believing in fictions which the same text has set out so self-consciously to problematize. Instead of providing a character to come on and tell as much, Shakespeare makes us experience for ourselves the paradoxes and self-contradictions which are implicit in any representation of death. For he organizes *The Winter's Tale* in such a way as to make us experience the pleasure of Hermione's revival as if it were for real. But, as the play's title has been hinting from the beginning, the consoling repeatability of death to be found in tragedy's *fort! da!* game is a consolation that's only to be found in art – only in plays, fictions, stories, tales, and lies. That's the only kind of consolation we're left with. In which case, he leaves us wondering, is it any kind of consolation at all?

References

(References relate in all cases to the texts and editions cited in the bibliography)

INTRODUCTION

p.iii   *theoretical man*, Nietzsche, *The Birth of Tragedy*, p.92.

p.iv   *grand metaphysical illusion,* Nietzsche, *The Birth of Tragedy*, p.93.

p.iv   *ghastly absurdity of existence,* Nietzsche, *The Birth of Tragedy*, p.51.

p.v   *developed play,* Freud, *Jokes and Their Relation to the Unconscious*, p.179.

CHAPTER ONE – OF GAMBLING, CREATIVITY, AND GOD

p.8   *Let us imagine*, Borges, 'The Babylonian Lottery', pp.63-4.

p.8   *all the faculties of men*, Borges, 'The Babylonian Lottery', p.60.

p.14   *agreeable or even indifferent*, Freud, *Beyond the Pleasure Principle*, p.15.

p.15   *great cultural achievement*, Freud, *Beyond the Pleasure Principle*, p.15.

p.18   *hand as lawgiver*, Schiller, *Aesthetic Education*, p.209.

p.18   *abstracting from man's physical character*, Schiller, *Aesthetic Education*, p.15.

p.18   *man only plays*, Schiller, *Aesthetic Education*, p.107.

p.19   *regulated like a noble game*, Huizinga, *The Waning of the Middle Ages*, p.38.

p.19   *like a babe*, Huizinga, *Homo Ludens*, p.198.

p.20   *inside the play-ground*, Huizinga, *Homo Ludens*, p.29.

p.20   *first and supreme instrument*, Huizinga, *Homo Ludens*, p.22.

p.23   *the world evolution*, Caillois, *Man, Play, and Games*, pp.102-3.

p.23   *third joyous kingdom*, Schiller, *Aesthetic Education,* p.215.

p.24   *caught on*, Winnicott, *Playing and Reality*, p.40.

p.25   *immense shock*, Winnicott, *Playing and Reality*, p.71.

p.25   *the infant's transition*, Winnicott, *Playing and Reality*, pp.14-5.

p.25   *first 'not-me' possession*, Winnicott, *Playing and Reality*, p.1.

p.25   *potential space*, Winnicott, *Playing and Reality*, p.107.

p.25   *so to receive*, Schiller, *Aesthetic Education*, p.97.

p.26   *a third area*, Winnicott, *Playing and Reality*, p.102.

p.26   *consummates the will*, Schiller, *Aesthetic Education*, p.215.

p.26   *on the wane*, Huizinga, *Homo Ludens*, p.233.

p.26   *outside the sphere of equals*, Huizinga, *Homo Ludens*, p.111.

p.28   *seriousness for serious things*, Plato, *Laws*, pp.187-8.

p.30   *highest and holiest expression*, Huizinga, *Homo Ludens*, p.36.

p.33   *not real gods*, Augustine, *City of God*, p.61.

p.34   *this ridiculous world*, Ralegh, *History of the World*, p.70.

p.34   *author of all our tragedies*, Ralegh, *History of the World*, p.70.

p.37   *fuller understanding*, von Neumann and Morgenstern, *Theory of Games*, p.20.

p.38   *useless, only a craft*, Pascal, quoted in David, *Games, Gods and Gambling*, p.252.

p.39   *God is, or is not*, Pascal, *Pensées*, p.153.

CHAPTER TWO – OF THE DEATH OF GOD, DECONSTRUCTION, AND PLAY

p.43   *contest is necessary*, Nietzsche, 'Homer's Contest', *Portable Nietzsche*, p.36.

p.43   *new social order*, Caillois, *Man, Play, and Games*, p.157.

p.44   *man of theory*, Nietzsche, *The Birth of Tragedy*, p.109.

p.44   *theoretical culture*, Nietzsche, *The Birth of Tragedy*, p.110.

p.46   *you are worth knowing*, Nietzsche, *The Birth of Tragedy*, p.108.

p.48   *a world in which we can live*, Nietzsche, *The Gay Science*, p.177.

p.48   *common net of knowledge*, Nietzsche, *The Birth of Tragedy*, pp.93-4.

p.48   *weave the net*, Nietzsche, *The Birth of Tragedy*, p.95.

p.49   *acquired habituation*, Nietzsche, *Human, All Too Human*, p.109.

p.49   *function of the herd*, Nietzsche, *The Gay Science*, p.174.

p.49   *an artistic fiction*, Nietzsche, *The Birth of Tragedy*, p.10.

p.49   *total character of the world*, Nietzsche, *The Gay Science*, p.168.

p.50   *a god who begets children*, Nietzsche, *Human, All Too Human*, p.66.

p.50   *error, deception, simulation*, Nietzsche, *The Gay Science*, p.282.

p.51   *mode of redemption*, Nietzsche, *The Birth of Tragedy*, p.10.

p.51   *art, nothing but art*, Nietzsche, *The Will to Power*, p.452.

p.51   *Dionysiac drama*, Nietzsche, *The Genealogy of Morals*, pp.156-7.

p.51   *chess-like*, Nietzsche, *The Birth of Tragedy*, p.71.

p.52   *third mode of existence*, Nietzsche, *The Birth of Tragedy*, p.125.

p.52   *laughter I declare to be blessed*, Nietzsche, *The Birth of Tragedy*, p.15.

p.52   *Homeric laughter*, Nietzsche, *Human, All Too Human*, p.20.

p.52   *a new beginning*, Nietzsche, *Thus Spoke Zarathustra*, p.55.

p.52   *a work of art that gives birth to itself*, Nietzsche, *The Will to Power*, p.419.

p.53   *pretentious lie of civilization*, Nietzsche, *The Birth of Tragedy*, p.53.

p.53   *game of blindman's bluff*, Nietzsche, 'On Truth and Lie', *Portable Nietzsche*, p.43

p.55   *significance of language*, Nietzsche, *Human, All Too Human*, p.16.

p.55   *tremendous error*, Nietzsche, *Human, All Too Human*, p.16.

p.55   *what, then, is truth?* Nietzsche, 'On Truth and Lie', *Portable Nietzsche*, pp.46-7.

p.57   *decorative display of what-goes-without-saying*, Barthes, *Mythologies*, p.11.

p.57   *transforms history into nature*, Barthes, *Mythologies*, p.140.

p.58   *perfect intelligibility of reality*, Barthes, *Mythologies*, p.26.

p.58   *an ideal understanding of things*, Barthes, *Mythologies*, p.26.

p.59   *pleasure of the sentence*, Barthes, *The Pleasure of the Text*, p.51.

p.60   *goes without saying*, Bourdieu, *Outline of a Theory of Practice*, p.167.

p.60   *that which is undiscussed*, Bourdieu, *Outline of a Theory of Practice*, p.170.

p.60   *hither side of all inquiry*, Bourdieu, *Outline of a Theory of Practice*, p.168.

p.61   *history turned into nature*, Bourdieu, *Outline of a Theory of Practice*, p.78.

REFERENCES

p.61   *immediately intelligible*, Bourdieu, *Outline of a Theory of Practice*, p.80.

p.61   *shock, disturbance, even loss*, Barthes, *The Pleasure of the Text*, p.19.

p.61   *euphoria, fulfilment, comfort*, Barthes, *The Pleasure of the Text*, p.19.

p.61   *sincere fiction*, Bourdieu, *Outline of a Theory of Practice*, p.171.

p.62   *nothing other than the habitus*, Bourdieu, *Outline of a Theory of Practice*, p.83.

p.62   *construction of reality*, Bourdieu, *Outline of a Theory of Practice*, p.165.

p.62   *ideology of the dominant class*, Barthes, *The Pleasure of the Text*, p.32.

p.62   *material and symbolic means*, Bourdieu, *Outline of a Theory of Practice*, p.169

p.63   *the sentence is a body*, Barthes, *The Pleasure of the Text*, p.51.

p.63   *text of bliss*, Barthes, *The Pleasure of the Text*, p.14.

p.63   *text of pleasure*, Barthes, *The Pleasure of the Text*, p.14.

p.63   *a logical, closed measure*, Barthes, *The Pleasure of the Text*, p.33.

p.63   *textual body*, Barthes, *The Pleasure of the Text*, p.34.

p.63   *ordered significances of realistic fiction*, Bersani, *The Freudian Body*, p.82.

p.63   *fundamental political strategy*, Bersani, *The Freudian Body*, p.83.

p.64   *play havoc with theoretical accounts*, Bersani, *The Freudian Body*, p.4.

p.64   *the intelligible and the unintelligible*, Bersani, *The Freudian Body*, p.114.

p.64   *most resolutely superficial*, Bersani, *The Freudian Body*, p.110.

p.65   *elaborated forms of self-enjoyment*, Bersani, *The Culture of Redemption*, p.43.

p.66   *only possible mode of redemption*, Nietzsche, *The Birth of Tragedy*, p.10.

p.66   *conceptual centre*, Bersani, *The Culture of Redemption*, p.2.

p.66   *philosophical condensation*, Bersani, *The Culture of Redemption*, p.87.

p.66   *dissolving of the boundaries*, Bersani, *The Culture of Redemption*, p.92.

p.66   *figure dissolving its own figured state*, Bersani, *The Culture of Redemption*, p.94.

p.67   *art plays with these boundaries*, Bersani, *The Culture of Redemption*, p.101.

p.67   *express our relief*, Bersani, *The Culture of Redemption*, p.116.

p.72   *cynical distance, laughter, irony*, Žižek, *The Sublime Object of Ideology*, p.28.

p.73   *proceeds within certain limits of time and space*, Huizinga, *Homo Ludens*, p.154.

p.74   *pedantic, totally meaningless mythology*, Caillois, *Man, Play, and Games*, p.13.

p.74   *discovery and description of 'the truth'*, Burke, *A Grammar of Motives*, p.503.

p.74   *I could make an interpretation*, Winnicott, *Playing and Reality*, p.36.

p.80   *species of sensation*, Hume, *A Treatise of Human Nature*, p.103.

p.80   *not solely in poetry and music*, Hume, *A Treatise of Human Nature*, p.103.

p.81   *a kind of cause*, Hume, *A Treatise of Human Nature*, p.180.

p.81   *most curious operations*, Hume, *A Treatise of Human Nature*, p.128

p.82   *a false reason and none at all*, Hume, *A Treatise of Human Nature*, p.268.

p.82   *the conduct of a man*, Hume, *A Treatise of Human Nature*, p.273.

CHAPTER THREE – JOKING AND ITS DISCONTENTS

p.85   *immense number*, Freud, *Three Essays on the Theory of Sexuality*, p.191.
p.85   *chamber of maiden-thought*, quoted in Gittings, *John Keats*, p.314.
p.85   *infant or thoughtless chamber*, quoted in Gittings, *John Keats*, p.313.
p.86   *developed play*, Freud, *Jokes and Their Relation to the Unconscious*, p.179.
p.87   *cannot be doubted*, Freud, *Jokes*, p.125.
p.87   *rebellion against the compulsion of logic and reality*, Freud, *Jokes*, p.126.
p.87   *spectator of an act of sexual aggression*, Freud, *Jokes*, p.97.
p.88   *voice within us that rebels*, Freud, *Jokes*, p.110.
p.89   *euphoria which we endeavour to reach*, Freud, *Jokes*, p.236.
p.89   *rebellion against authority as a merit*, Freud, *Jokes*, p.105.
p.91   *a person appears comic to us*, Freud, *Jokes*, pp.195-6.
p.92   *comparison between the adult's ego and the child's ego*, Freud, *Jokes*, p.225.
p.92   *we rediscover the child's helplessness*, Freud, *Jokes*, p.226.
p.92   *not proper for an adult*, Freud, *Jokes*, p.227.
p.92   *restriction of our muscular work*, Freud, *Jokes*, p.195.
p.93   *a joke is made, the comic is found*, Freud, *Jokes*, p.181.
p.94   *treating himself like a child*, Freud, 'Humour', p.164.
p.94   *tiny and all its interests trivial*, Freud, 'Humour', p.164.
p.95   *something liberating about it*, Freud, 'Humour', p.162.
p.95   *something of grandeur and elevation*, Freud, 'Humour', p.162.
p.95   *kindly words of comfort*, Freud, 'Humour', p.166.
p.95   *repudiating reality and serving an illusion*, Freud, 'Humour', p.166.
p.95   *without rightly knowing why*, Freud, 'Humour', p.166.
p.96   *thrift, thrift, Horatio!*, *Hamlet*, I.ii.180.
p.96   *quite famillionairely*, Freud, *Jokes*, p.16.
p.96   *you've not paid for the liqueur*, Freud, *Jokes*, p.60.
p.96   *but, where's the Saviour?*, Freud, *Jokes*, p.74.
p.97   *the way in which some housewives economize*, Freud, *Jokes*, p.44.
p.98   *some 'psychical expenditure' is required*, Freud, *Jokes*, p.118.
p.99   *disjecta membra*, Freud, *Jokes*, p.14.
p.99   *organic whole*, Freud, *Jokes*, p.14.
p.100   *what these jokes whisper may be said aloud*, Freud, *Jokes*, p.110.
p.101   *one noble and truly human occupation*, Nietzsche, *The Birth of Tragedy*,
        p.94.
p.103   *sudden glory*, Hobbes, *Treatise of Human Nature*, p.46.
p.104   *humour has something liberating about it*, Freud, 'Humour', p.162.
p.104   *something of grandeur and elevation*, Freud, 'Humour', p.162
p.104   *a great deal to learn about the nature of the superego*, Freud, 'Humour',
        p.166.
p.104   *incomprehensible*, Freud, *Jokes*, p.188.
p.104   *oscillation of attention backwards and forwards*, Freud, *Jokes*, p.188.
p.108   *as a result of its efforts*, Freud, *The Interpretation of Dreams*, p.490.
p.108   *already interpreted once*, Freud, *The Interpretation of Dreams*, p.490.
p.108   *the purposes of our interpretation*, Freud, *The Interpretation of Dreams*,
        p.500.
p.109   *in just the same way*, Freud, *The Interpretation of Dreams*, p.499.

REFERENCES

p.109   *a first interpretation*, Freud, *The Interpretation of Dreams*, p.500.

p.109   *only with the greatest difficulty*, Freud, *The Interpretation of Dreams*, p.523.

p.111   *ingenious and amusing*, Freud, *The Interpretation of Dreams*, p.298n.

p.111   *must, at least in some essential respect, be identical*, Freud, *Jokes*, p.165.

p.111   *no one can be content*, Freud, *Jokes*, p.143.

p.112   *binding on it*, Freud, *Jokes*, p.179.

p.112   *indefinable feeling*, Freud, *Jokes*, p.167.

p.112   *absence*, Freud, *Jokes*, p.167.

p.112   *plunge*, Freud, *Jokes*, p.169

p.112   *make an effort*, Freud, *Jokes*, p.148

p.112   *part of the work which has created the joke*, Freud, *Jokes*, p.54.

p.113   *substance and value*, Freud, *Jokes*, p.131.

p.113   *have come about unintentionally*, Freud, *Jokes*, p.132.

p.113   *underlying construction of the joke,* Freud, *Jokes*, p.132.

p.113   *never happens of its own accord*, Freud, *Jokes*, p.220.

p.113   *objective certainty*, Freud, *Jokes*, p.156.

p.113   *not relevant for our present purposes*, Freud, *Jokes*, p.164.

p.114   *incompleteness*, Freud, *Jokes*, p.167

p.114   *astonishing*, Freud, *Civilization and its Discontents*, p.86.

p.114   *the individual's dangerous desire*, Freud, *Civilization and its Discontents*,
         p.124.

p.115   *ambivalence*, Freud, *Civilization and its Discontents*, p.132.

p.115   *the instinct of life*, Freud, *Civilization and its Discontents*, p.122.

p.115   *so patently infantile*, Freud, *Civilization and its Discontents*, p.74.

p.115   *the picture of the real world*, Freud, *Civilization and its Discontents*, p.84.

p.115   *scientific work is the only road*, Freud, *The Future of an Illusion*, p.31.

p.115   *its numerous and important successes*, Freud, *The Future of an Illusion*,
         p.55.

p.115   *our science is no illusion*, Freud, *The Future of an Illusion*, p.56.

p.115   *religious systems*, Freud, *Civilization and its Discontents*, p.94.

p.115   *speculations of philosophy*, Freud, *Civilization and its Discontents*, p.94.

p.115   *powerful deflections*, Freud, *Civilization and its Discontents*, p.75.

p.116   *shifting the instinctual aims*, Freud, *Civilization and its Discontents*, p.79.

p.116   *if we assume quite generally*, Freud, *Civilization and its Discontents*, p.94.

p.116   *narcissistic man*, Freud, *Civilization and its Discontents*, p.83.

p.116   *internal mental processes*, Freud, *Civilization and its Discontents*, p.84.

p.116   *it was discovered that*, Freud, *Civilization and its Discontents*, p.87.

p.116   *scientific activity*, Freud, *Civilization and its Discontents*, p.75.

p.117   *less the explicitly proposed antagonism*, Bersani, *The Freudian Body*, pp.12-
         13.

p.117   *may have spoilt the structure*, Freud, *Civilization and its Discontents*, p.134.

p.118   *careless manner*, Hume, *A Treatise on Human Nature*, p.273.

p.119   *opposite case*, Kris, *Psychoanalytic Explorations in Art*, p.177.

p.119   *controlled*, Kris, *Psychoanalytic Explorations in Art*, p.202.

p.119   *voluntary*, Kris, *Psychoanalytic Explorations in Art*, p.206.

p.119   *in the service of the ego*, Kris, *Psychoanalytic Explorations in Art*, p.177.

p.119   *as a defect*, Kris, *Psychoanalytic Explorations in Art*, p.197

p.119   *a valuable achievement*, Kris, *Psychoanalytic Explorations in Art*, p.197.

p.120   *the magic spring of the primary process*, Gombrich, 'Freud's Aesthetics',
        p.134.
p.120   *the whole field of art*, Kris, *Psychoanalytic Explorations in Art*, p.177.
p.120   *behind the surface*, Kris, *Psychoanalytic Explorations in Art*, p.190.
p.120   *innermost essence of reality*, Kris, *Psychoanalytic Explorations in Art*,
        p.190.
p.120   *controlled use*, Kris, *Psychoanalytic Explorations in Art*, p.198.
p.120   *sake of a deeper truth*, Kris, *Psychoanalytic Explorations in Art*, p.198.
p.120   *century of the Great Masters*, Kris, *Psychoanalytic Explorations in Art*,
        p.198.
p.120   *unlike the dream*, Kris, *Psychoanalytic Explorations in Art*, p.196.
p.121   *let themselves go*, Kris, *Psychoanalytic Explorations in Art*, p.203.
p.121   *dominating power of the ego*, Kris, *Psychoanalytic Explorations in Art*,
        p.203.
p.121   *pleasurable*, Kris, *Psychoanalytic Explorations in Art*, p.207.
p.121   *sense of mastery*, Kris, *Psychoanalytic Explorations in Art*, p.211.
p.121   *feeling of pleasure*, Kris, *Psychoanalytic Explorations in Art*, pp.212-13.
p.121   *master the tension*, Kris, *Psychoanalytic Explorations in Art*, p.185.
p.121   *pedagogic restraint*, Kris, *Psychoanalytic Explorations in Art*, p.208.
p.121   *attack*, Kris, *Psychoanalytic Explorations in Art*, p.226.
p.121   *victorious fight*, Kris, *Psychoanalytic Explorations in Art*, p.227.
p.121   *moderate joy*, Kris, *Psychoanalytic Explorations in Art*, p.229.
p.122   *most unchallengeable . . . most transparent*, Lacan, *Écrits*, p.60.
p.122   *the logic that is merely a lure*, Lacan, *Écrits*, p.60.
p.122   *something foreign to me in what I found*, Lacan, *Écrits*, p.60.
p.123   *truth of the subject*, Lacan, *Four Fundamental Concepts of Psychoanalysis*,
        p.5.
p.123   *game*, Lacan, *Four Fundamental Concepts of Psychoanalysis*, p.4.
p.123   *comedy*, Lacan, *Four Fundamental Concepts of Psychoanalysis*, p.4.
p.123   *laughing matter*, Lacan, *Four Fundamental Concepts of Psychoanalysis*, p.4.
p.123   *with good reason*, Lacan, *Écrits*, p.59.
p.124   *a kind of joke played by the unconscious*, Weber, *The Legend of Freud*, p.11.
p.124   *a laughingstock out of the theory*, Weber, *The Legend of Freud*, p.86.
p.124   *no appropriate name*, Freud, *Jokes*, p.139n.
p.124   *life is a suspension bridge*, Freud, *Jokes*, p.139n.
p.125   *narcissistic striving of the ego*, Weber, *The Legend of Freud*, p.114.
p.125   *shaggy fleece*, Weber, *The Legend of Freud*, p.116.
p.125   *overcome by the idea*, Freud, 'Dora', p.34.
p.126   *strongest unconscious current in her mental life*, Freud, 'Dora', p.120n.
p.126   *paraphernalia of handbooks*, Huizinga, *Homo Ludens*, p.225.
p.126   *enormous amount of mental energy*, Huizinga, *Homo Ludens*, p.225.
p.126   *universal craze*, Huizinga, *Homo Ludens*, p.225.
p.126   *private bridge circles*, Forrester and Appignanesi, *Freud's Women*, p.167.
p.126   *across the years*, Forrester and Appignanesi, *Freud's Women*, p.167.
p.127   *to laugh at the efforts of doctors*, Freud, 'Dora', p.22.

REFERENCES

CHAPTER FOUR – THE POINT OF PUNS

p.129   *during the period*, Freud, *Jokes*, p.125.
p.129   *little by little*, Freud, *Jokes*, p.125.
p.129   *organic whole*, Freud, *Jokes*, p.127.
p.129   *all the techniques of jokes*, Freud, *Jokes*, p.14.
p.130   *serious use of words*, Freud, *Jokes*, p.119.
p.130   *serious thought*, Freud, *Jokes*, p.120.
p.130   *intellectual work that pursues serious aims*, Freud, *Jokes*, p.219.
p.130   *no place whatever left for the comic*, Freud, *Jokes*, p.219.
p.130   *labelled by him as 'Jewish'*, Gilman, *Difference and Pathology*, p.187.
p.130   *nodal points of numerous ideas*, Freud, *The Interpretation of Dreams*,
            pp.340-1.
p.131   *sober method of expression*, Freud, *The Interpretation of Dreams*, p.341.
p.131   *play – let us keep to that name*, Freud, *Jokes*, p.128.
p.131   *whole ingenuity of the joke-work*, Freud, *Jokes*, p.129.
p.131   *the old play with words*, Freud, *Jokes*, p.130.
p.131   *withstand the scrutiny of criticism*, Freud, *Jokes*, p.130.
p.132   *two fixed points*, Freud, *Jokes*, p.131.
p.132   *set straight by the third person's understanding*, Freud, *Jokes*, p.179.
p.132   *developed play*, Freud, *Jokes*, p.179.
p.133   *substance and value*, Freud, *Jokes*, p.131.
p.133   *illustration to a point*, quoted in Simon, *The Labyrinth of the Comic*, p.228.
p.133   *when they had a special point*, quoted in Oring, *The Jokes of Sigmund
            Freud*, p.11
p.133   *he liked to illustrate a point*, quoted in Oring, *The Jokes of Sigmund Freud*,
            p.2.
p.133   *most serious psychological problems*, Reik, *Surprise and the Psychoanalyst*,
            p.62
p.134   *the process of interpretation*, Reik, *Surprise and the Psychoanalyst*, p.67.
p.134   *rarely*, Reik, *Surprise and the Psychoanalyst*, p.70.
p.134   *special circumstances*, Reik, *Surprise and the Psychoanalyst*, p.70.
p.134   *overcoming the temptation*, Reik, *Surprise and the Psychoanalyst*, p.70.
p.135   *home-roulade*, Freud, *Jokes*, pp.121n, 94.
p.135   *clearly recall*, Freud, *Jokes*, p.95.
p.135   *merely intended to protect that pleasure*, Freud, *Jokes*, p.131.
p.135   *joking envelope*, Freud, *Jokes*, p.132.
p.136   *more significant and more valuable*, Freud, *Jokes*, p.132.
p.136   *for its own end*, quoted in Simon, *The Labyrinth of the Comic*, p.228.
p.137   *first and supreme instrument*, Huizinga, *Homo Ludens*, p.22.
p.139   *unascertained origin*, *Oxford English Dictionary*.
p.139   *this trope which many consider illegitimate*, Redfern, *Puns*, p.16.
p.139   *bastards, immigrants, barbarians*, Redfern, *Puns*, p.4.
p.139   *why bastard? wherefore base?*, *King Lear*, I.ii.6.
p.139   *manly strokes*, Addison, 'The history of the pun', p.262.
p.140   *luminous vapours*, Johnson, *Preface to Shakespeare*, p.74.
p.140   *fatal Cleopatra*, Johnson, *Preface to Shakespeare*, p.74.
p.140   *fundum*, Swift, *A Modest Defence of Punning*, p.205.

PLAY IN A GODLESS WORLD

p.142   *likely to impede understanding*, Saussure, *Course in General Linguistics*, p.124n.

p.142   *diction becomes distinguished*, Aristotle, *Poetics*, pp.2333-34.

p.143   *stages of advancing logical disorder*, Empson, *Seven Types of Ambiguity*, p.69.

p.143   *subdued conceits and ambiguities*, Empson, *Seven Types of Ambiguity*, p.195.

p.144   *exemplary product of language*, Culler, *On Puns*, p.4.

p.145   *serene linguistic landscape*, Felperin, *Beyond Deconstruction*, p.186.

p.145   *spirit (ie. 'sprit')*, Felperin, *Beyond Deconstruction*, p.188.

p.145   *trains of meaning*, Felperin, *Beyond Deconstruction*, p.192.

p.146   *now sleeps in port*, Pope, *The Dunciad*, Book IV, lines 199-202.

p.147   *a slumber did my spirit steal*, quoted in Hartman, *Easy Pieces*, p.149.

p.147   Eco's objection, Eco, 'Over-interpreting texts', pp.45-66.

p.150   *O Eve, in evil hour*, Milton, *Paradise Lost*, Book IX, lines 1067-98.

p.151   *O much deceived*, Milton, *Paradise Lost*, Book IX, lines 404-7.

p.153   *and from this testimony of your own sex*, *Measure for Measure*, II.iv.131-35.

p.153   *to the dreadful summit of the cliff*, *Hamlet*, I.iv.70-71.

p.153   *it waves me still*, *Hamlet*, I.iv.78.

p.154   *let four captains*, *Hamlet*, V.ii.395-403.

p.154   *secret jeer*, Empson, *The Structure of Complex Words*, p.66.

p.154   *more obvious nonsense*, Empson, *The Structure of Complex Words*, p.66.

p.154   *moving and wholehearted*, Empson, *The Structure of Complex Words*, p.66.

p.154   *high on a stage*, *Hamlet*, V.ii.378.

p.154   *letting his machine run away*, Empson, *The Structure of Complex Words*, p.68.

p.154   *avoid noticing it*, Empson, *The Structure of Complex Words*, p.68.

p.155   *hugger mugger*, *Hamlet*, IV.v.84.

p.155   *maimèd rites*, *Hamlet*, V.i.219.

p.155   *canonized bones, hearsed in death*, *Hamlet*, I.iv.47-48.

p.155   *harrows me with fear and wonder*, *Hamlet*, I.i.44.

p.155   *would harrow up thy soul*, *Hamlet*, I.v.15-16.

p.156   *nodal points*, Freud, *The Interpretation of Dreams*, p.340.

p.156   *the sound of which*, Freud, *The Interpretation of Dreams*, p.340.

p.156   *set straight by the third person's understanding*, Freud, *Jokes*, p.179.

p.156   *immediately comprehensible*, Freud, *Interpretation of Dreams*, p.277.

p.157   *obsessional ideas*, Freud, 'Rat Man', p.186.

p.157   *purely external association*, Freud, 'Rat Man', p.188.

p.157   *obnoxious*, Freud, 'Rat Man', p.188.

p.158   *complex stimulus-word*, Freud, 'Rat Man', p.216.

p.158   *coined himself a regular rat currency*, Freud, 'Rat Man', p.213.

p.159   *the patient's rat delirium disappeared*, Freud, 'Rat Man', p.220.

p.159   *complete restoration of the patient's personality*, Freud, 'Rat Man', p.155.

p.159   *forced himself to understand*, Freud, 'Rat Man', p.190.

p.160   *objectionable or superficial*, Freud, *The Interpretation of Dreams*, p.530.

p.160   *superficial associations*, Freud, *The Interpretation of Dreams*, p.531.

p.160   *basic pillars,* Freud, *The Interpretation of Dreams,* p.531.

p.160   *most thoroughly interpreted dream,* Freud, *The Interpretation of Dreams,*
          p.525.

p.160   *tangle of dream-thoughts,* Freud, *The Interpretation of Dreams,* p.525.

p.161   *nothing arbitrary about them,* Freud, *The Interpretation of Dreams,* p.514.

p.163   *the signifier and the signified are knotted together,* Lacan, *The Psychoses,*
          p.268.

p.163   *I don't know how many there are,* Lacan, *The Psychoses,* pp.268-69.

p.164   *triumphant jubilation and playful discovery,* Lacan, *Écrits,* p.18.

p.164   *series of gestures,* Lacan, *Écrits,* p.1.

p.164   *drama,* Lacan, *Écrits,* p.4.

p.164   *insufficiency to anticipation,* Lacan, *Écrits,* p.4.

p.165   *two opposed fields of contest,* Lacan, *Écrits,* p.5.

p.165   *an ideal unity, a salutary imago,* Lacan, *Écrits,* p.19.

p.166   *something derisory is going on in front of the mirror,* Bowie, *Lacan,* p.23.

p.166   *threshold of the visible world,* Lacan, *Écrits,* p.3.

p.166   *specular image,* Lacan, *Écrits,* p.2.

p.166   *specular I,* Lacan, *Écrits,* p.5.

p.166   *spectacular captation,* Lacan, *Écrits,* p.18.

p.166   *spectacular absorption,* Lacan, *Écrits,* p.20.

p.166   *punned into a spectacle,* Bowie, *Lacan,* p.36.

p.168   *pair of sounds modulated on presence and absence,* Lacan, *Écrits,* p.65.

p.168   *small number of these phonemic oppositions,* Lacan, *Écrits,* p.73.

p.168   *an infantile cry,* Lacan, *Écrits,* p.31.

p.168   *first stammerings of speech,* Lacan, *Écrits,* p.31.

p.168   *game of occultation,* Lacan, *Écrits,* p.103.

p.169   *entire discourse about the seriousness of Beyond,* Derrida, *The Post Card,*
          p.377.

p.169   *most interesting and spectacular case,* Derrida, *The Post Card,* p.377.

p.169   *what follows is speculation,* Freud, *Beyond the Pleasure Principle,* p.24.

p.169   *the 'properly Freudian' usage,* Derrida, *The Post Card,* p.283.

p.169   *specular reflection,* Derrida, *The Post Card,* p.284.

p.169   *the production of surplus value,* Derrida, *The Post Card,* p.284.

p.169   *the given of the gift,* Derrida, *The Post Card,* p.284.

p.169   *come to deride all those,* Derrida, *The Post Card,* p.408.

CHAPTER FIVE – SHAKESPEARE'S PLAY

p.170   *quite a business,* Freud, *Beyond the Pleasure Principle,* p.14.

p.170   *the complete game,* Freud, *Beyond the Pleasure Principle,* p.15.

p.170   *obvious,* Freud, *Beyond the Pleasure Principle,* p.15.

p.171   *all right, then, go away!,* Freud, *Beyond the Pleasure Principle,* p.16.

p.171   *instinct for mastery,* Freud, *Beyond the Pleasure Principle,* p.16.

p.171   *great cultural achievement,* Freud, *Beyond the Pleasure Principle,* p.15.

p.171   *play begins,* Huizinga, *Homo Ludens,* p.28.

p.172   *world of durability,* Arendt, *The Human Condition,* p.236.

p.172   *almost no effect,* Freud, *Beyond the Pleasure Principle,* p.35.

p.172   *playground, laboratory,* Berger, *Second World and Green World,* pp.11-12.

p.173   *suffering of every kind,* Freud, 'Psychopathic Characters on the Stage',
         p.307.
p.173   *more deeply,* Freud, 'Psychopathic Characters on the Stage', p.306.
p.174   *regular, norm-governed social life,* Turner, *From Ritual to Theatre,* p.92.
p.174   *taken in by the eye,* Aristotle, *Poetics,* p.2322.
p.174   *what we actually see with the eye,* Schiller, *Aesthetic Education,* p.195.
p.174   *enjoy through the eye,* Schiller, *Aesthetic Education,* p.195.
p.174   *already aesthetically free,* Schiller, *Aesthetic Education,* p.195.
p.175   *interested spectator,* Freud, 'Psychopathic Characters on the Stage', p.305.
p.175   *complete in itself,* Aristotle, *Poetics,* p.2321.
p.175   *proper,* Aristotle, *Poetics,* p.2326.
p.175   *the moment of survival,* Canetti, *Crowds and Power,* p.265.
p.175   *more demands repetition,* Canetti, *Crowds and Power,* p.265.
p.175   *no doubt that the greater pleasure,* Freud, *Beyond the Pleasure Principle,*
         p.15.
p.176   *haply you think, The Spanish Tragedy,* IV.iv.76-84.
p.176   *for instance, in tragedy,* Freud, *Beyond the Pleasure Principle,* p.17.
p.176   *highly enjoyable,* Freud, *Beyond the Pleasure Principle,* p.17.
p.177   *system of aesthetics,* Freud, *Beyond the Pleasure Principle,* p.17.
p.177   *compensate,* Freud, 'Psychopathic Characters on the Stage', p.307.
p.177   *a crucial assumption,* Bersani, *The Culture of Redemption,* p.1.
p.177   *plumb the farthest abysses of being,* Nietzsche, *The Birth of Tragedy,* p.93.
p.178   *grand metaphysical illusion,* Nietzsche, *The Birth of Tragedy,* p.93.
p.178   *modern writers,* Freud, 'Psychopathic Characters on the Stage', p.307.
p.178   *aversion,* Freud, 'Psychopathic Characters on the Stage', p.309.
p.178   *superior patching function,* Bersani, *The Culture of Redemption,* p.1.
p.179   *catastrophes of history,* Bersani, *The Culture of Redemption,* p.1.
p.179   *agreeable or even indifferent,* Freud, *Beyond the Pleasure Principle,* p.15.
p.179   *soon mended,* Winnicott, *Playing and Reality,* p.97.
p.179   *we must assume,* Winnicott, *Playing and Reality,* p.97.
p.180   *after 'recovery' from x + y + z deprivation,* Winnicott, *Playing and Reality,*
         p.97.
p.180   *dealing with a fear of separation,* Winnicott, *Playing and Reality,* p.17.
p.180   *symbol of union,* Winnicott, *Playing and Reality,* p.43.
p.181   *already organized,* Winnicott, *Playing and Reality,* p.28.
p.181   *instinct for mastery,* Freud, *Beyond the Pleasure Principle,* p.16.
p.182   *mysterious masochistic trends,* Freud, *Beyond the Pleasure Principle,* p.14.
p.182   *compulsion to repeat,* Freud, *Beyond the Pleasure Principle,* p.20.
p.182   *daemonic,* Freud, *Beyond the Pleasure Principle,* p.21.
p.182   *remarkable,* Freud, *Beyond the Pleasure Principle,* p.20.
p.182   *no lesson has been learnt,* Freud, *Beyond the Pleasure Principle,* p.21.
p.183   *passivity of the experience,* Freud, *Beyond the Pleasure Principle,* p.17.
p.183   *more primitive, more elementary,* Freud, *Beyond the Pleasure Principle,*
         p.23.
p.183   *an urge inherent in organic life,* Freud, *Beyond the Pleasure Principle,* p.36.
p.184   *die only in its own fashion,* Freud, *Beyond the Pleasure Principle,* p.39.
p.184   *level of intellectual achievement,* Freud, *Beyond the Pleasure Principle,*
         p.42.

REFERENCES

p.184   *benevolent illusion*, Freud, *Beyond the Pleasure Principle*, p.42.

p.184   *all that is most precious*, Freud, *Beyond the Pleasure Principle*, p.42.

p.185   *even in analytic circles*, Freud, *Civilization and its Discontents*, p.119.

p.185   *more serviceable*, Freud, *Civilization and its Discontents*, p.119.

p.185   *kind of compulsion to repeat*, Freud, *Civilization and its Discontents*, p.93.

p.185   *powerful deflections*, Freud, *Civilization and its Discontents*, p.75.

p.185   *I have not the courage*, Freud, *Civilization and its Discontents*, p.145.

p.186   *ghastly absurdity of existence*, Nietzsche, *The Birth of Tragedy*, p.51.

p.186   *the instinct of life*, Freud, *Civilization and its Discontents*, p.122.

p.186   *vacillating rhythm*, Freud, *Beyond the Pleasure Principle*, p.41.

p.186   *speculator's indefatigable motion*, Derrida, *The Post Card*, p.295.

p.186   *mimes walking*, Derrida, *The Post Card*, p.269.

p.187   *it may be asked*, Freud, *Beyond the Pleasure Principle*, p.59.

p.187   *repeatedly combining*, Freud, *Beyond the Pleasure Principle*, p.59.

p.187   *playing so seriously*, Derrida, *The Post Card*, p.302.

p.187   *cool benevolence*, Freud, *Beyond the Pleasure Principle*, p.59.

p.187   *benevolent illusion*, Freud, *Beyond the Pleasure Principle*, p.42.

p.187   *peculiar pleasure*, Freud, *Jokes*, p.117.

p.188   *peculiar tension*, Freud, *Beyond the Pleasure Principle*, p.63.

p.188   *either pleasurable or unpleasurable*, Freud, *Beyond the Pleasure Principle*, p.63.

p.188   *make a fresh start*, Freud, *Beyond the Pleasure Principle*, p.41.

p.188   *to no good end*, Freud, *Beyond the Pleasure Principle*, p.64.

p.188   *tragedy is the most perverse*, Barthes, *The Pleasure of the Text*, pp.47-48.

p.189   *put to the sword*, Yeats, 'Lapis Lazuli', line 27.

p.189   *hysterical women*, Yeats, 'Lapis Lazuli', line 1.

p.189   *all perform their tragic play*, Yeats, 'Lapis Lazuli', lines 9-24.

p.189   *mournful melodies*, Yeats, 'Lapis Lazuli', line 53.

p.191   *all true rites and lawful ceremonies*, Julius Caesar, III.i.241.

p.191   *savage spectacle*, Julius Caesar, III.i.223.

p.191   *piece of work*, Julius Caesar, II.i.327.

p.191   *piteous spectacle*, Julius Caesar, III.ii.198.

p.191   *stoop, Romans, stoop*, Julius Caesar, III.i.105-16.

p.194   *disrobe the images*, Julius Caesar, I.i.64-65.

p.194   *hence! home, you idle creatures*, Julius Caesar, I.i.1.

p.194   *common laughter*, Julius Caesar, I.ii.72.

p.194   *tag-rag people*, Julius Caesar, I.ii.258.

p.195   *mere foolery*, Julius Caesar, I.ii.236, 287.

p.195   *would be crown'd*, Julius Caesar, II.i.12.

p.196   *bad verses*, Julius Caesar, III.iii.30.

p.196   *jigging*, Julius Caesar, IV.iii.137.

p.196   *seal'd compact*, Hamlet, I.i.86-87.

p.197   *gage*, Hamlet, I.i.91.

p.197   *inextricable complex*, Huizinga, *Homo Ludens*, p.113.

p.197   *rite of war*, Hamlet, V.ii.399.

p.197   *amiss*, Hamlet, V.ii.402.

p.197   *high on a stage*, Hamlet, V.ii.378.

p.197   *out of frame*, Hamlet, I.ii.20.

p.197   *out of joint, Hamlet,* I.v.188.

p.197   *foul play, Hamlet,* I.ii.255.

p.198   *auspicious . . . dropping, Hamlet,* I.ii.11.

p.198   *hugger mugger, Hamlet,* IV.v.84.

p.198   *maimèd rites, Hamlet,* V.i.219.

p.198   *seems, Hamlet,* I.ii.76.

p.198   *actions that a man might play, Hamlet,* I.ii.84.

p.199   *artistic failure,* Eliot, 'Hamlet', p.47.

p.199   *piece of work, Hamlet,* III.ii.46.

p.199   *in jest, Hamlet,* III.ii.234.

p.199   *in sport, Julius Caesar,* III.i.114.

p.200   *piece of work, Hamlet,* II.ii.303.

p.200   *O, what a rogue and peasant slave am I!, Hamlet,* II.ii.550-62.

p.201   *the play's the thing, Hamlet,* II.ii.604-5.

p.201   *I have heard, Hamlet,* II.ii.588.

p.202   *for if the king like not the comedy, Hamlet,* III.ii.293-94.

p.202   *near, Hamlet,* III.ii.76.

p.202   *something like, Hamlet,* II.ii.595.

p.202   *who calls me villain, Hamlet,* II.ii.572-75.

p.202   *bloody, bawdy villain!, Hamlet,* II.ii.580-81.

p.202   *foul play, Hamlet,* V.ii.198, 207.

p.203   *miching mallecho, Hamlet,* III.ii.137.

p.203   *imperious show, Antony and Cleopatra,* IV.xv.23.

p.203   *eternal, Antony and Cleopatra,* V.i.66.

p.203   *perish'd like a blaze,* Jonson, *Hymenai,* p.209.

p.204   *window'd in great Rome, Antony and Cleopatra,* IV.xiv.72-75.

p.204   *would not see, Antony and Cleopatra,* IV.xiv.77.

p.204   *shouting varlotry, Antony and Cleopatra,* V.ii.56.

p.204   *Alexandrian revels, Antony and Cleopatra,* V.ii.218.

p.204   *I'll never see it!, Antony and Cleopatra,* V.ii.223-24.

p.204   *extemporally, Antony and Cleopatra,* V.ii.217.

p.204   *high event, Antony and Cleopatra,* V.ii.360.

p.204   *play till doomsday, Antony and Cleopatra,* V.ii.232.

p.204   *your crown's awry, Antony and Cleopatra,* V.ii.318-19.

p.205   *like a queen, Antony and Cleopatra,* V.ii.227.

p.205   *public eye, Antony and Cleopatra,* III.vi.11.

p.205   *again for Cydnus, Antony and Cleopatra,* V.ii.228.

p.205   *gaze, Antony and Cleopatra,* II.ii.217.

p.205   *the barge she sat in, Antony and Cleopatra,* II.ii.191-92.

p.205   *a seeming mermaid steers, Antony and Cleopatra,* II.ii.209.

p.205   *a strange invisible perfume hits the sense, Antony and Cleopatra,* II.ii.212.

p.206   *nay, but this dotage of our general's, Antony and Cleopatra,* I.i.1-6.

p.206   *infinite variety, Antony and Cleopatra,* II.ii.235.

p.206   *the istoria which merits both praise and admiration,* Alberti, *On Painting,* p.75.

p.206   *would I had never seen her!, Antony and Cleopatra,* I.ii.152.

p.206   *left unseen a wonderful piece of work, Antony and Cleopatra,* I.ii.154.

p.206   *ass unpolicied, Antony and Cleopatra,* V.ii.307-8.

REFERENCES

p.207   *sweet dependency, Antony and Cleopatra*, V.ii.26.
p.207   *conqu'ring hand, Antony and Cleopatra*, III.xiii.75.
p.207   *doctrine of obedience, Antony and Cleopatra*, V.ii.31.
p.207   *all's but naught, Antony and Cleopatra*, IV.xv.78.
p.208   *now, Iras, what think'st thou?, Antony and Cleopatra*, V.ii.207-21.
p.210   *eternal moment of disclosed presence*, Bryson, *Vision and Painting*, p.94.
p.210   *stag'd to th'show, Antony and Cleopatra*, III.xiii.30.
p.211   *the king's daughter, The Winter's Tale*, V.ii.23.
p.211   *the queen, the queen, The Winter's Tale*, III.ii.200-202.
p.212   *saint-like, The Winter's Tale*, V.i.2.
p.212   *upon them shall the causes of their death appear, The Winter's Tale*,
         III.ii.236-38.
p.212   *recreation, The Winter's Tale*, III.ii.240.
p.212   *sad tale, The Winter's Tale*, II.i.25.
p.212   *in winter's tedious nights, Richard II*, V.i.40-42.
p.212   *thy mother plays, The Winter's Tale*, I.ii.187-89.
p.213   *play'd to take spectators, The Winter's Tale*, III.ii.36-37.
p.213   *in the level of your dreams, The Winter's Tale*, III.ii.81.
p.213   *jest, The Winter's Tale*, I.ii.249.
p.213   *sport, The Winter's Tale*, II.i.58.
p.213   *better than nature*, Sidney, *Apology for Poetry*, p.100.
p.213   *forms such as never were in nature*, Sidney, *Apology for Poetry*, p.100.
p.213   *bestow a Cyrus upon the world*, Sidney, *Apology for Poetry*, p.101.
p.213   *wholly imaginative*, Sidney, *Apology for Poetry*, p.101.
p.213   *stormie winter*, Sidney, *Apology for Poetry*, p.143.
p.213   *winter in storm perpetual, The Winter's Tale*, III.ii.212-13.
p.213   *disgrac'd a part, The Winter's Tale*, I.ii.188.
p.215   *thou in our wonder and astonishment*, Milton, 'On Shakespeare', lines 7-14.
p.215   *it is owing to their wonder*, Aristotle, *Metaphysics*, p.1554.
p.215   *a man who is puzzled and wonders*, Aristotle, *Metaphysics*, p.1554.
p.216   *were it but told you, should be hooted at, The Winter's Tale*, V.iii.116-17.
p.216   *drollery*, Jonson, *Bartholomew Fair*, p.16.
p.217   *holdeth children from play*, Sidney, *Apology for Poetry*, p.113.
p.217   *is it true, think you?, The Winter's Tale*, IV.iv.266.
p.217   *it was told me I should be rich by the fairies, The Winter's Tale*, III.iii.117-
         18.
p.217   *I have heard (but not believ'd), The Winter's Tale*, III.iii.16-17.
p.217   *indeed the issue of king Polixenes, The Winter's Tale*, III.iii.43-44.
p.217   *a swain's wearing, The Winter's Tale*, IV.iv.9.
p.217   *not appearing what we are, The Winter's Tale*, IV.ii.47-48.
p.217   *scene, The Winter's Tale*, IV.iv.593.
p.217   *what a fool honesty is, The Winter's Tale*, IV.iv.595.

Bibliography

Joseph Addison, 'The history of the pun', *The Spectator* 10 May 1711, in *The Spectator*, ed. Donald F. Bond (Oxford: Clarendon Press, 1965), 5 vols., vol.i.

Leon Battista Alberti, *On Painting*, ed. and trans. John R. Spencer (New Haven: Yale University Press, revised ed. 1966).

Lisa Appignanesi and John Forrester, *Freud's Women* (London: Virago, 1992).

Hannah Arendt, *The Human Condition* (Chicago: Chicago University Press, 1958).

Aristotle, *The Complete Works of Aristotle*, ed. Jonathan Barnes (Princeton, N.J.: Princeton University Press, 1984), 2 vols.

— *Poetics,* vol.ii.

— *Metaphysics,* vol.ii.

Derek Attridge *Peculiar Language: Literature as Difference from the Renaissance to James Joyce* (London: Methuen, 1988).

Augustine, *City of God*, trans. Henry Bettenson (Harmondsworth: Penguin, 1972).

Roland Barthes, *Mythologies*, trans. Annette Lavers (London: Paladin Books, 1973).

— *The Pleasure of the Text*, trans. Richard Miller (Oxford: Blackwell, 1990).

Anne Barton, *Shakespeare and the Idea of the Play* (Westport CT.: Greenwood Press, 1962).

Gregory Bateson, *Steps To An Ecology of Mind* (London: Intertext Books, 1972).

Harry Berger, *Second World and Green World: Studies in Renaissance Fiction-Making* (Berkeley: University of California Press, 1988).

Henri Bergson, *Laughter*, ed. Wylie Sypher (Baltimore: Johns Hopkins University Press, 1956).

Peter L. Bernstein, *Against the Gods: The Remarkable Story of Risk* (New York: John Wiley, 1996).

Leo Bersani, *The Freudian Body: Psychoanalysis and Art* (New York: Columbia University Press, 1986).

— *The Culture of Redemption* (Cambridge, Mass.: Harvard University Press, 1990).

— and Ulysse Dutoit, *Arts of Impoverishment: Beckett, Rothko, Resnais* (Cambridge, Mass.: Harvard University Press, 1993).

R. Howard Bloch *Etymologies and Genealogies: A Literary Anthropology of the French Middle Ages* (Chicago: University of Chicago Press, 1983).

Jorge Luis Borges, 'The Babylonian Lottery', in *Fictions*, ed. and trans. Anthony Kerrigan (London: Calder, 1985).

Pierre Bourdieu, *Outline of a Theory of Practice*, trans. Richard Nice (Cambridge: Cambridge University Press, 1977).

Malcolm Bowie, *Lacan* (London: Fontana, 1991).

Norman Bryson, *Vision and Painting: The Logic of the Gaze* (London: Macmillan, 1983).

Kenneth Burke, *A Grammar of Motives* (London: Prentice Hall, 1945).

Roger Caillois, *Man, Play, and Games*, trans. Meyer Barash (New York: Free Press, 1961).

— *L'Homme et le Sacré* (Paris: Gallimard, 1961).

Elias Canetti, *Crowds and Power*, trans. Carol Stewart (Harmondsworth: Penguin, revised ed. 1973).

Stanley Cavell, *Disowning Knowledge in Six Plays of Shakespeare* (Cambridge: Cambridge University Press, 1987).

Jonathan Culler, *Structuralist Poetics: Structuralism, Linguistics, and the Study of Literature* (London: Routledge and Kegan Paul, 1975).

— ed., *On Puns: The Foundation of Letters* (Oxford: Blackwell, 1988).

F. N. David, *Games, Gods and Gambling* (London: Charles Griffin, 1962).

Jacques Derrida, *The Post Card: From Socrates to Freud and Beyond*, trans. Alan Bass (Chicago: University of Chicago Press, 1987).

— *Points . . . interviews 1974-1994*, ed. Elisabeth Weber, trans. Peggy Kamuf et al (Stanford: Stanford University Press, 1995).

Gilles Deleuze, *Difference and Repetition*, trans. Paul Patton (London: Athlone Press, 1994).

Mary Douglas, *Purity and Danger: An Analysis of the Concepts of Pollution and Taboo* (London: Routledge and Kegan Paul, 1966).

— *Implicit Meanings: Essays in Anthropology* (London: Routledge and Kegan Paul, 1975).

Terry Eagleton, *The Ideology of the Aesthetic* (Oxford: Blackwell, 1990).

Umberto Eco, *The Limits of Interpretation* (Bloomington I.A.: Indiana University Press, 1990).

— 'Overinterpreting texts', in *Interpretation and Overinterpretation*, ed. Stefan Collini (Cambridge: Cambridge University Press, 1992), pp.45-66.

Nobert Elias, *The Civilizing Process*, trans. Edmund Jephcott (Oxford: Blackwell, 1982), 2 vols.

T. S. Eliot, 'Hamlet', in *Selected Prose*, ed. Frank Kermode (London: Faber, 1975).

William Empson, *The Structure of Complex Words* (London: Hogarth Press, 1985).

— *Seven Types of Ambiguity* (3rd ed., repr. Harmondsworth: Penguin, 1995).

Howard Felperin, *Beyond Deconstruction: The Uses and Abuses of Literary Theory* (Oxford: Clarendon Press, 1985).

Sigmund Freud, *The Standard Edition of the Complete Psychological Works of Sigmund Freud*, ed. and trans. James Strachey (London: The Hogarth Press, 1960), 24 vols.

— *The Interpretation of Dreams* (1900), vols. iv and v.

— *The Psychopathology of Everyday Life* (1901), vol. vi.

— *Jokes and Their Relation to the Unconscious* (1905), vol. viii.

— *Three Essays on the Theory of Sexuality* (1905), vol. vii.

— *Fragment of an Analysis of a Case of Hysteria* ('Dora') (1905), vol. vii.

— 'Psychopathic Characters on the Stage' (unpublished), vol. vii.

— 'Creative Writers and Day-Dreaming' (1908), vol. ix.

— *Notes upon a Case of Obsessional Neurosis* ('The Rat Man'), vol. x.

— *Beyond the Pleasure Principle* (1920), vol. xviii.

— *The Ego and the Id* (1923), vol. xix.

— 'Humour' (1927), vol. xxi.

— *The Future of an Illusion* (1927), vol. xxi.

— *Civilization and its Discontents* (1930), vol. xxi.

— *New Introductory Lectures on Psychoanalysis* (1933), vol. xxii.

Northrop Frye, *Anatomy of Criticism* (Princeton: Princeton University Press, 1957).

Sander Gilman, *Difference and Pathology: Stereotypes of Sexuality, Race, and Madness* (Ithaca: Cornell University Press, 1985).

Robert Gittings, *John Keats* (Harmondsworth: Penguin, 1968).

E. H. Gombrich, 'Freud's Aesthetics', repr. in *Literature and Psychoanalysis*, ed. Edith Kurzweil and William Phillips (New York: Columbia University Press, 1983), pp.132-45.

Ian Hacking, *The Emergence of Probability* (Cambridge: Cambridge University Press, 1975).

Geoffrey Hartman, *Easy Pieces* (New York: Columbia University Press, 1985).

Carl Hill, *The Soul of Witz: Joke Theory from Grimm to Freud* (Lincoln and London: University of Nebraska Press, 1993).

Thomas Hobbes, *The English Works of Thomas Hobbes*, ed. Sir William Molesworth (London: Bohn, 1839-45, reprinted by Routledge and Thoemmes Press, 1992), 12 vols.

— *Treatise of Human Nature*, vol.iv.

Norman N. Holland, in *Laughing: A Psychology of Humour* (Ithaca: Cornell University Press, 1982).

David Hume, *A Treatise of Human Nature*, ed. L. A. Selby-Bigge, rev. P. H. Nidditch (Oxford: Oxford University Press, 2nd ed. 1978).

Johan Huizinga, *The Waning of the Middle Ages*, trans. F. Hopman (Harmondsworth: Penguin, 1955).

— *Homo Ludens: A Study of the Play Element in Culture* (London: Temple Smith, 1970).

Samuel Johnson, *The Yale Edition of the Works of Samuel Johnson* (New Haven: Yale University Press, 1958-1990) 16 vols.

— *Preface to Shakespeare,* vol.vii.

— *Dictionary of the English Language* (1755).

Ernest Jones, *Sigmund Freud: Life and Work* (London: Hogarth Press, 1957), 3 vols.

Ben Jonson, *Ben Jonson*, ed. C. H. Herford and Percy Simpson (Oxford: Clarendon Press, 1925-52), 11 vols.

— *Hymenai*, vol.vii.

— *Bartholomew Fair*, vol.vi.

Søren Kierkegaard, *Fear and Trembling; Repetition*, ed. and trans. Howard V. Hong and Edna H. Hong (Princeton, NJ: Princeton University Press, 1983).

Arthur Koestler, *The Act of Creation* (London: Hutchinson, 1964).

Ernst Kris, *Psychoanalytic Explorations in Art* (London: Allen and Unwin, 1953).

Thomas Kyd, *The Spanish Tragedy*, ed. Philip Edwards (Manchester: Manchester University Press, 1959).

Jacques Lacan, *Écrits: A Selection*, trans. Alan Sheridan (London: Routledge, 1977).

— 'The mirror stage as formative of the function of the I', *Écrits*, pp.1-7.

— 'Aggressivity in psychoanalysis', *Écrits*, pp.8-29.

— 'The function and field of speech and language in psychoanalysis', *Écrits*, pp.30-113.

— *The Psychoses: The Seminar of Jacques Lacan, Book III, 1955-56*, ed. Jacques-Alain Miller, trans. Russell Grigg (London: Routledge, 1993).

— *The Four Fundamental Concepts of Psychoanalysis*, ed. Jacques-Alain Miller, trans. Alan Sheridan (Harmondsworth: Penguin, 1979).

Candace D. Lang, *Irony/Humour: Critical Paradigms* (Baltimore: Johns Hopkins University Press, 1988).

Allan Megill, *Prophets of Extremity: Nietzsche, Heidegger, Foucault, Derrida* (Berkeley: University of California Press, 1985).

John Milton, *Paradise Lost*, ed. Alastair Fowler (London: Longman, 1971).

— *Complete Shorter Poems*, ed. John Carey (London: Longman, 1968).

Friedrich Nietzsche, *The Birth of Tragedy and The Genealogy of Morals*, trans. Francis Golffing (New York: Anchor Books, 1956).
— *The Portable Nietzsche*, ed. and trans. W. Kaufmann (New York: Viking Penguin, 1954).
— 'Homer's Contest', *Portable Nietzsche*, pp.32-39.
— 'On Truth and Lie in an Extra-Moral Sense', *Portable Nietzsche*, pp.42-47.
— *Human, All Too Human*, trans. R. J. Hollingdale (Cambridge: Cambridge University Press, 1986).
— *The Gay Science*, trans. Walter Kaufmann (New York: Vintage, 1974).
— *The Will to Power*, trans. Walter Kaufmann and R. J. Hollingdale (New York: Vintage, 1967).
The Oxford English Dictionary, second edition.
Elliott Oring, *The Jokes of Sigmund Freud: A Study in Humour and Jewish Identity* (Philadelphia: University of Pennsylvania Press, 1984).
Blaise Pascal, *Pensées and other writings*, ed. and trans. Honor Levi (Oxford: Oxford University Press, 1995).
Adam Phillips, *On Flirtation* (London: Faber, 1994).
— *Terrors and Experts* (London: Faber, 1995).
Plato, *Laws*, trans. A. E. Taylor (London: Dent, 1960).
Alexander Pope, *The Twickenham Edition of the Poems of Alexander Pope*, ed. John Butt (London: Methuen, 1961-67), 10 vols.
— *The Dunciad*, vol.iv.
Sir Walter Ralegh, *The History of the World*, ed. C. A. Patrides (London: Macmillan, 1971).
Walter Redfern, *Puns* (Oxford: Blackwell, 1984).
Theodor Reik, *Surprise and the Psychoanalyst: On the Conjecture and Comprehension of Unconscious Processes*, trans. Margaret M. Green (London: Kegan Paul, Trench and Trubner, 1936).
Ferdinand de Saussure, *Course in General Linguistics*, ed. Charles Bally and Albert Sechehaye, trans. Roy Harris (London: Duckworth, 1983).
Friedrich Schiller, *On the Aesthetic Education of Man*, ed. and trans. Elizabeth M. Wilkinson and L. A. Willoughby (Oxford: Clarendon Press, 1967).
William Shakespeare, *The Riverside Shakespeare*, ed. G. Blakemore Evans (Boston: Houghton Mifflin, 2nd ed., 1997).
— *King Lear*.
— *Richard II*.
— *Measure for Measure*.
— *Julius Caesar*.
— *Hamlet*.
— *Antony and Cleopatra*.
— *The Winter's Tale*.

Sir Philip Sidney, *An Apology for Poetry*, ed. Geoffrey Shepherd (Manchester: Manchester University Press, 1973).

Richard Keller Simon, *The Labyrinth of the Comic: Theory and Practice from Fielding to Freud* (Tallahasee: Florida State University Press, 1985).

Jonathan Swift, *The Prose Works of Jonathan Swift*, ed. Herbert Davis, *et al* (Oxford: Blackwell, 1965-74), 16 vols.

— *A Modest Defence of Punning*, vol.iv.

Lionel Trilling, *Beyond Culture: Essays on Literature and Learning* (Oxford: Oxford University Press, 1980).

Victor Turner, *From Ritual to Theatre: The Human Seriousness of Play* (New York: PAJ Publications, 1982).

Giorgio Vasari, *The Lives of the Artists*, ed. and trans. Julia and Peter Bondanella (Oxford: Oxford University Press, 1991).

Max Weber, *The Protestant Ethic and the Spirit of Capitalism*, trans. Talcott Parsons (London: Unwin, 1985).

John von Neumann and Oskar Morgenstern, *Theory of Games and Economic Behaviour* (Princeton: Princeton University Press, 1953).

Samuel Weber, *The Legend of Freud* (Minneapolis: University of Minnesota Press, 1982).

D. W. Winnicott, *Playing and Reality* (London: Tavistock Publications, 1971; reprinted by Routledge, 1991).

— *Through Paediatrics to Psychoanalysis* (London: Karnac, 1984).

— *The Maturational Processes and the Facilitating Environment* (London: Karnac, 1990).

W. B. Yeats, *Collected Poems* (London: Macmillan, 2nd. ed. 1950).

Slavoj Žižek, *The Sublime Object of Ideology* (London and New York: Verso, 1989).

Index